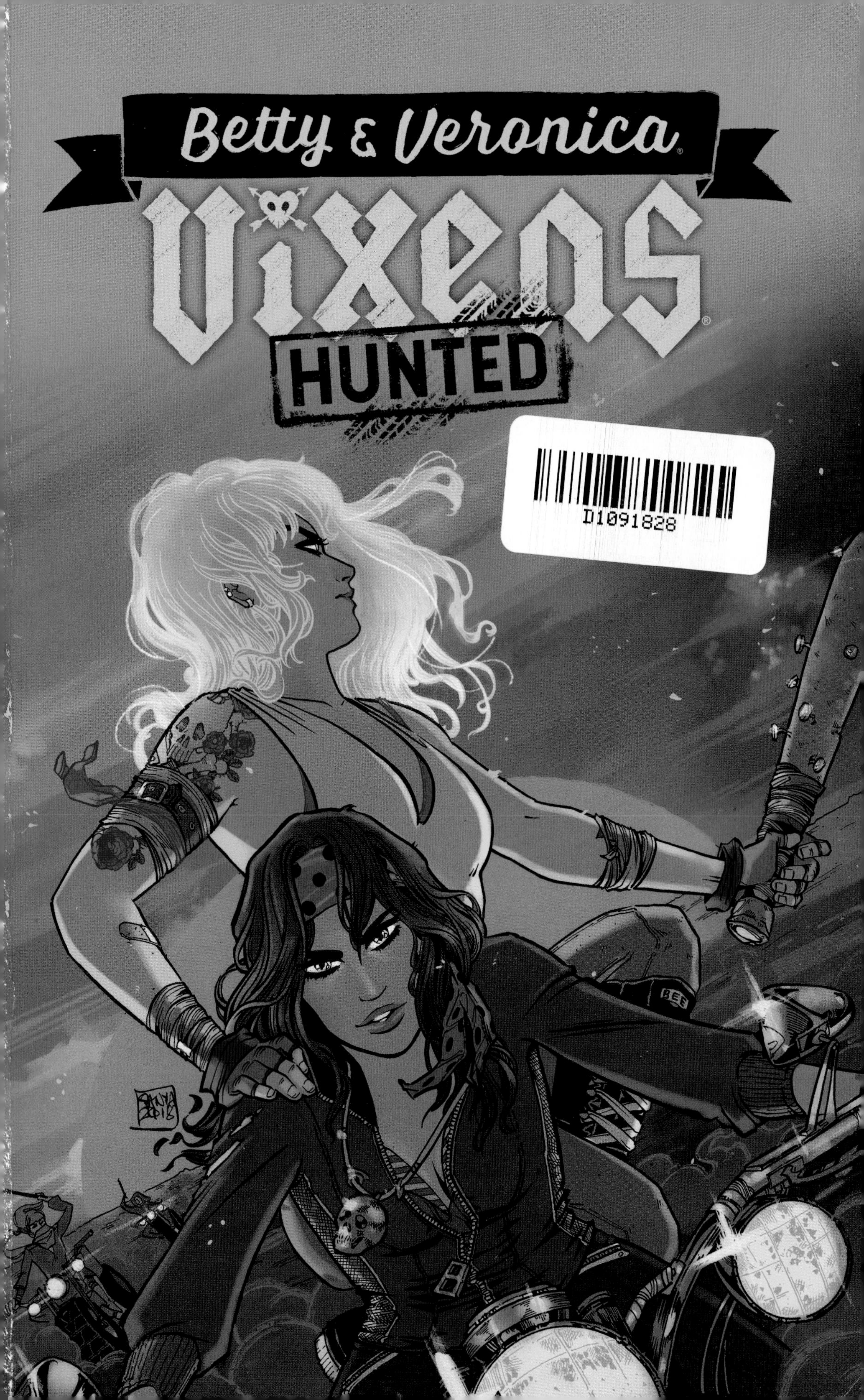
Betty & Veronica®
Vixens®
HUNTED

Betty & Veronica

Vixens
HUNTED

story by
JAMIE LEE ROTANTE

colors by
ELAINA UNGER and
MATT HERMS

editors
ALEX SEGURA and
VINCENT LOVALLO

associate editor
STEPHEN OSWALD

editor-in-chief
VICTOR GORELICK

publisher
JON GOLDWATER

art by
JEN VAUGHN (ISSUES 6-7)
SANYA ANWAR (ISSUES 8, 10)
EVA CABRERA (ISSUE 9)

letters by
RACHEL DEERING

cover art by
SANYA ANWAR

graphic designer
KARI MCLACHLAN

This second volume of *Betty & Veronica: Vixens* that you hold in your hands right now completes the series. That's ten issues in total. That's ten issues of Betty & Veronica leading an all-female motorcycle gang. That's ten issues of Betty & Veronica kicking asses and taking names. That's ten more issues of a Betty & Veronica comic than I ever imagined I'd someday write.

Getting the opportunity to tell this story is nothing short of amazing—an honor I'll forever be grateful for. And getting the chance to work with a team of immensely talented female artists was like a dream come true. But I've already gushed enough about how amazing it was to write this... now it's time to gush about the characters I was fortunate to get to write about.

Betty and Veronica aren't just two of Archie Comics' most famous characters—they're American icons. The quintessential yin and yang, the two BFFs show how sometimes the best friendships form when opposites attract. They're strong, independent and look out for one another—even when they're at odds with each other over Archie. Betty and Veronica have all the trappings of great comic heroes, and that was something I wanted to test and push to an extreme while still keeping it somewhat in the real world.

But I didn't want it to be only Betty and Veronica on this adventure—there are so many amazing female characters in our library that could also be included.

When assembled the Vixens had all the makings of a superhero group: Betty's the fearless All-American, good-girl-gone-bad leader, Veronica's the fierce one with the money to supply all their needs, Toni's the muscle, Midge is the regimented and by-the-book (though a bit flirty as well!) fighter, Ethel is the one whose potential has not yet been realized but has fight deep down inside her and Evelyn is the wildcard with some kind of trained-assassin-esque mysterious backstory. It didn't take a lot of stretching for the characters to fit these molds; these were all elements of their preexisting personalities. And those were just the main characters.

In addition to getting to write strong and likable female characters, I also got to interact with some amazing women in the real world—from motorcycle collectives to roller derby teams. *Vixens* isn't just a fictitious look at women taking charge, it's an account of what happens when females come together. Strong women are everywhere and I was lucky to get to tell a story that shows that.

Jamie Lee Rotante
Writer, BETTY & VERONICA: VIXENS

NOW LEAVING
RIVERDALE

1 MILE

Chapter Six

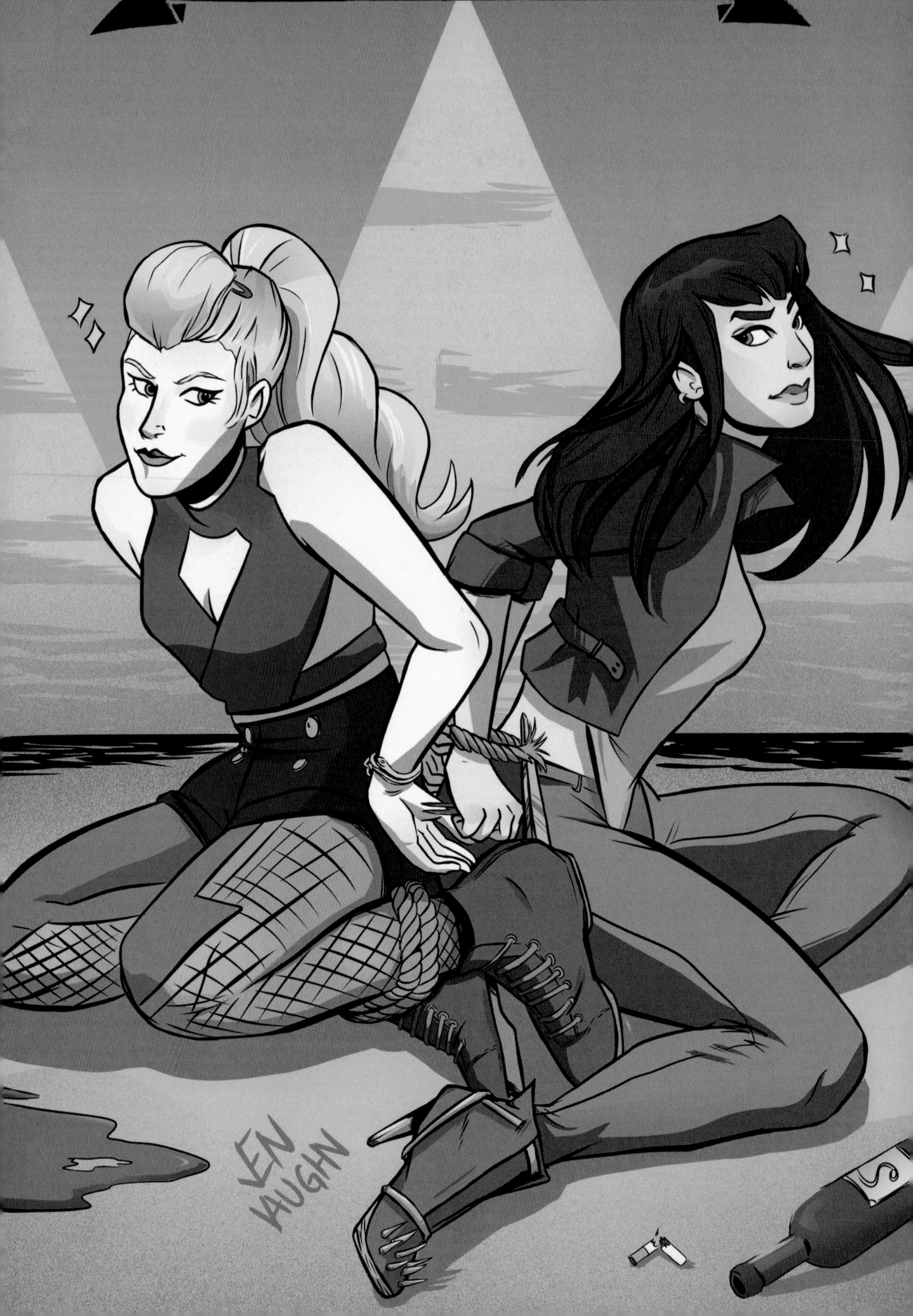

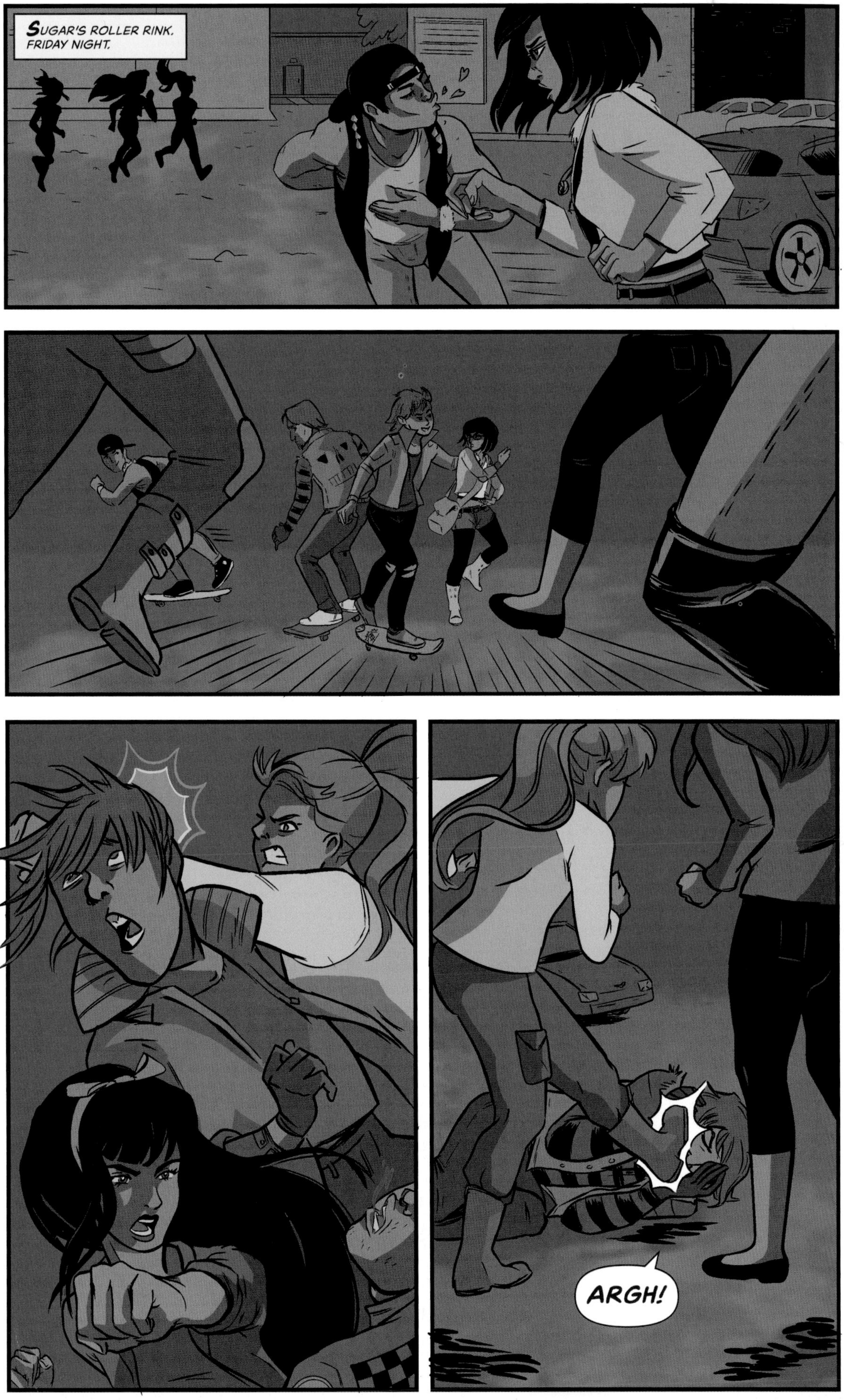
SUGAR'S ROLLER RINK.
FRIDAY NIGHT.
ARGH!

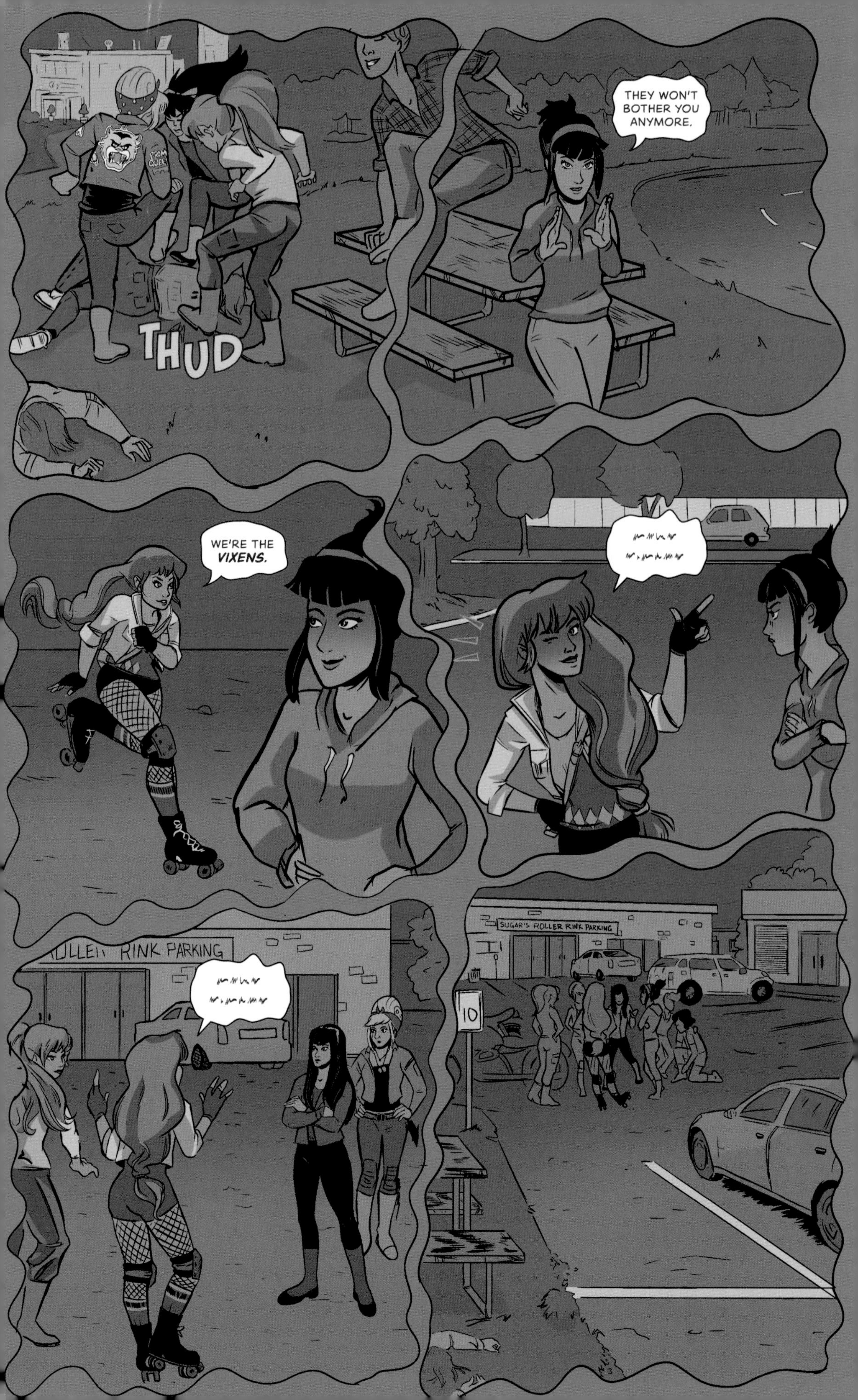
THUD
THEY WON'T BOTHER YOU ANYMORE.
WE'RE THE *VIXENS.*
SUGAR'S ROLLER RINK PARKING
ROLLER RINK PARKING
10

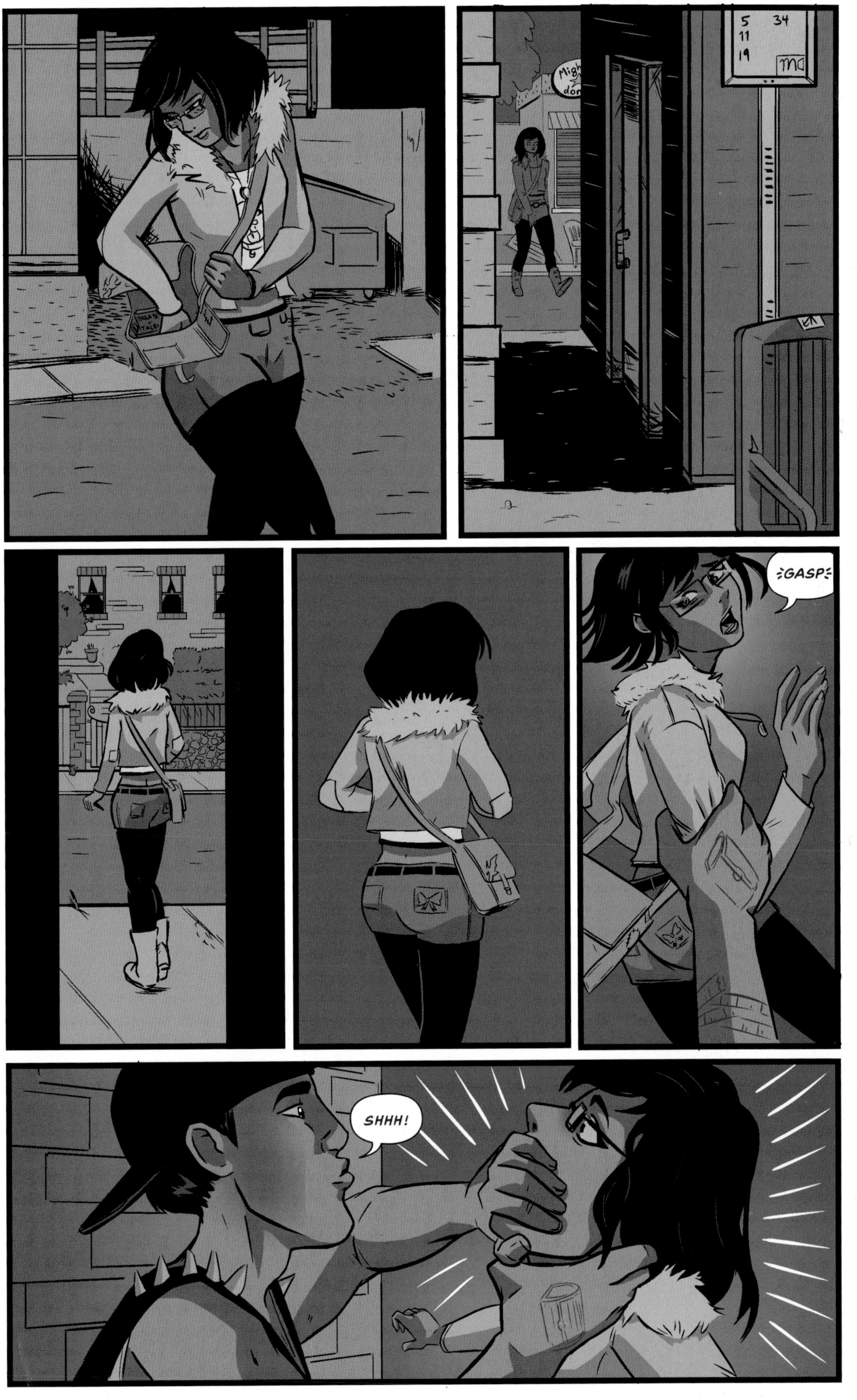
5 34
11
19
GASP
SHHH!

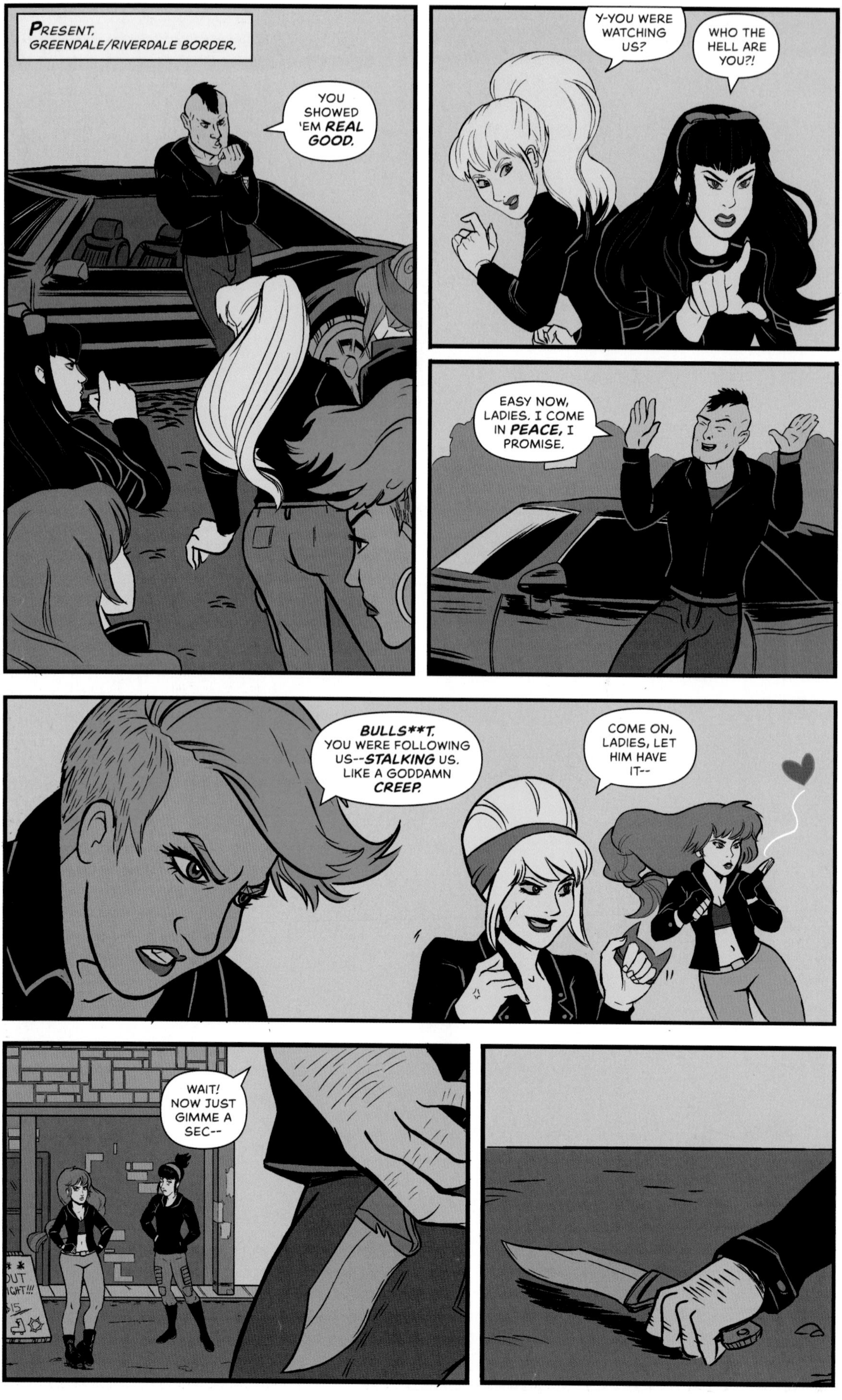
PRESENT.
GREENDALE/RIVERDALE BORDER.
YOU SHOWED 'EM REAL GOOD.
Y-YOU WERE WATCHING US?
WHO THE HELL ARE YOU?!
EASY NOW, LADIES. I COME IN PEACE, I PROMISE.
BULLS**T. YOU WERE FOLLOWING US--STALKING US. LIKE A GODDAMN CREEP.
COME ON, LADIES, LET HIM HAVE IT--
WAIT! NOW JUST GIMME A SEC--

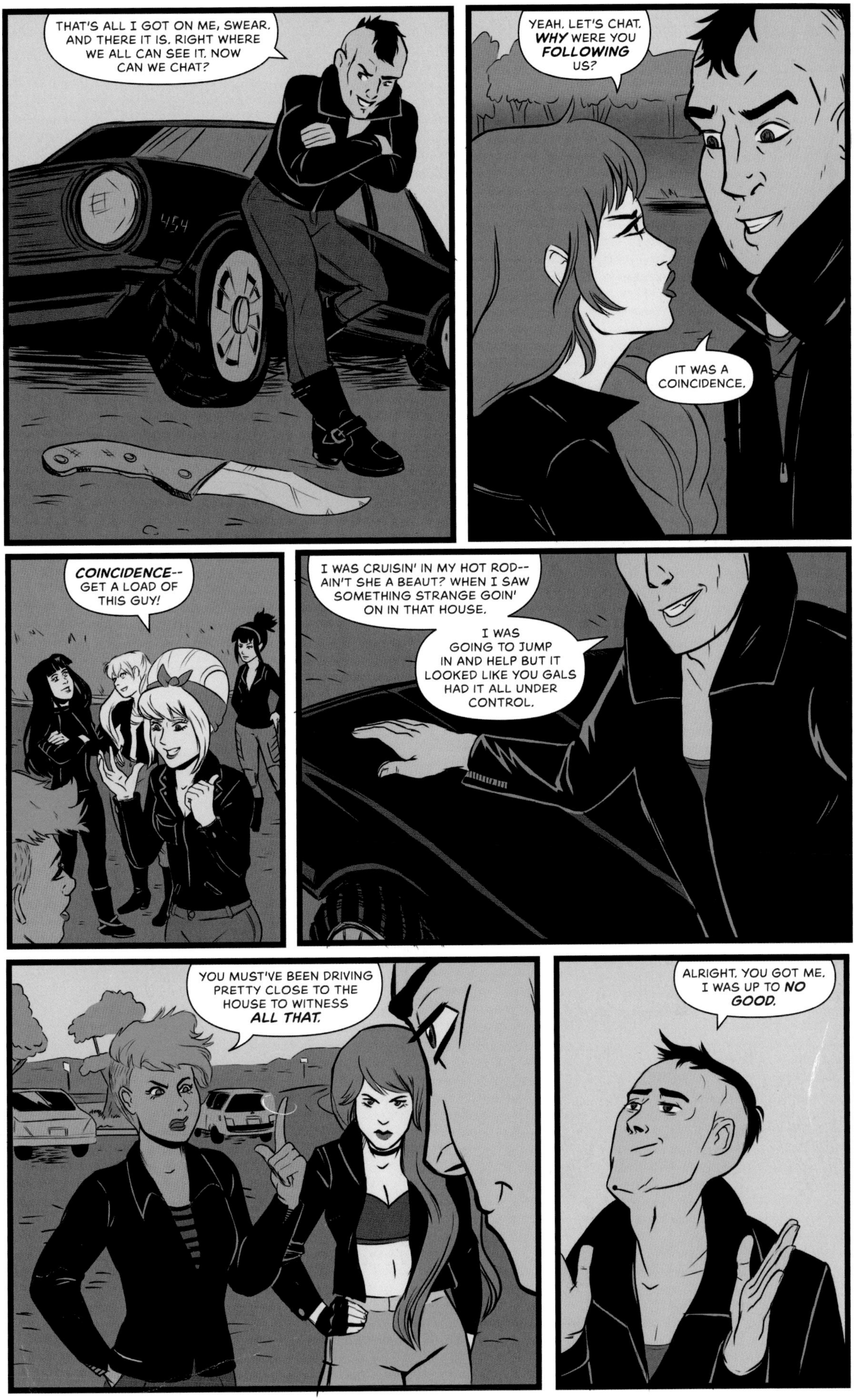
THAT'S ALL I GOT ON ME, SWEAR. AND THERE IT IS, RIGHT WHERE WE ALL CAN SEE IT. NOW CAN WE CHAT?
YEAH, LET'S CHAT. WHY WERE YOU FOLLOWING US?
IT WAS A COINCIDENCE.
COINCIDENCE-- GET A LOAD OF THIS GUY!
I WAS CRUISIN' IN MY HOT ROD-- AIN'T SHE A BEAUT? WHEN I SAW SOMETHING STRANGE GOIN' ON IN THAT HOUSE.
I WAS GOING TO JUMP IN AND HELP BUT IT LOOKED LIKE YOU GALS HAD IT ALL UNDER CONTROL.
YOU MUST'VE BEEN DRIVING PRETTY CLOSE TO THE HOUSE TO WITNESS ALL THAT.
ALRIGHT, YOU GOT ME. I WAS UP TO NO GOOD.

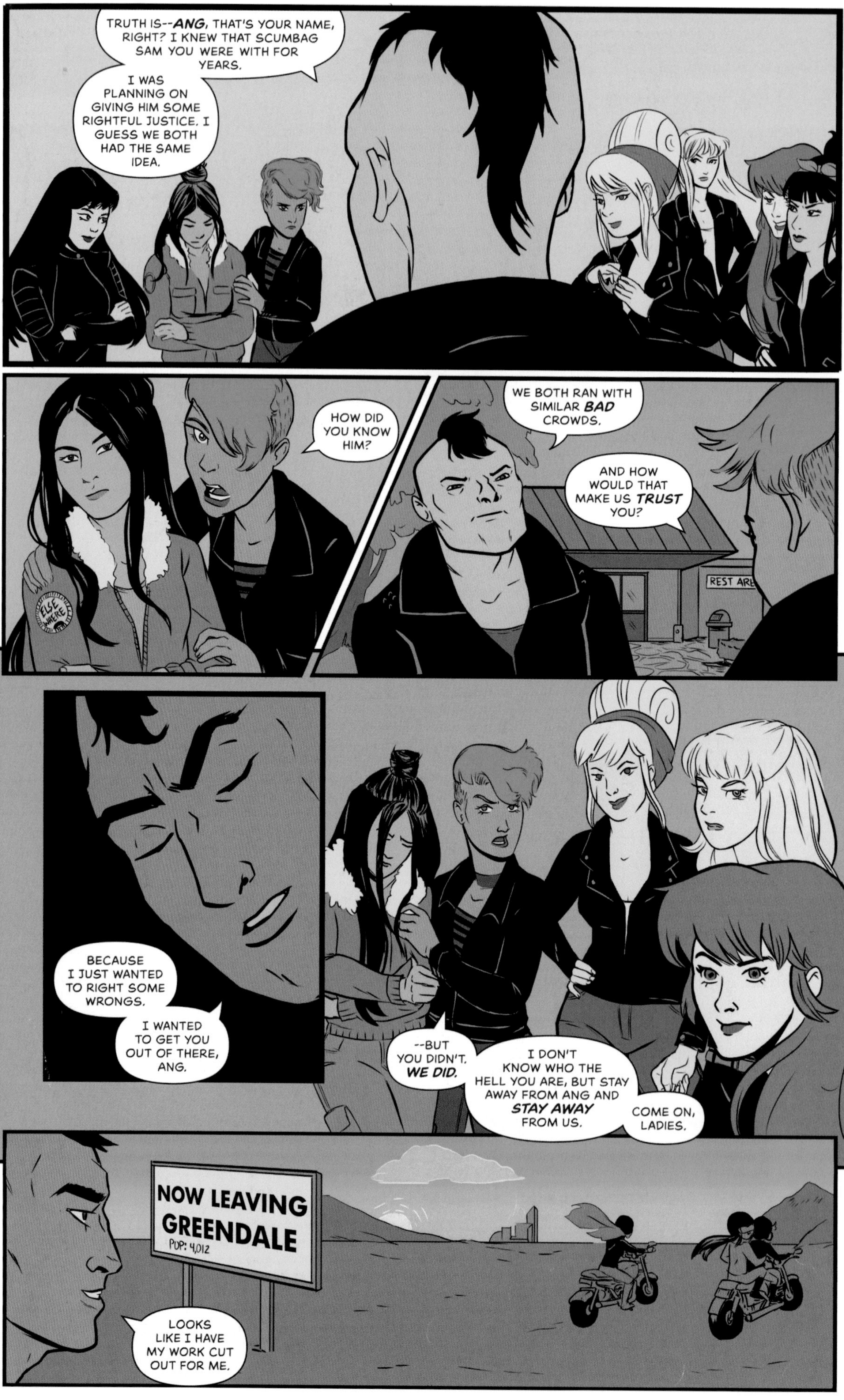
TRUTH IS--ANG, THAT'S YOUR NAME, RIGHT? I KNEW THAT SCUMBAG SAM YOU WERE WITH FOR YEARS.
I WAS PLANNING ON GIVING HIM SOME RIGHTFUL JUSTICE. I GUESS WE BOTH HAD THE SAME IDEA.
HOW DID YOU KNOW HIM?
WE BOTH RAN WITH SIMILAR BAD CROWDS.
AND HOW WOULD THAT MAKE US TRUST YOU?
ELSE WHERE
REST AR
BECAUSE I JUST WANTED TO RIGHT SOME WRONGS.
I WANTED TO GET YOU OUT OF THERE, ANG.
--BUT YOU DIDN'T. WE DID.
I DON'T KNOW WHO THE HELL YOU ARE, BUT STAY AWAY FROM ANG AND STAY AWAY FROM US.
COME ON, LADIES.
NOW LEAVING GREENDALE
POP: 4,012
LOOKS LIKE I HAVE MY WORK CUT OUT FOR ME.

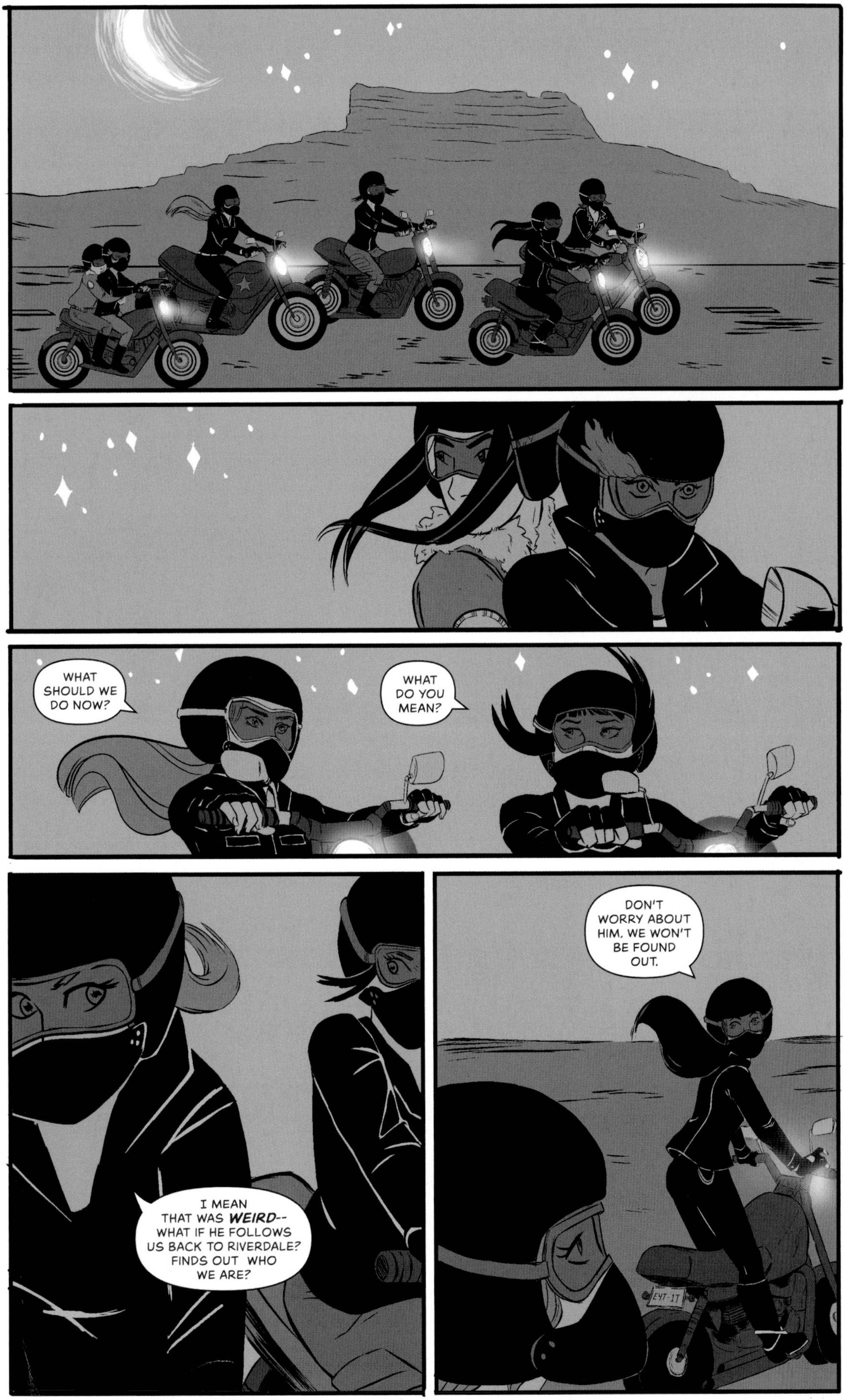
WHAT SHOULD WE DO NOW?
WHAT DO YOU MEAN?
I MEAN THAT WAS ***WEIRD***-- WHAT IF HE FOLLOWS US BACK TO RIVERDALE? FINDS OUT WHO WE ARE?
DON'T WORRY ABOUT HIM. WE WON'T BE FOUND OUT.

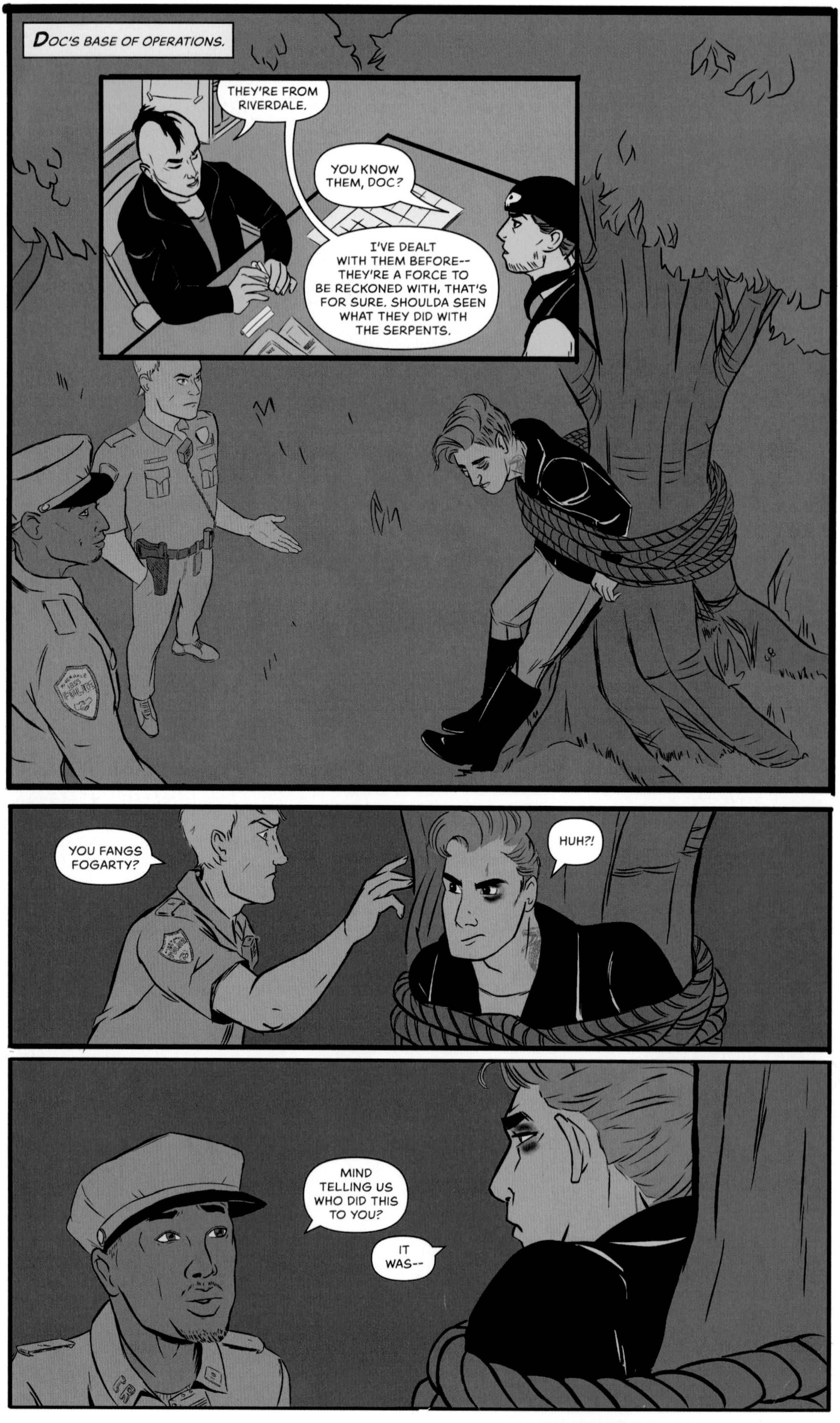
DOC'S BASE OF OPERATIONS.
THEY'RE FROM RIVERDALE.
YOU KNOW THEM, DOC?
I'VE DEALT WITH THEM BEFORE-- THEY'RE A FORCE TO BE RECKONED WITH, THAT'S FOR SURE. SHOULDA SEEN WHAT THEY DID WITH THE SERPENTS.
YOU FANGS FOGARTY?
HUH?!
MIND TELLING US WHO DID THIS TO YOU?
IT WAS--

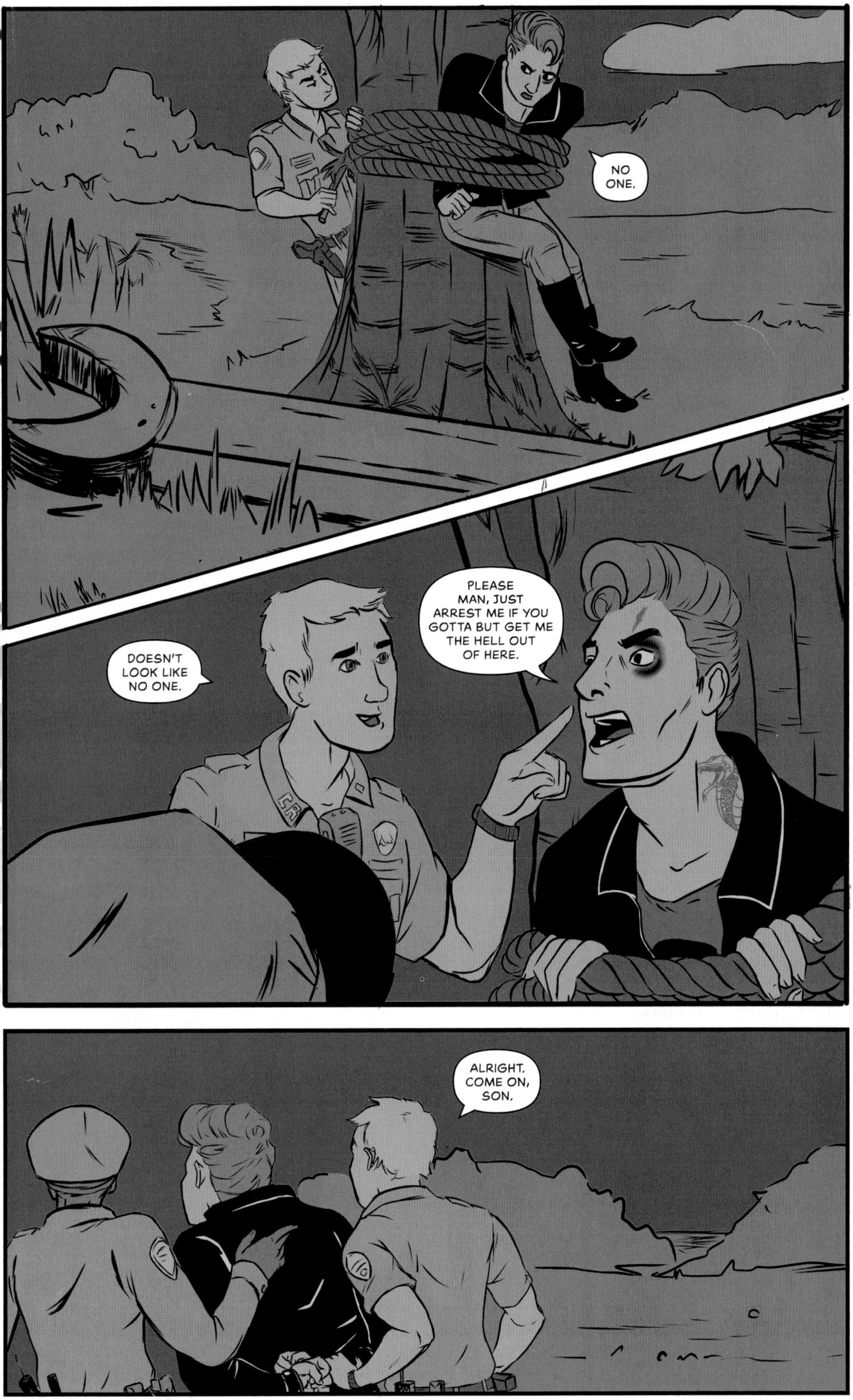
NO ONE.
DOESN'T LOOK LIKE NO ONE.
PLEASE MAN, JUST ARREST ME IF YOU GOTTA BUT GET ME THE HELL OUT OF HERE.
ALRIGHT. COME ON, SON.

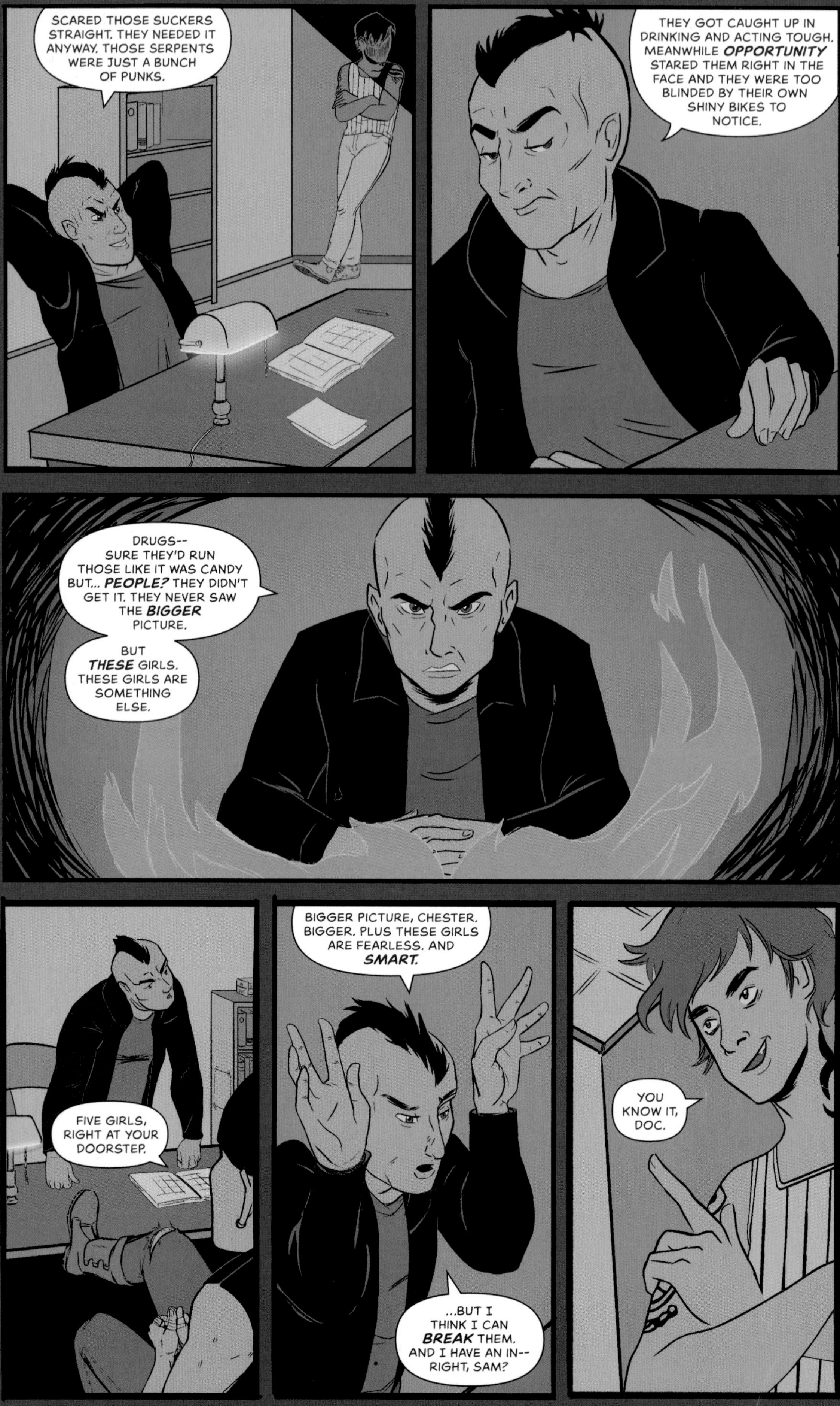
SCARED THOSE SUCKERS STRAIGHT. THEY NEEDED IT ANYWAY. THOSE SERPENTS WERE JUST A BUNCH OF PUNKS.
THEY GOT CAUGHT UP IN DRINKING AND ACTING TOUGH. MEANWHILE OPPORTUNITY STARED THEM RIGHT IN THE FACE AND THEY WERE TOO BLINDED BY THEIR OWN SHINY BIKES TO NOTICE.
DRUGS-- SURE THEY'D RUN THOSE LIKE IT WAS CANDY BUT... PEOPLE? THEY DIDN'T GET IT. THEY NEVER SAW THE BIGGER PICTURE.
BUT THESE GIRLS. THESE GIRLS ARE SOMETHING ELSE.
FIVE GIRLS, RIGHT AT YOUR DOORSTEP.
BIGGER PICTURE, CHESTER. BIGGER. PLUS THESE GIRLS ARE FEARLESS. AND SMART.
...BUT I THINK I CAN BREAK THEM. AND I HAVE AN IN-- RIGHT, SAM?
YOU KNOW IT, DOC.

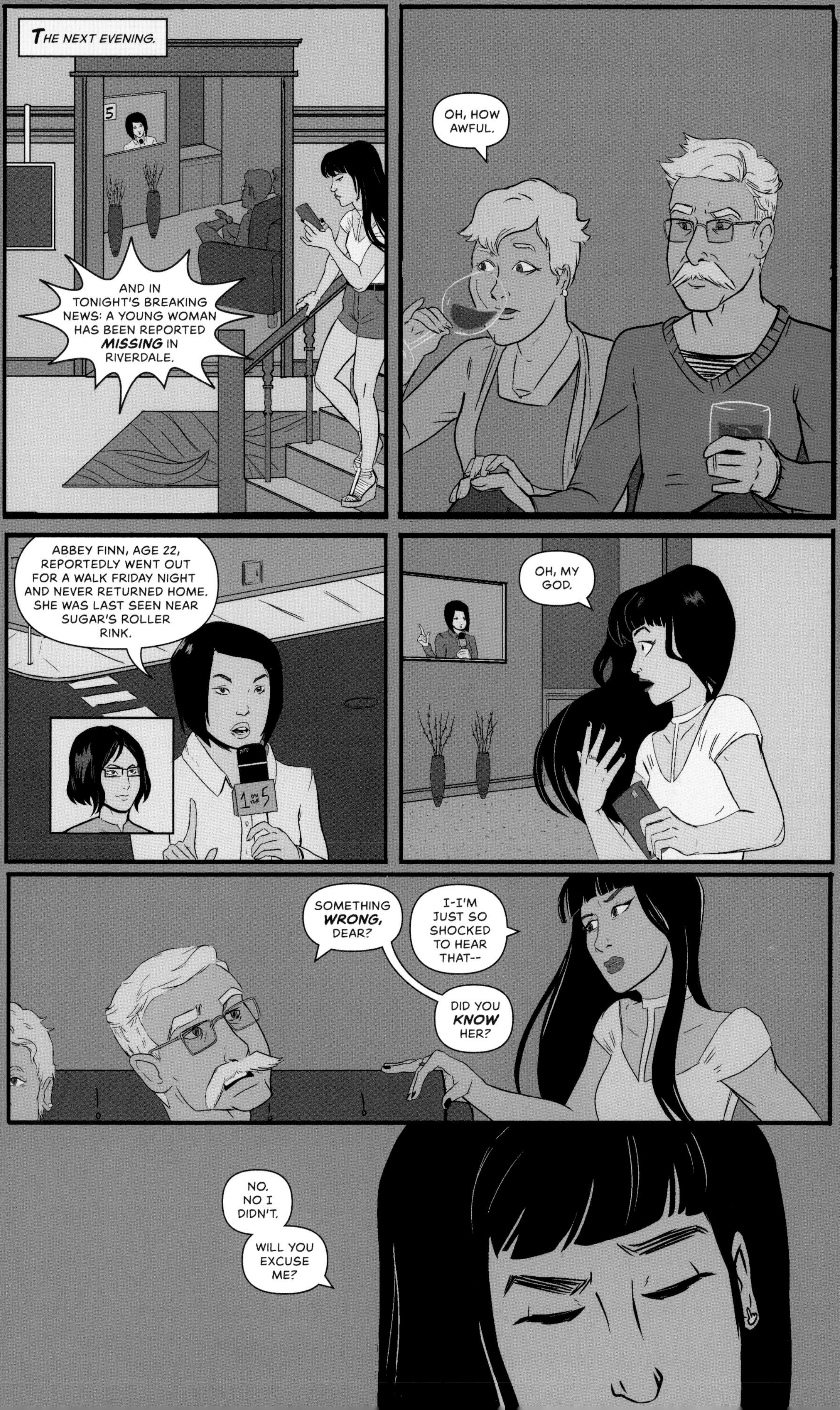
THE NEXT EVENING.
5
AND IN TONIGHT'S BREAKING NEWS: A YOUNG WOMAN HAS BEEN REPORTED MISSING IN RIVERDALE.
OH, HOW AWFUL.
ABBEY FINN, AGE 22, REPORTEDLY WENT OUT FOR A WALK FRIDAY NIGHT AND NEVER RETURNED HOME. SHE WAS LAST SEEN NEAR SUGAR'S ROLLER RINK.
1 ON THE 5
OH, MY GOD.
SOMETHING WRONG, DEAR?
I-I'M JUST SO SHOCKED TO HEAR THAT--
DID YOU KNOW HER?
NO. NO I DIDN'T.
WILL YOU EXCUSE ME?

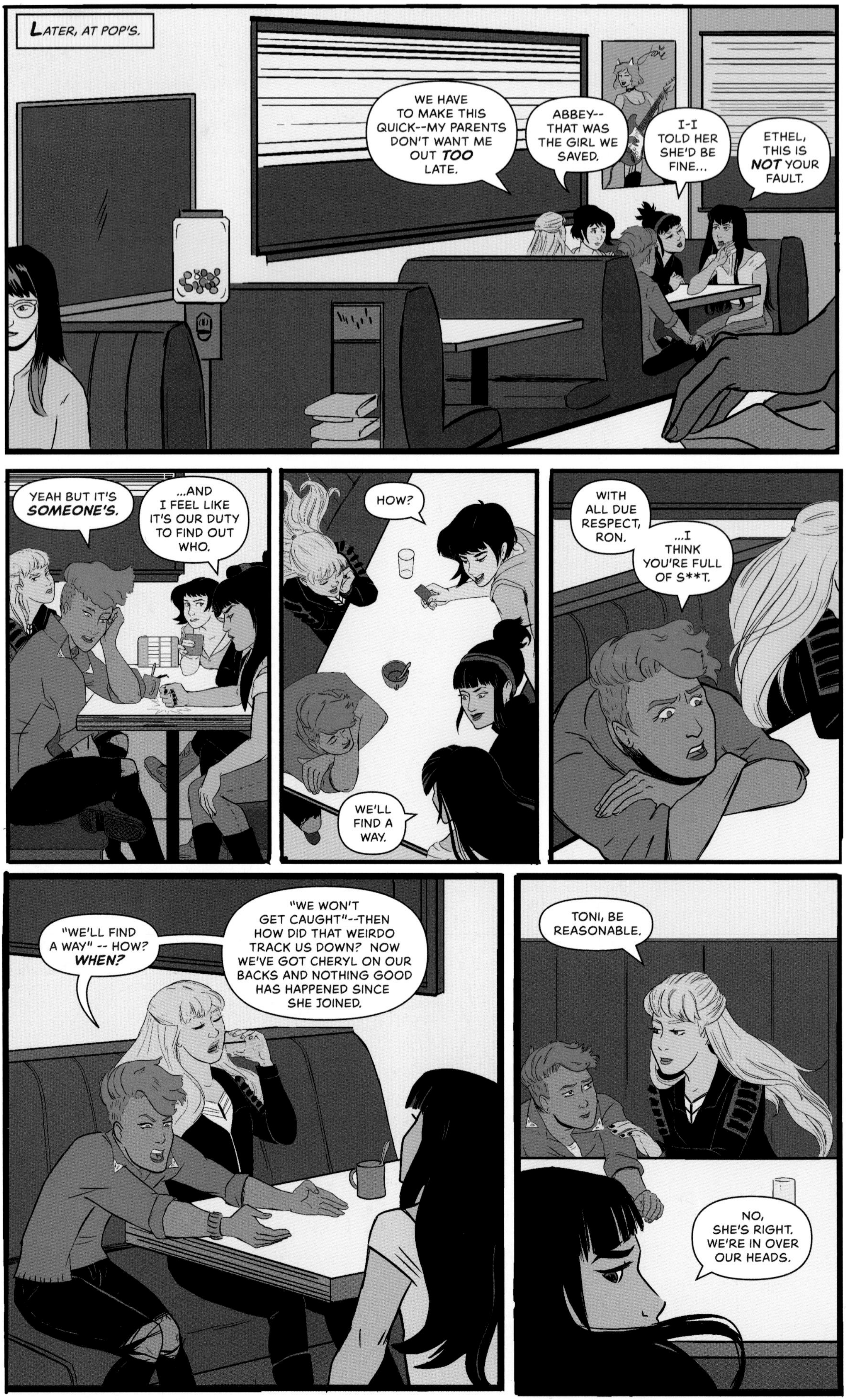
LATER, AT POP'S.
WE HAVE TO MAKE THIS QUICK--MY PARENTS DON'T WANT ME OUT **TOO** LATE.
ABBEY-- THAT WAS THE GIRL WE SAVED.
I-I TOLD HER SHE'D BE FINE...
ETHEL, THIS IS **NOT** YOUR FAULT.
YEAH BUT IT'S **SOMEONE'S.**
...AND I FEEL LIKE IT'S OUR DUTY TO FIND OUT WHO.
HOW?
WE'LL FIND A WAY.
WITH ALL DUE RESPECT, RON.
...I THINK YOU'RE FULL OF S**T.
"WE'LL FIND A WAY" -- HOW? **WHEN?**
"WE WON'T GET CAUGHT"--THEN HOW DID THAT WEIRDO TRACK US DOWN? NOW WE'VE GOT CHERYL ON OUR BACKS AND NOTHING GOOD HAS HAPPENED SINCE SHE JOINED.
TONI, BE REASONABLE.
NO, SHE'S RIGHT. WE'RE IN OVER OUR HEADS.

AND NOW SOMEONE WE THOUGHT WE HELPED IS MISSING. THIS IS **ALL** WRONG.

RONNIE...

...YOU WANT TO GIVE UP NOW? IS THAT WHAT YOU'RE SAYING?

SOMEONE'S IN TROUBLE AND WE'RE GOING TO TURN OUR BACKS ON HER BECAUSE THE GOING GOT TOUGH? I THOUGHT THIS WAS ABOUT MORE THAN THE SERPENTS.

WE GOT SO CAUGHT UP IN OUR OWN VICTORY WE DIDN'T NOTICE THAT SHE WALKED AWAY. BETTY, **WE SCREWED UP.**

AND NOW WE HAVE TO MAKE IT **RIGHT.** JUST LIKE YOU SAID.

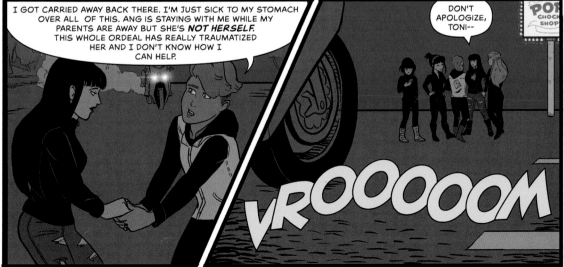

I GOT CARRIED AWAY BACK THERE. I'M JUST SICK TO MY STOMACH OVER ALL OF THIS. ANG IS STAYING WITH ME WHILE MY PARENTS ARE AWAY BUT SHE'S **NOT HERSELF.** THIS WHOLE ORDEAL HAS REALLY TRAUMATIZED HER AND I DON'T KNOW HOW I CAN HELP.

DON'T APOLOGIZE, TONI--

VROOOOOM

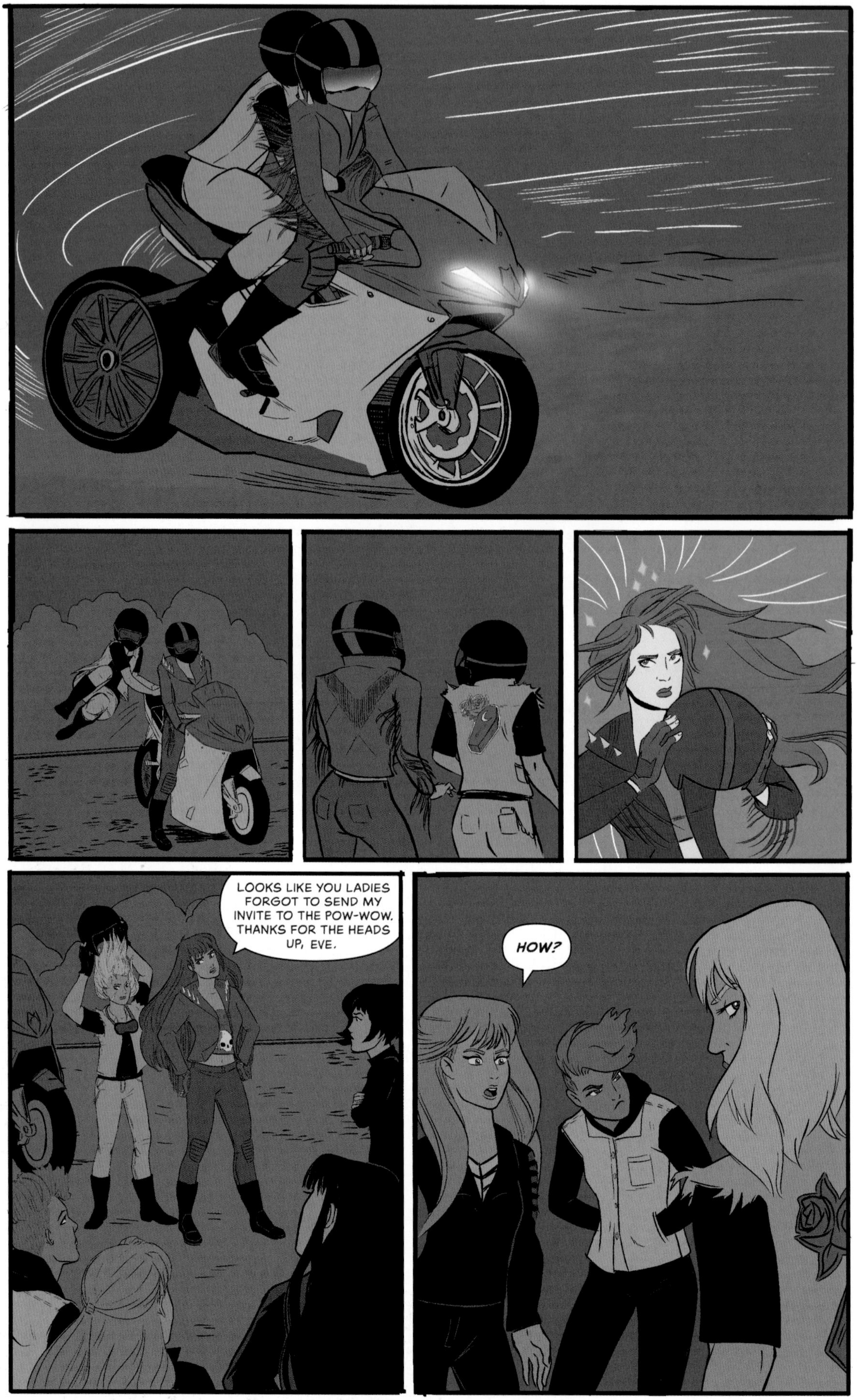
LOOKS LIKE YOU LADIES FORGOT TO SEND MY INVITE TO THE POW-WOW. THANKS FOR THE HEADS UP, EVE.
HOW?

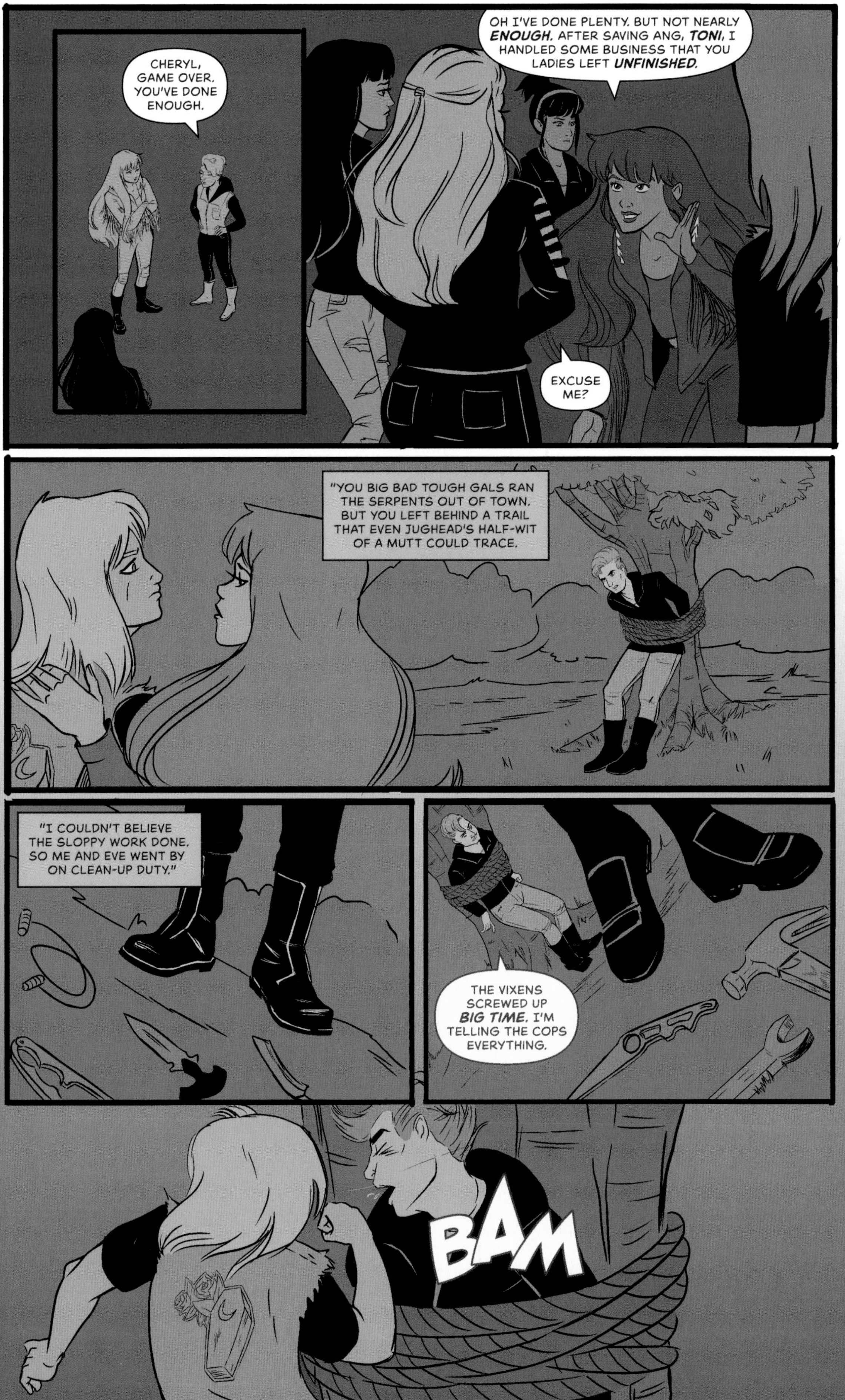
CHERYL, GAME OVER. YOU'VE DONE ENOUGH.
OH I'VE DONE PLENTY. BUT NOT NEARLY ENOUGH. AFTER SAVING ANG, TONI, I HANDLED SOME BUSINESS THAT YOU LADIES LEFT UNFINISHED.
EXCUSE ME?
"YOU BIG BAD TOUGH GALS RAN THE SERPENTS OUT OF TOWN. BUT YOU LEFT BEHIND A TRAIL THAT EVEN JUGHEAD'S HALF-WIT OF A MUTT COULD TRACE.
"I COULDN'T BELIEVE THE SLOPPY WORK DONE, SO ME AND EVE WENT BY ON CLEAN-UP DUTY."
THE VIXENS SCREWED UP BIG TIME. I'M TELLING THE COPS EVERYTHING.
BAM

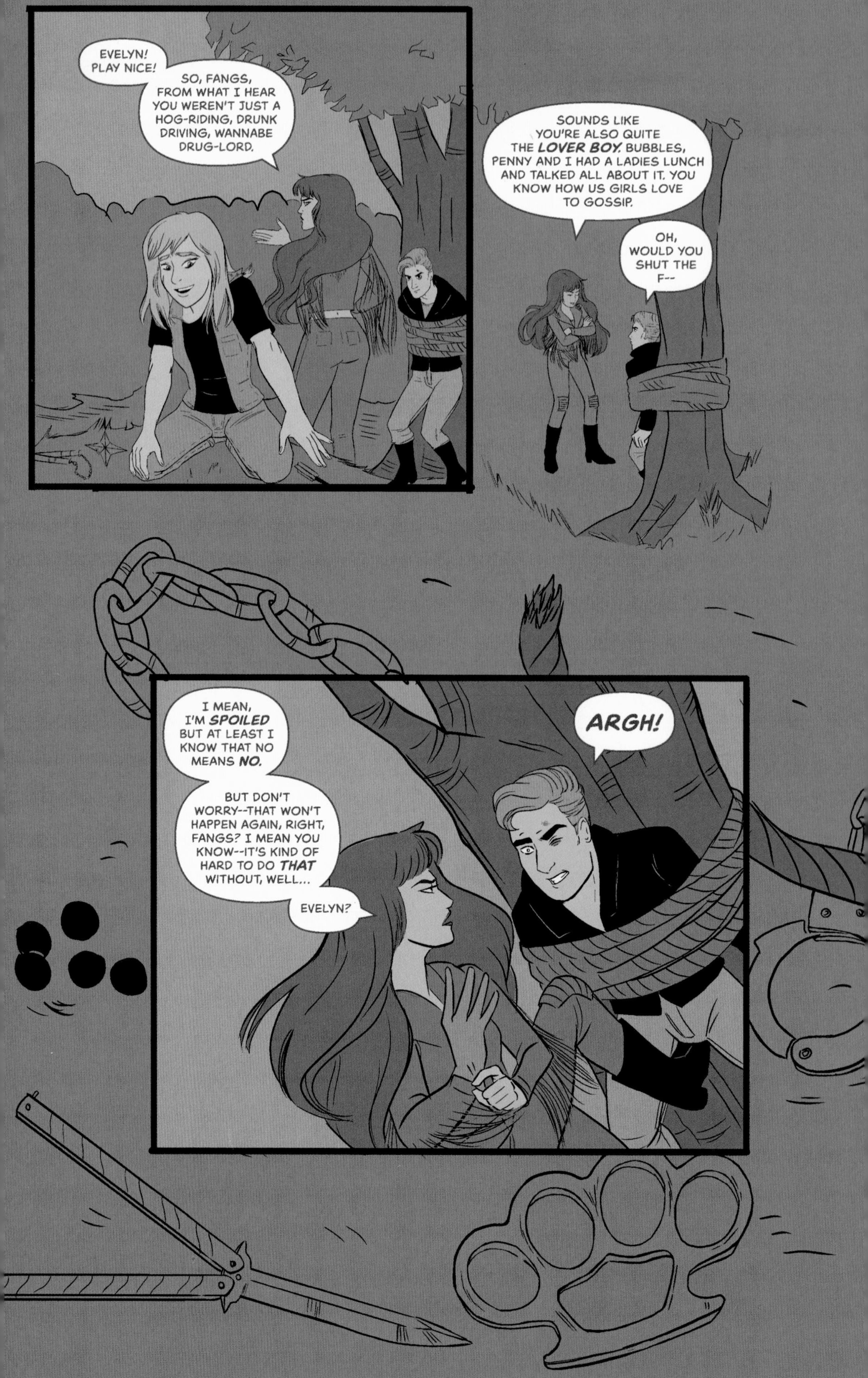
EVELYN! PLAY NICE!
SO, FANGS, FROM WHAT I HEAR YOU WEREN'T JUST A HOG-RIDING, DRUNK DRIVING, WANNABE DRUG-LORD.
SOUNDS LIKE YOU'RE ALSO QUITE THE **LOVER BOY.** BUBBLES, PENNY AND I HAD A LADIES LUNCH AND TALKED ALL ABOUT IT. YOU KNOW HOW US GIRLS LOVE TO GOSSIP.
OH, WOULD YOU SHUT THE F--
I MEAN, I'M **SPOILED** BUT AT LEAST I KNOW THAT NO MEANS **NO.**
BUT DON'T WORRY--THAT WON'T HAPPEN AGAIN, RIGHT, FANGS? I MEAN YOU KNOW--IT'S KIND OF HARD TO DO **THAT** WITHOUT, WELL...
ARGH!
EVELYN?

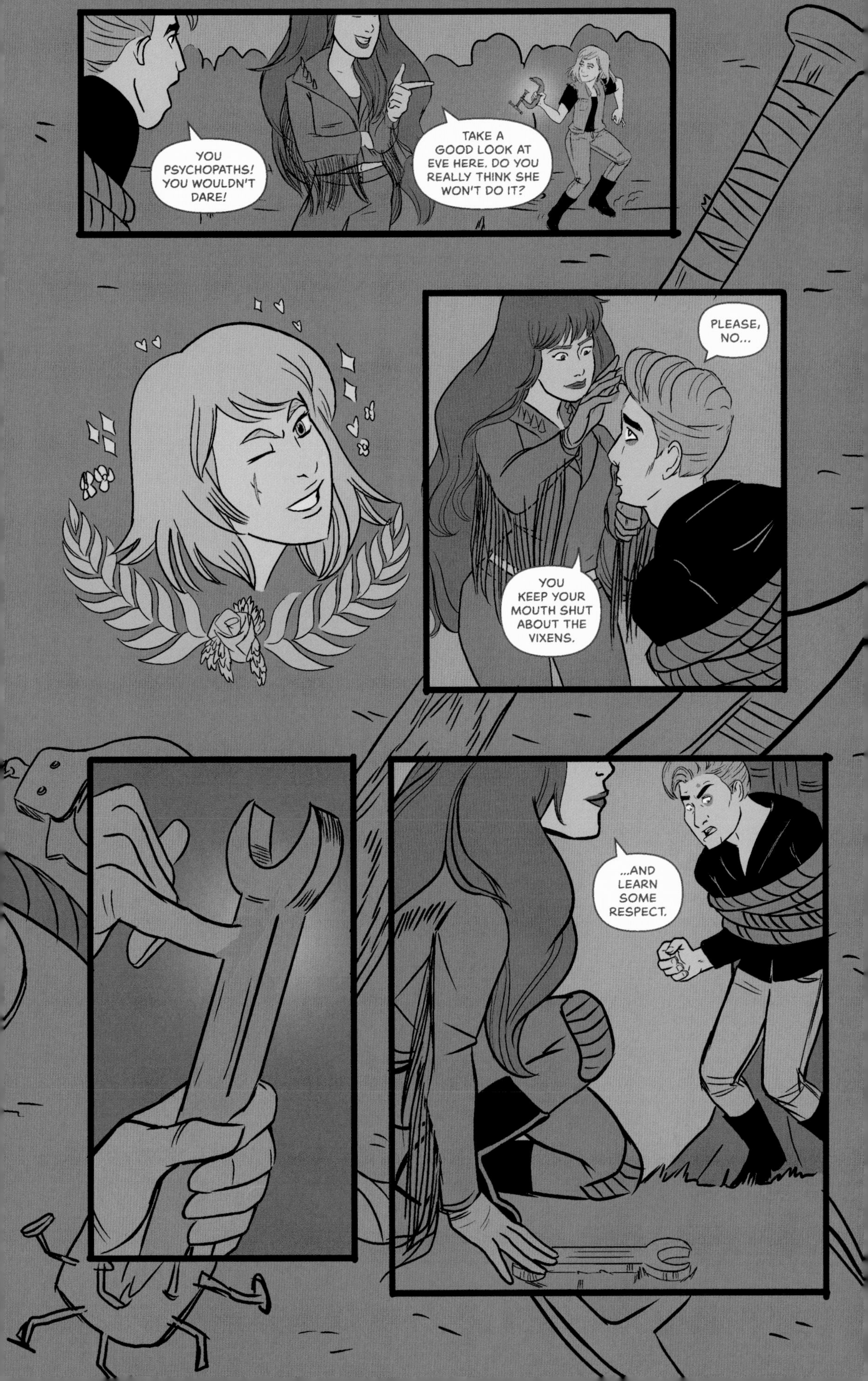
YOU PSYCHOPATHS! YOU WOULDN'T DARE!
TAKE A GOOD LOOK AT EVE HERE. DO YOU REALLY THINK SHE WON'T DO IT?
PLEASE, NO...
YOU KEEP YOUR MOUTH SHUT ABOUT THE VIXENS.
...AND LEARN SOME RESPECT.

JESUS, CHERYL.

FACE IT, LADIES. YOU **NEED** ME. SO NOW ABOUT THAT EX OF YOURS-- WHERE IS SHE?

ANG WENT TO A KICKBOXING CLASS I SIGNED HER UP FOR.

YOU LET HER GO OUT **ALONE?!** YOU GIRLS REALLY **DON'T** KNOW WHAT YOU'RE DOING.

INSTEAD OF INSULTING US WHY DON'T YOU TRY WORKING **WITH US?**

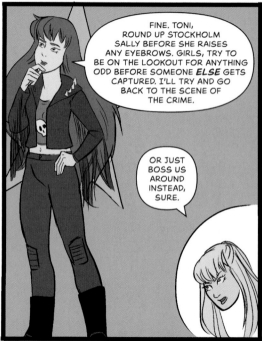

FINE, TONI, ROUND UP STOCKHOLM SALLY BEFORE SHE RAISES ANY EYEBROWS. GIRLS, TRY TO BE ON THE LOOKOUT FOR ANYTHING ODD BEFORE SOMEONE **ELSE** GETS CAPTURED. I'LL TRY AND GO BACK TO THE SCENE OF THE CRIME.

OR JUST BOSS US AROUND INSTEAD, SURE.

YOU MAKE IT **REALLY** HARD TO LIKE YOU, BLOSSOM.

GOOD.

NOW MOVE IT.

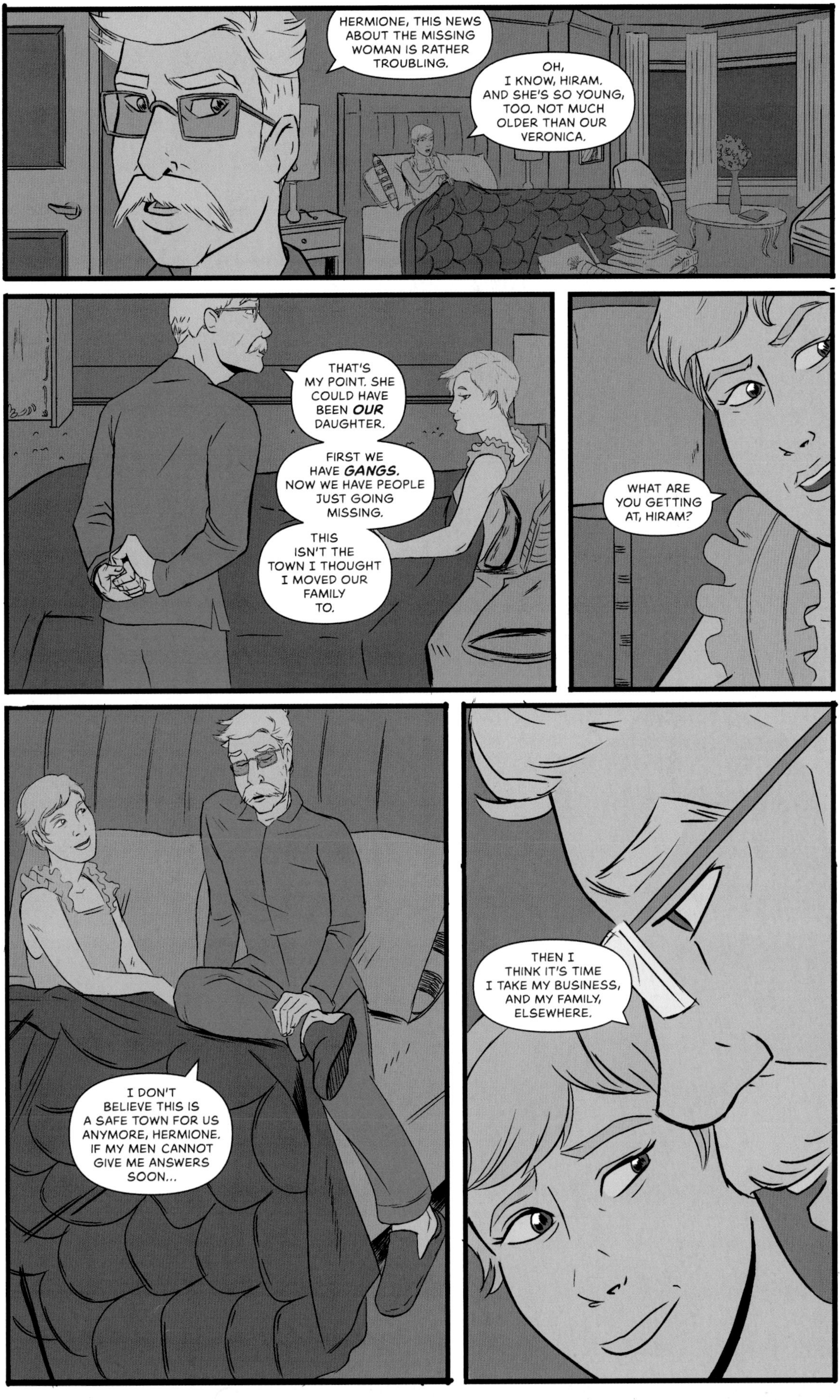
HERMIONE, THIS NEWS ABOUT THE MISSING WOMAN IS RATHER TROUBLING.
OH, I KNOW, HIRAM. AND SHE'S SO YOUNG, TOO. NOT MUCH OLDER THAN OUR VERONICA.
THAT'S MY POINT. SHE COULD HAVE BEEN **OUR** DAUGHTER.
FIRST WE HAVE **GANGS.** NOW WE HAVE PEOPLE JUST GOING MISSING.
THIS ISN'T THE TOWN I THOUGHT I MOVED OUR FAMILY TO.
WHAT ARE YOU GETTING AT, HIRAM?
I DON'T BELIEVE THIS IS A SAFE TOWN FOR US ANYMORE, HERMIONE. IF MY MEN CANNOT GIVE ME ANSWERS SOON...
THEN I THINK IT'S TIME I TAKE MY BUSINESS, AND MY FAMILY, ELSEWHERE.

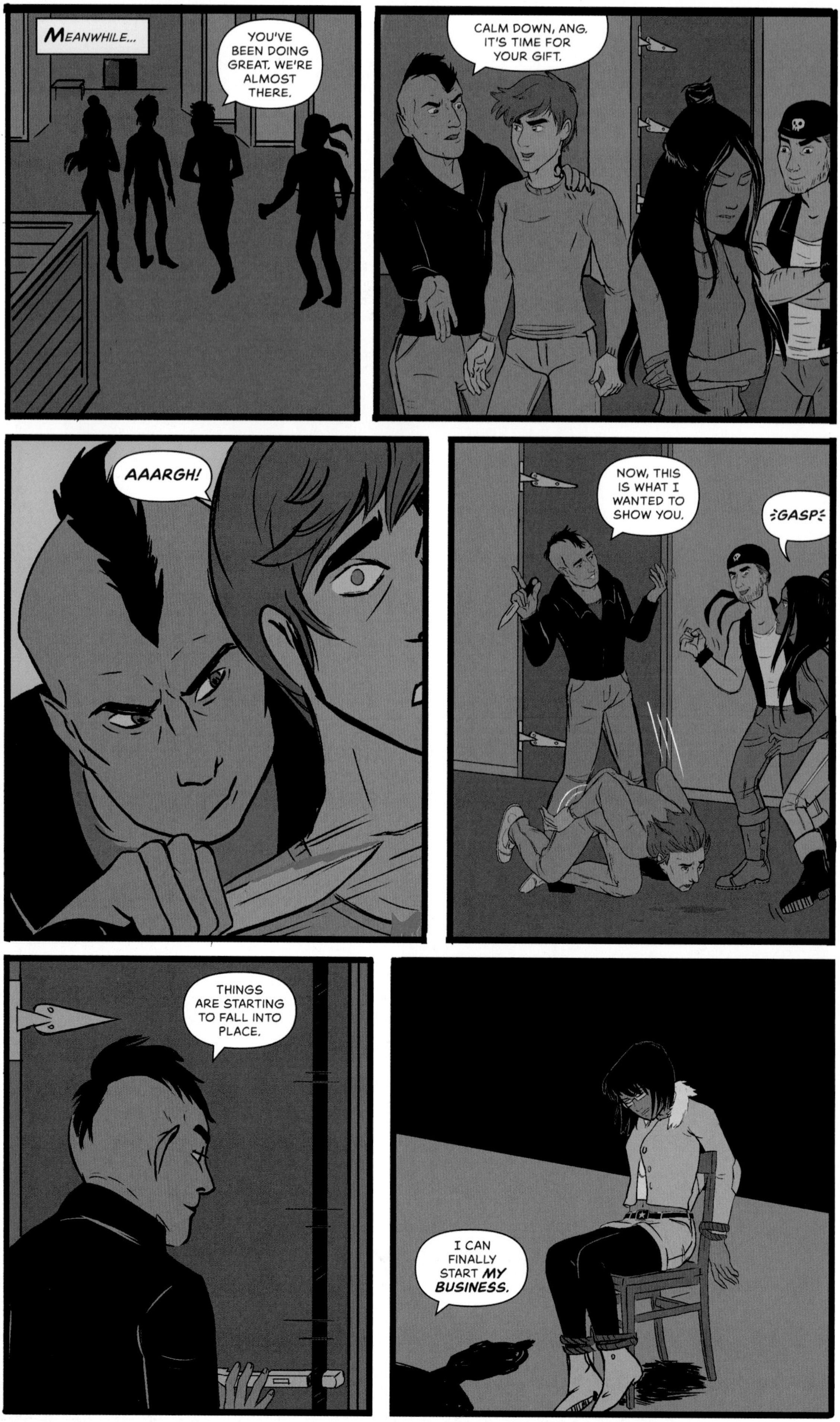
MEANWHILE...
YOU'VE BEEN DOING GREAT. WE'RE ALMOST THERE.
CALM DOWN, ANG. IT'S TIME FOR YOUR GIFT.
AAARGH!
NOW, THIS IS WHAT I WANTED TO SHOW YOU.
GASP
THINGS ARE STARTING TO FALL INTO PLACE.
I CAN FINALLY START MY BUSINESS.

to be continued...

Chapter Seven

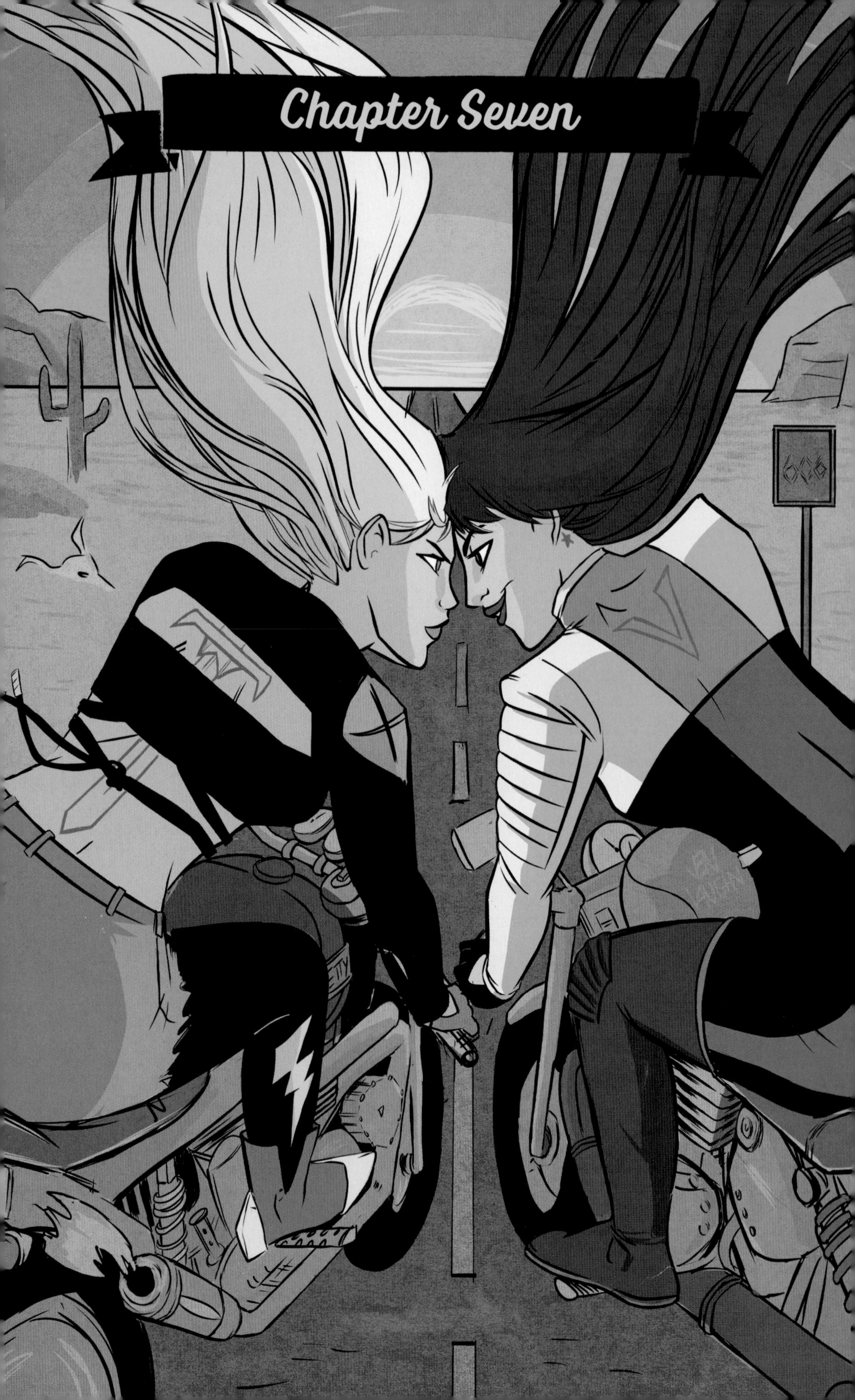

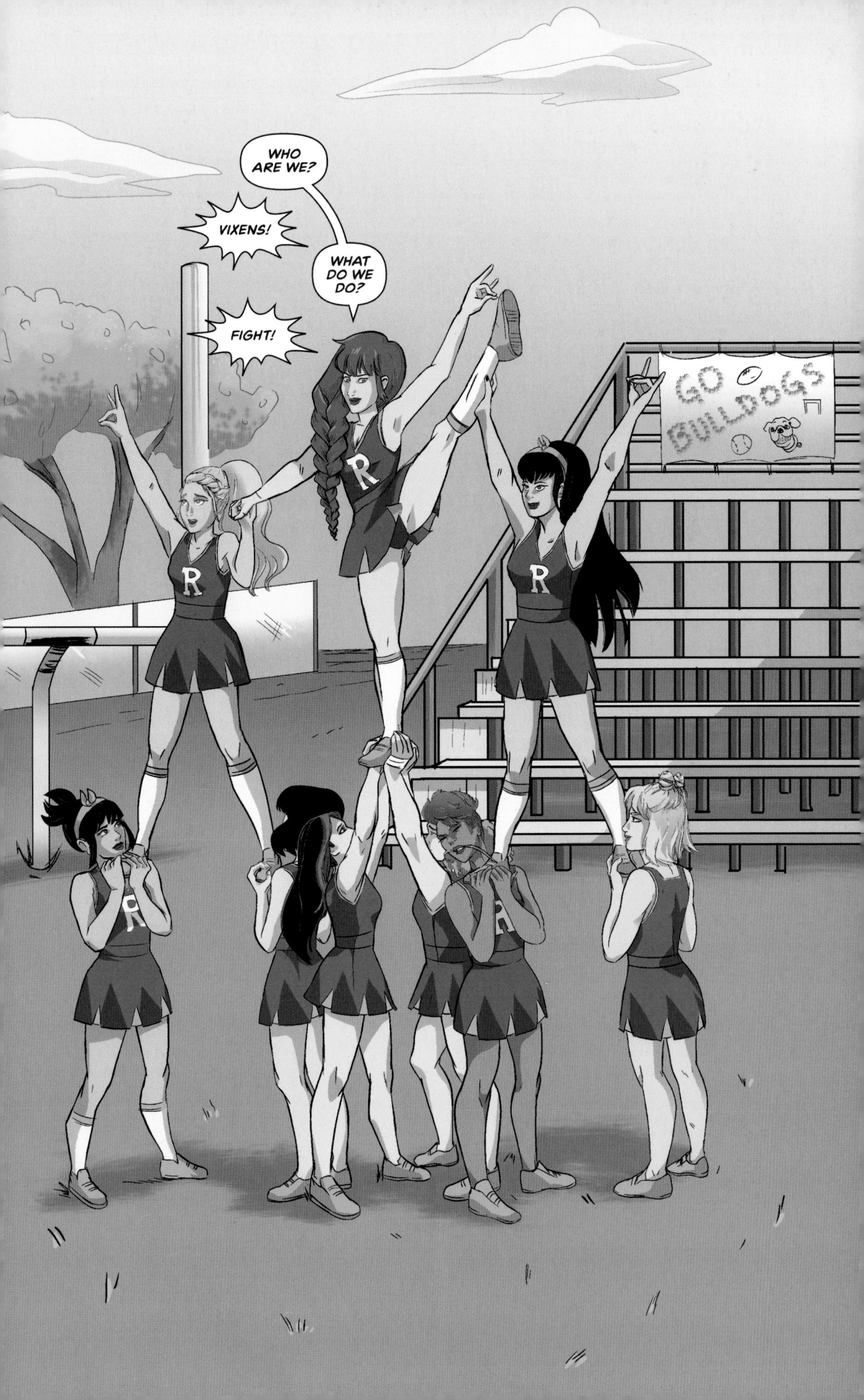
WHO ARE WE?
VIXENS!
WHAT DO WE DO?
FIGHT!
GO BULLDOGS

MEANWHILE, BORDER OF RIVERDALE/PEMBROOKE.

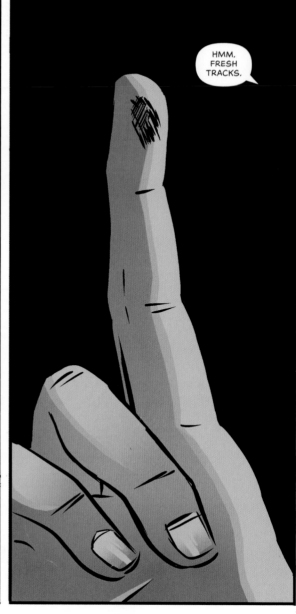

HMM. FRESH TRACKS.

GOOD PRACTICE, GIRLS. BUT, TONI, CAN YOU PUT IN A LITTLE MORE EFFORT NEXT TIME?
CHERYL THIS IS RIDICULOUS. I DO NOT WANT TO BE A CHEERLEADER.
BUT WE DO WANT TO GET TO KNOW EACH OTHER BETTER. AND WHAT BETTER WAY TO FORCE CAMARADERIE AMONGST US VIXENS?
THEN WHY NOT HAVE US ALL JOIN YOUR DERBY LEAGUE, BLOSSOM?
MAYBE YOU'RE NOT TOUGH ENOUGH.
I'M HEAD CHEERLEADER. WHAT I SAY GOES AND NO ONE QUESTIONS ME.
WELL I QUESTION EVERYTHING, LIKE YOUR MOTIVES.
HOW WAS MY FORMATION?
TERRIBLE, EVE. TERRIBLE.
DAMN.

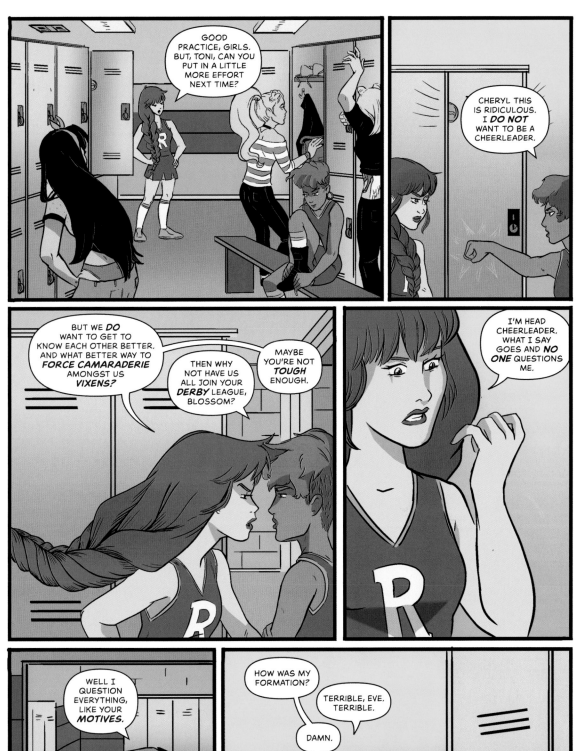

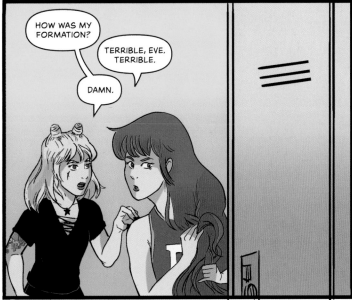

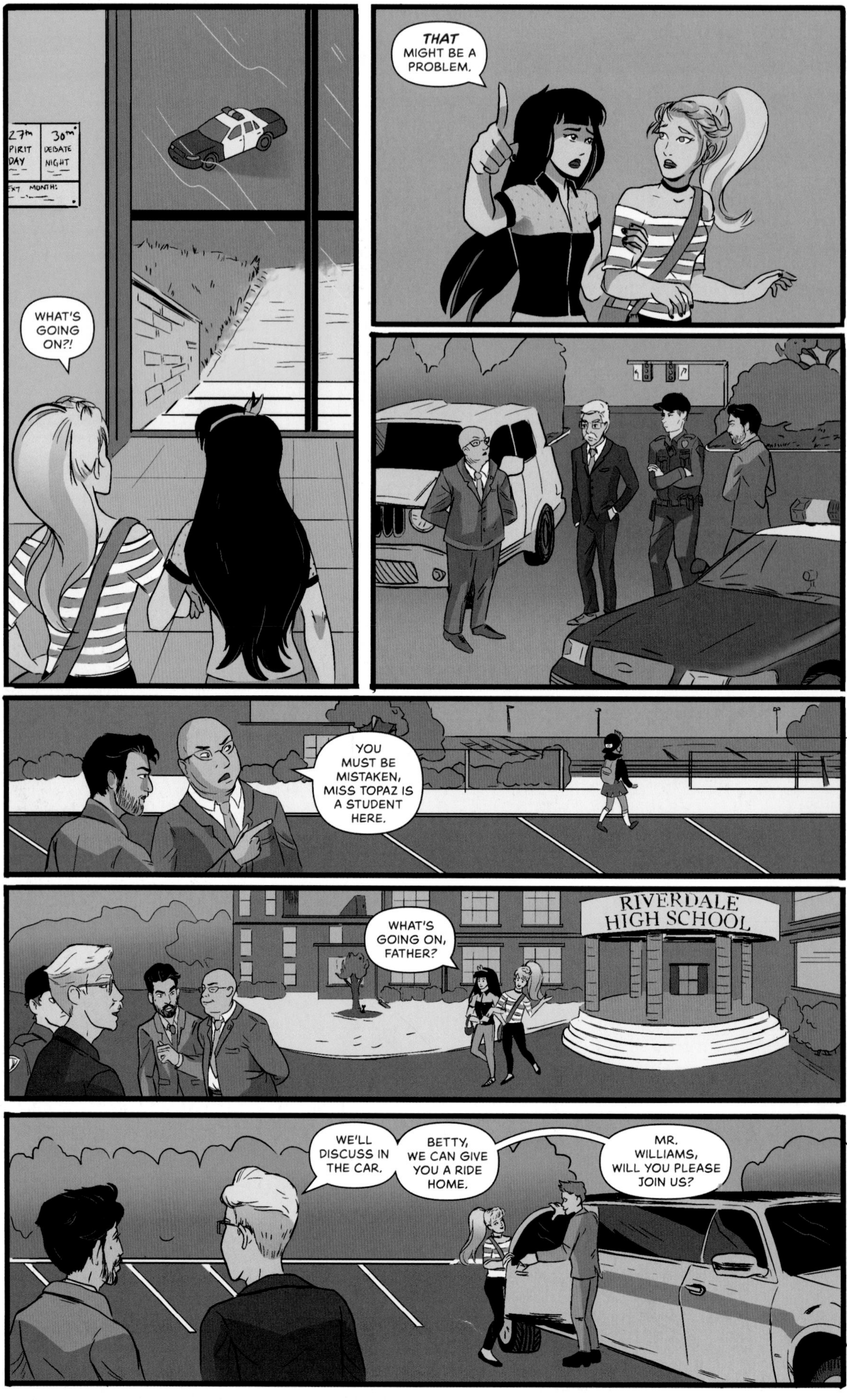
27th
30th
DEBATE
NIGHT
WHAT'S GOING ON?!
THAT MIGHT BE A PROBLEM.
YOU MUST BE MISTAKEN, MISS TOPAZ IS A STUDENT HERE.
RIVERDALE HIGH SCHOOL
WHAT'S GOING ON, FATHER?
WE'LL DISCUSS IN THE CAR.
BETTY, WE CAN GIVE YOU A RIDE HOME.
MR. WILLIAMS, WILL YOU PLEASE JOIN US?

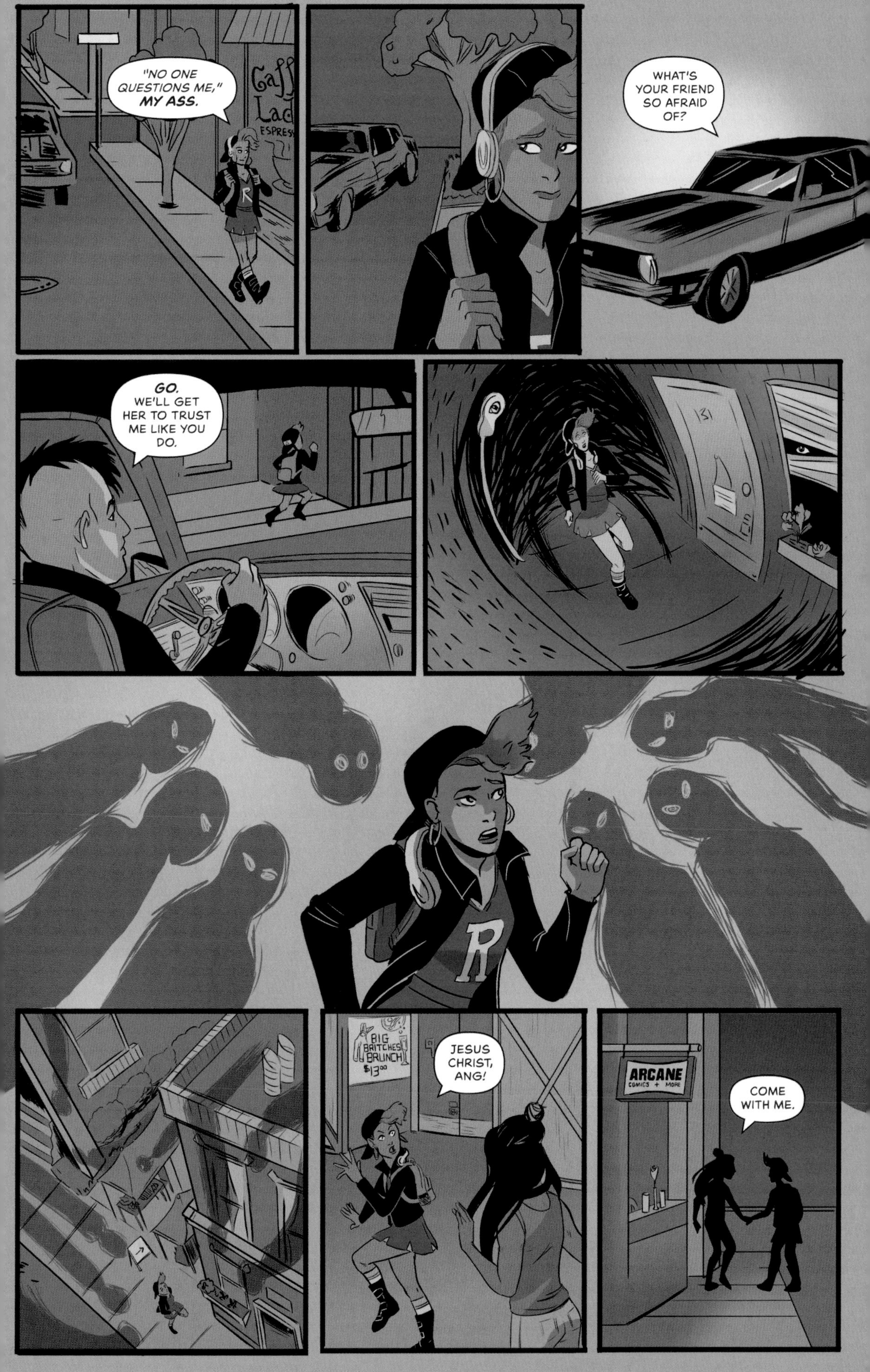
"NO ONE QUESTIONS ME," MY ASS.
Caff Lad ESPRESS
WHAT'S YOUR FRIEND SO AFRAID OF?
GO. WE'LL GET HER TO TRUST ME LIKE YOU DO.
BIG BRITCHES BRUNCH $13.00
JESUS CHRIST, ANG!
ARCANE COMICS + MORE
COME WITH ME.

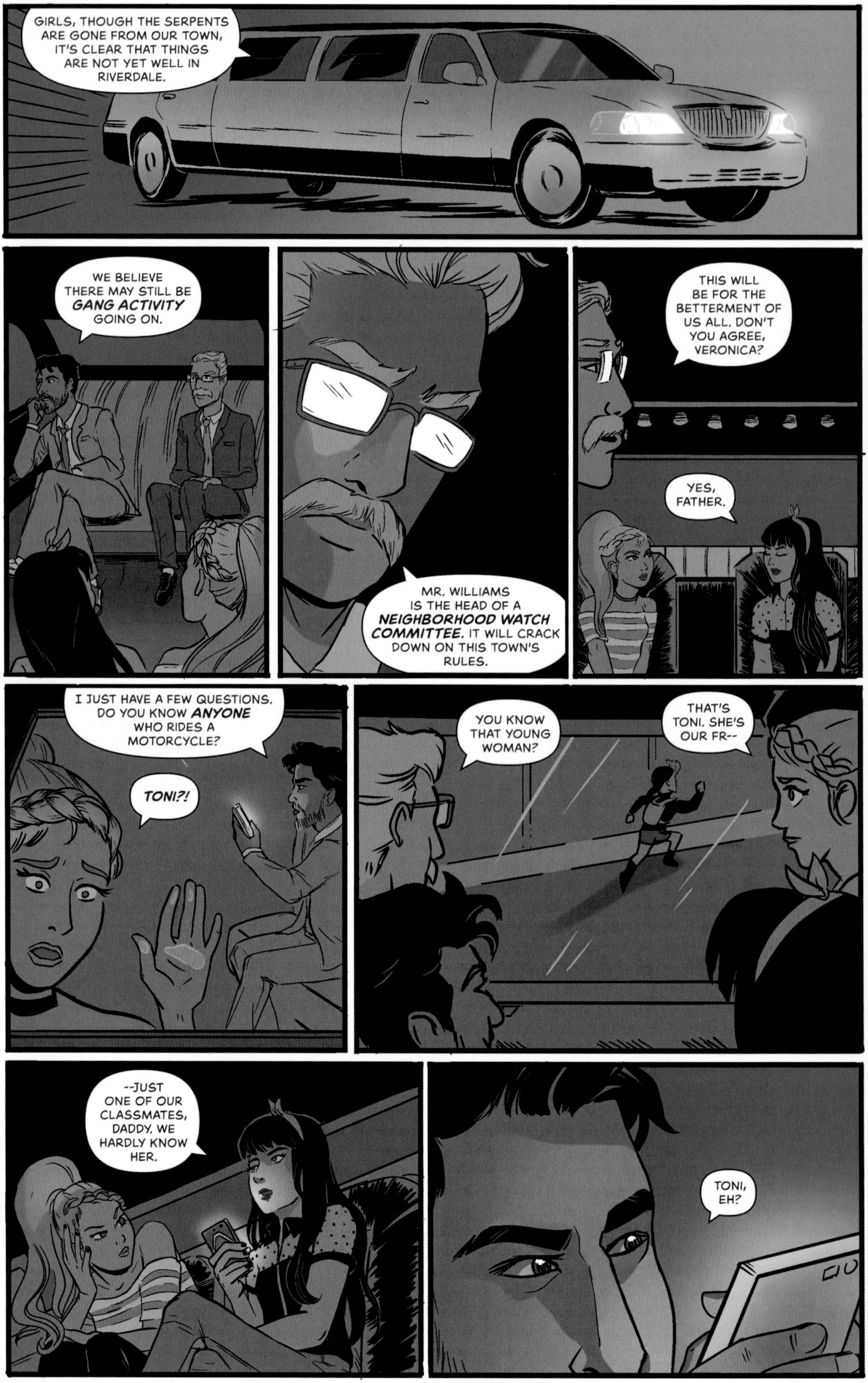
GIRLS, THOUGH THE SERPENTS ARE GONE FROM OUR TOWN, IT'S CLEAR THAT THINGS ARE NOT YET WELL IN RIVERDALE.
WE BELIEVE THERE MAY STILL BE GANG ACTIVITY GOING ON.
MR. WILLIAMS IS THE HEAD OF A NEIGHBORHOOD WATCH COMMITTEE. IT WILL CRACK DOWN ON THIS TOWN'S RULES.
THIS WILL BE FOR THE BETTERMENT OF US ALL. DON'T YOU AGREE, VERONICA?
YES, FATHER.
I JUST HAVE A FEW QUESTIONS. DO YOU KNOW ANYONE WHO RIDES A MOTORCYCLE?
TONI?!
YOU KNOW THAT YOUNG WOMAN?
THAT'S TONI. SHE'S OUR FR--
--JUST ONE OF OUR CLASSMATES, DADDY. WE HARDLY KNOW HER.
TONI, EH?

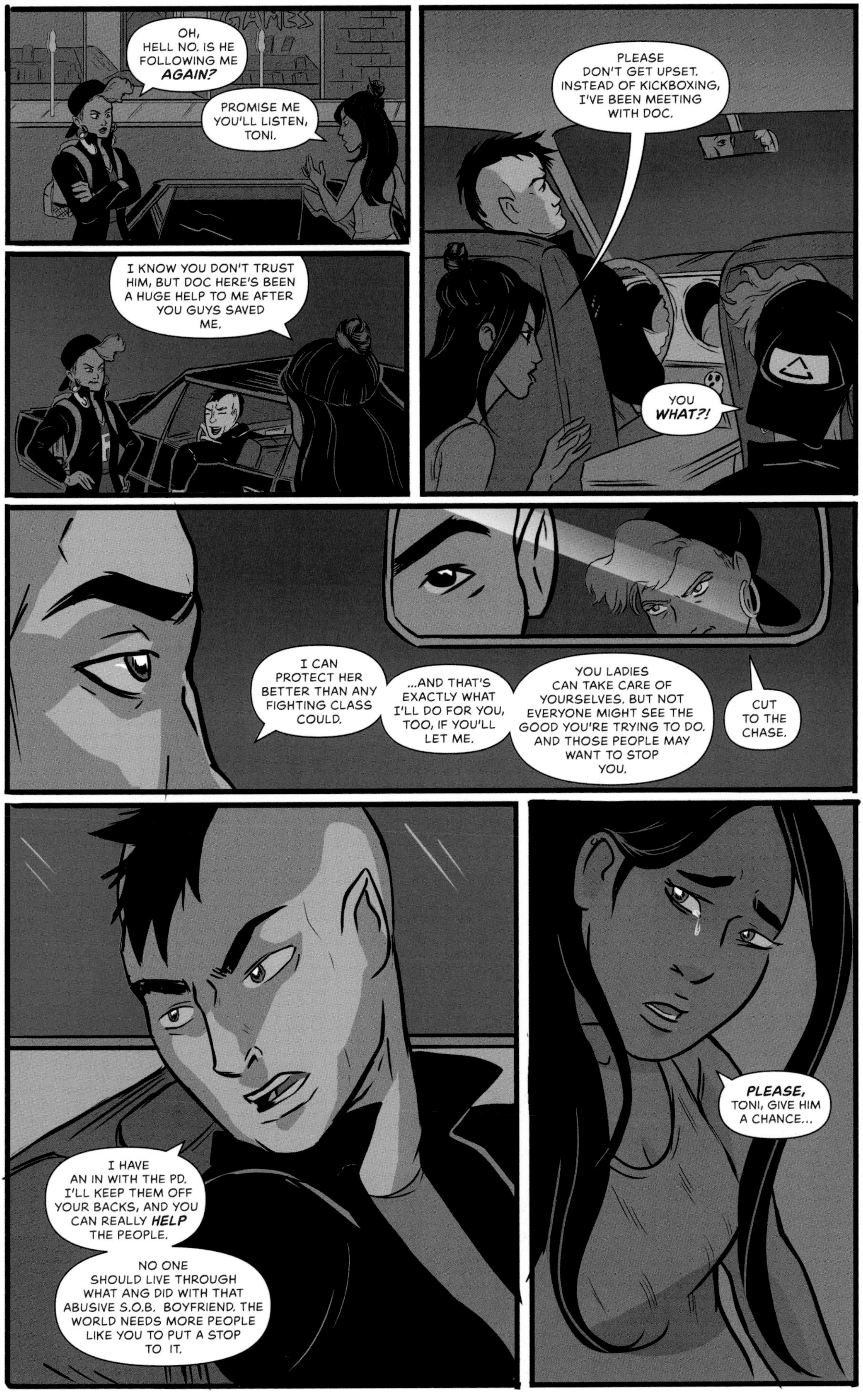
OH, HELL NO. IS HE FOLLOWING ME AGAIN?
PROMISE ME YOU'LL LISTEN, TONI.
I KNOW YOU DON'T TRUST HIM, BUT DOC HERE'S BEEN A HUGE HELP TO ME AFTER YOU GUYS SAVED ME.
PLEASE DON'T GET UPSET. INSTEAD OF KICKBOXING, I'VE BEEN MEETING WITH DOC.
YOU WHAT?!
I CAN PROTECT HER BETTER THAN ANY FIGHTING CLASS COULD.
...AND THAT'S EXACTLY WHAT I'LL DO FOR YOU, TOO, IF YOU'LL LET ME.
YOU LADIES CAN TAKE CARE OF YOURSELVES. BUT NOT EVERYONE MIGHT SEE THE GOOD YOU'RE TRYING TO DO. AND THOSE PEOPLE MAY WANT TO STOP YOU.
CUT TO THE CHASE.
I HAVE AN IN WITH THE PD. I'LL KEEP THEM OFF YOUR BACKS, AND YOU CAN REALLY HELP THE PEOPLE.
NO ONE SHOULD LIVE THROUGH WHAT ANG DID WITH THAT ABUSIVE S.O.B. BOYFRIEND. THE WORLD NEEDS MORE PEOPLE LIKE YOU TO PUT A STOP TO IT.
PLEASE, TONI, GIVE HIM A CHANCE...

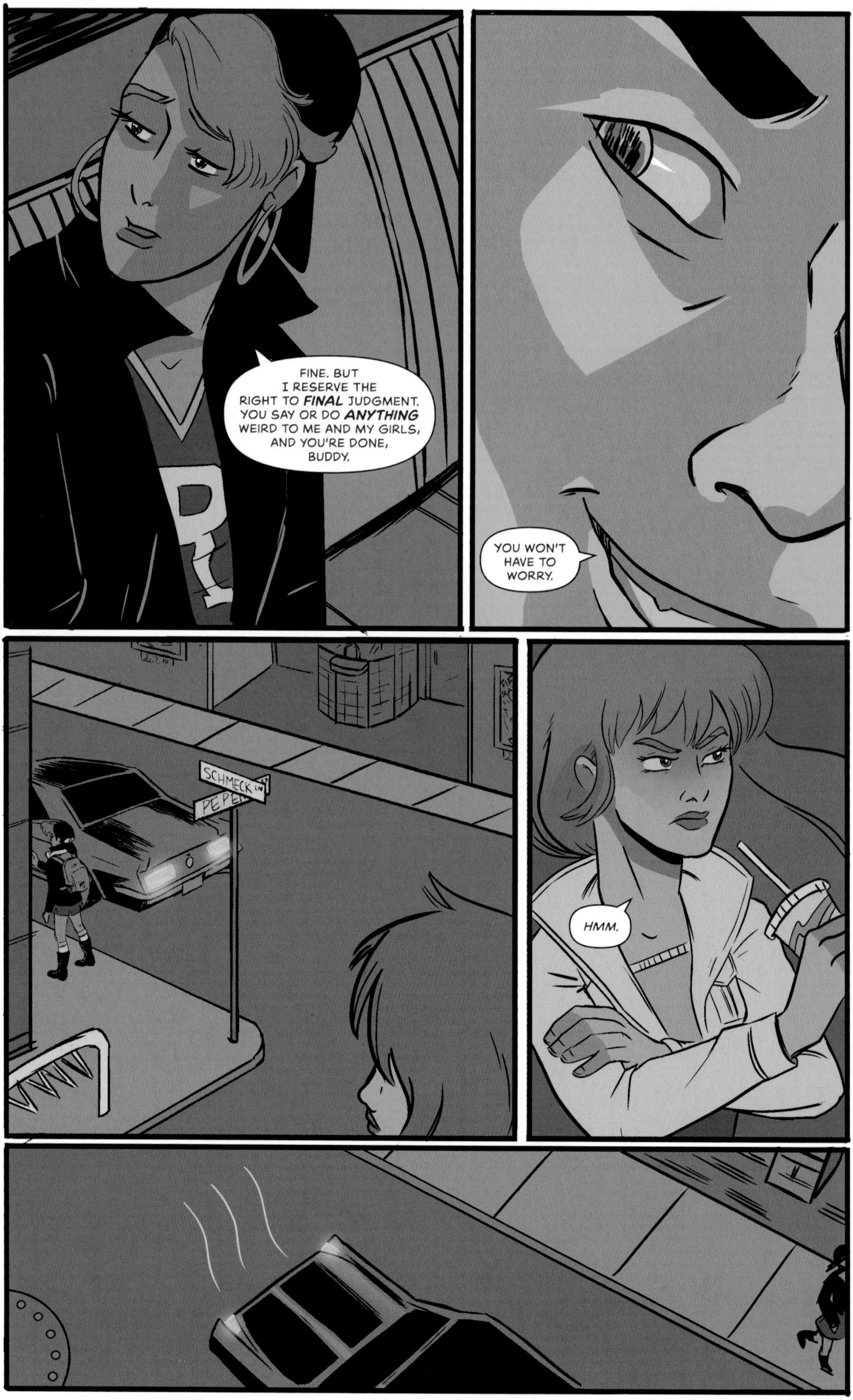
FINE. BUT I RESERVE THE RIGHT TO ***FINAL*** JUDGMENT. YOU SAY OR DO ***ANYTHING*** WEIRD TO ME AND MY GIRLS, AND YOU'RE DONE, BUDDY.
YOU WON'T HAVE TO WORRY.
SCHMECK LN
HMM.

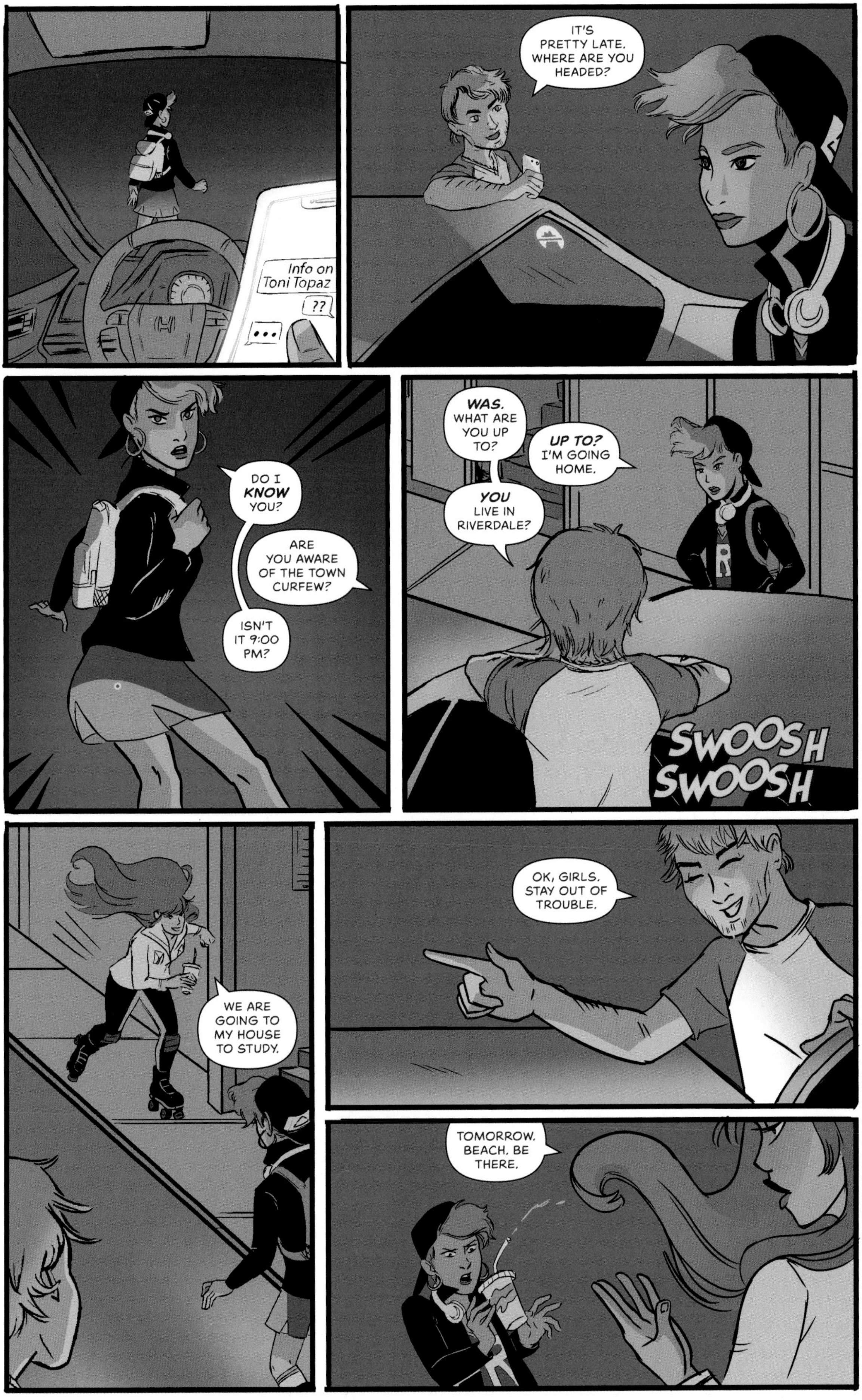
Info on Toni Topaz
??
IT'S PRETTY LATE. WHERE ARE YOU HEADED?
DO I KNOW YOU?
ARE YOU AWARE OF THE TOWN CURFEW?
ISN'T IT 9:00 PM?
WAS. WHAT ARE YOU UP TO?
UP TO? I'M GOING HOME.
YOU LIVE IN RIVERDALE?
SWOOSH SWOOSH
WE ARE GOING TO MY HOUSE TO STUDY.
OK, GIRLS. STAY OUT OF TROUBLE.
TOMORROW. BEACH. BE THERE.

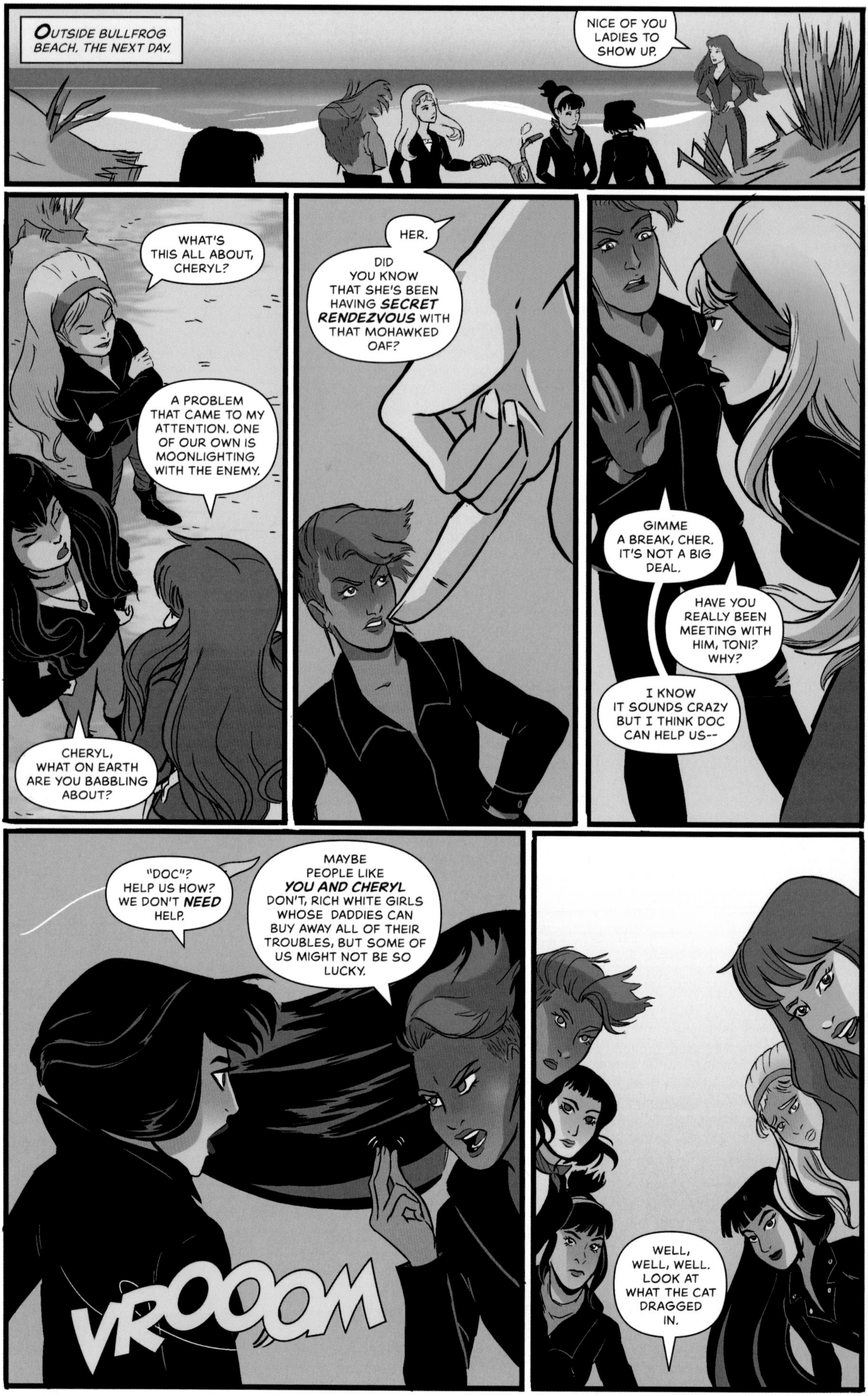
OUTSIDE BULLFROG BEACH, THE NEXT DAY.
NICE OF YOU LADIES TO SHOW UP.
WHAT'S THIS ALL ABOUT, CHERYL?
A PROBLEM THAT CAME TO MY ATTENTION. ONE OF OUR OWN IS MOONLIGHTING WITH THE ENEMY.
CHERYL, WHAT ON EARTH ARE YOU BABBLING ABOUT?
HER.
DID YOU KNOW THAT SHE'S BEEN HAVING SECRET RENDEZVOUS WITH THAT MOHAWKED OAF?
GIMME A BREAK, CHER. IT'S NOT A BIG DEAL.
HAVE YOU REALLY BEEN MEETING WITH HIM, TONI? WHY?
I KNOW IT SOUNDS CRAZY BUT I THINK DOC CAN HELP US--
"DOC"? HELP US HOW? WE DON'T NEED HELP.
MAYBE PEOPLE LIKE YOU AND CHERYL DON'T, RICH WHITE GIRLS WHOSE DADDIES CAN BUY AWAY ALL OF THEIR TROUBLES, BUT SOME OF US MIGHT NOT BE SO LUCKY.
VROOOM
WELL, WELL, WELL. LOOK AT WHAT THE CAT DRAGGED IN.

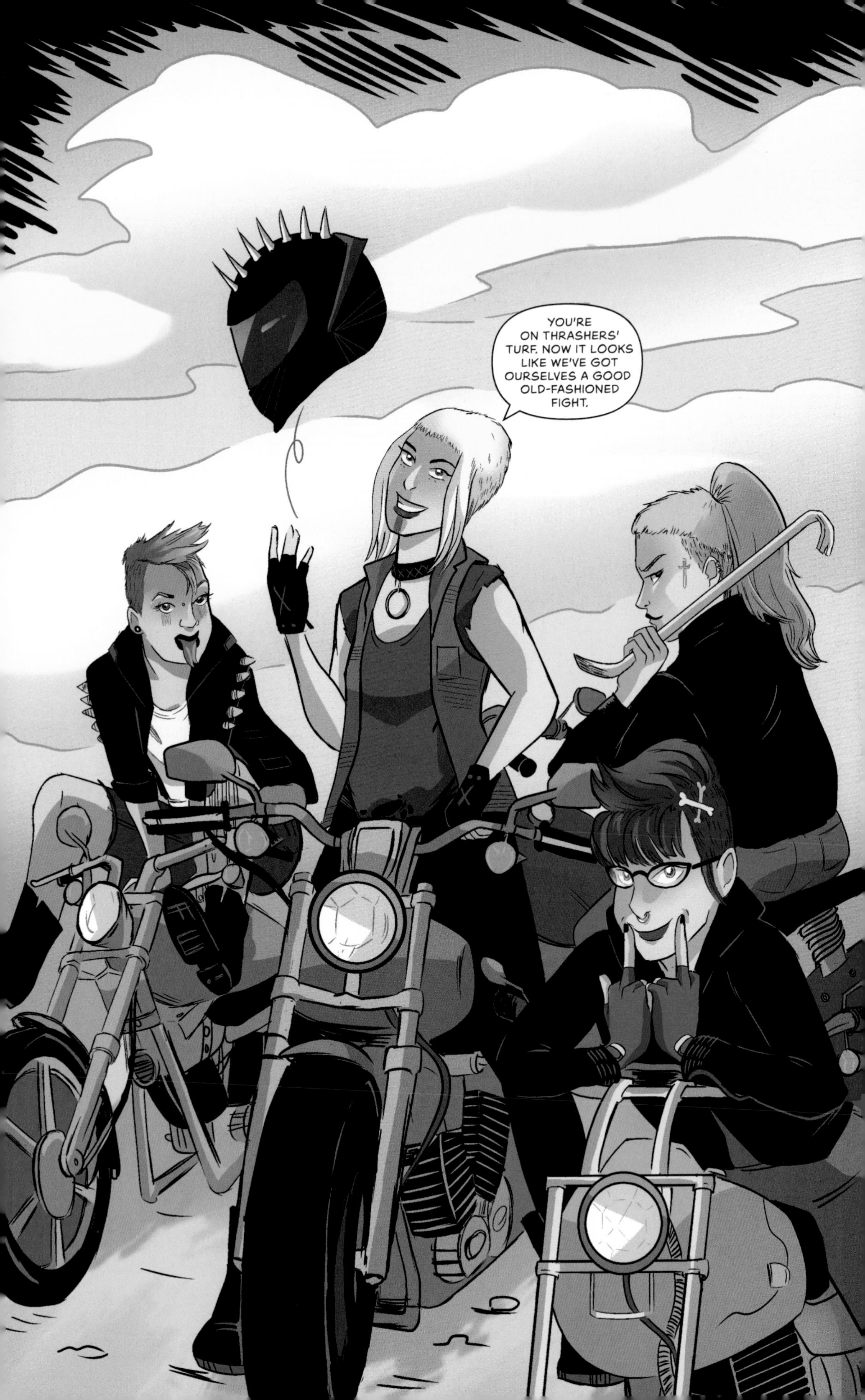
YOU'RE ON THRASHERS' TURF. NOW IT LOOKS LIKE WE'VE GOT OURSELVES A GOOD OLD-FASHIONED FIGHT.

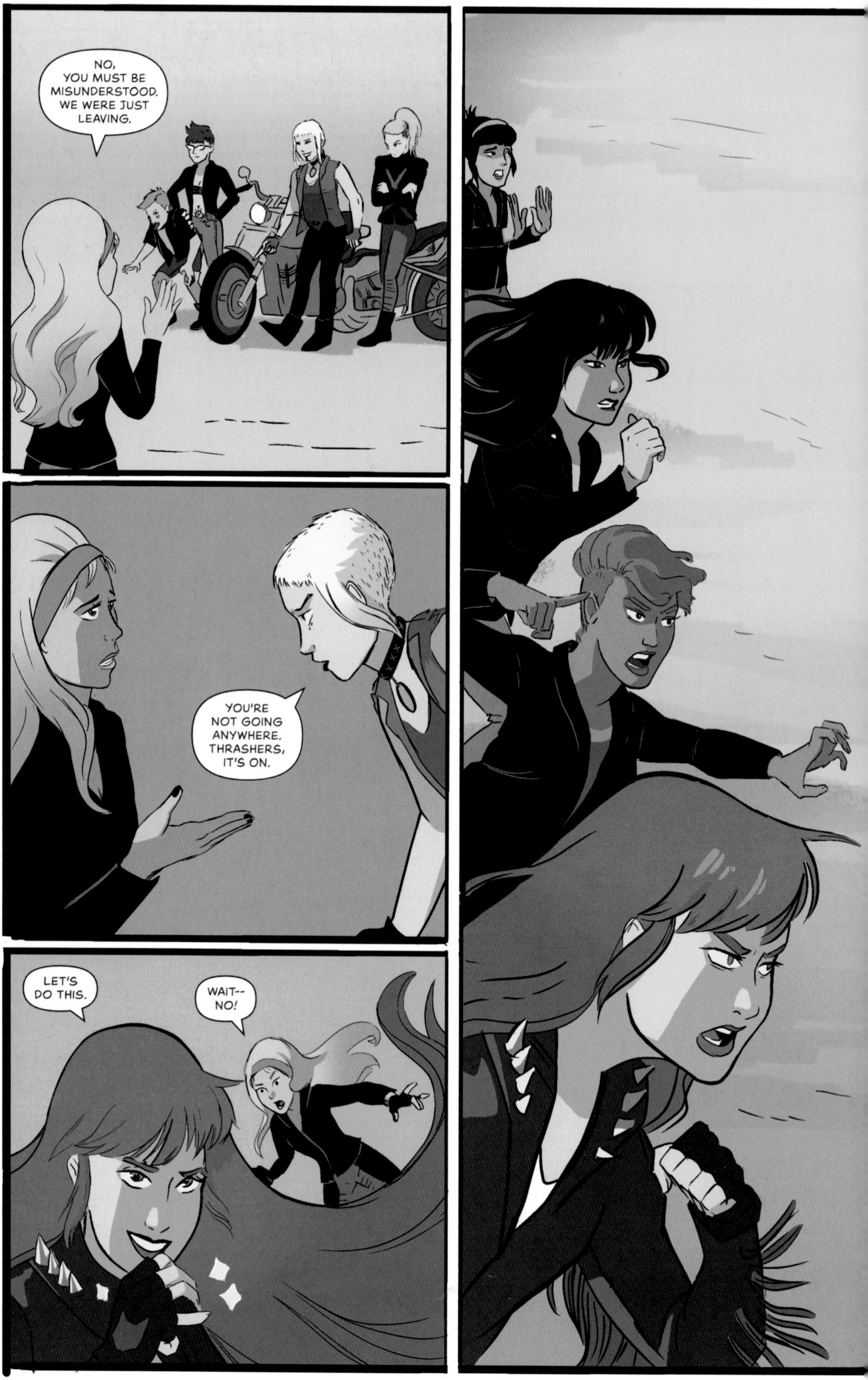
NO, YOU MUST BE MISUNDERSTOOD. WE WERE JUST LEAVING.
YOU'RE NOT GOING ANYWHERE. THRASHERS, IT'S ON.
LET'S DO THIS.
WAIT-- NO!

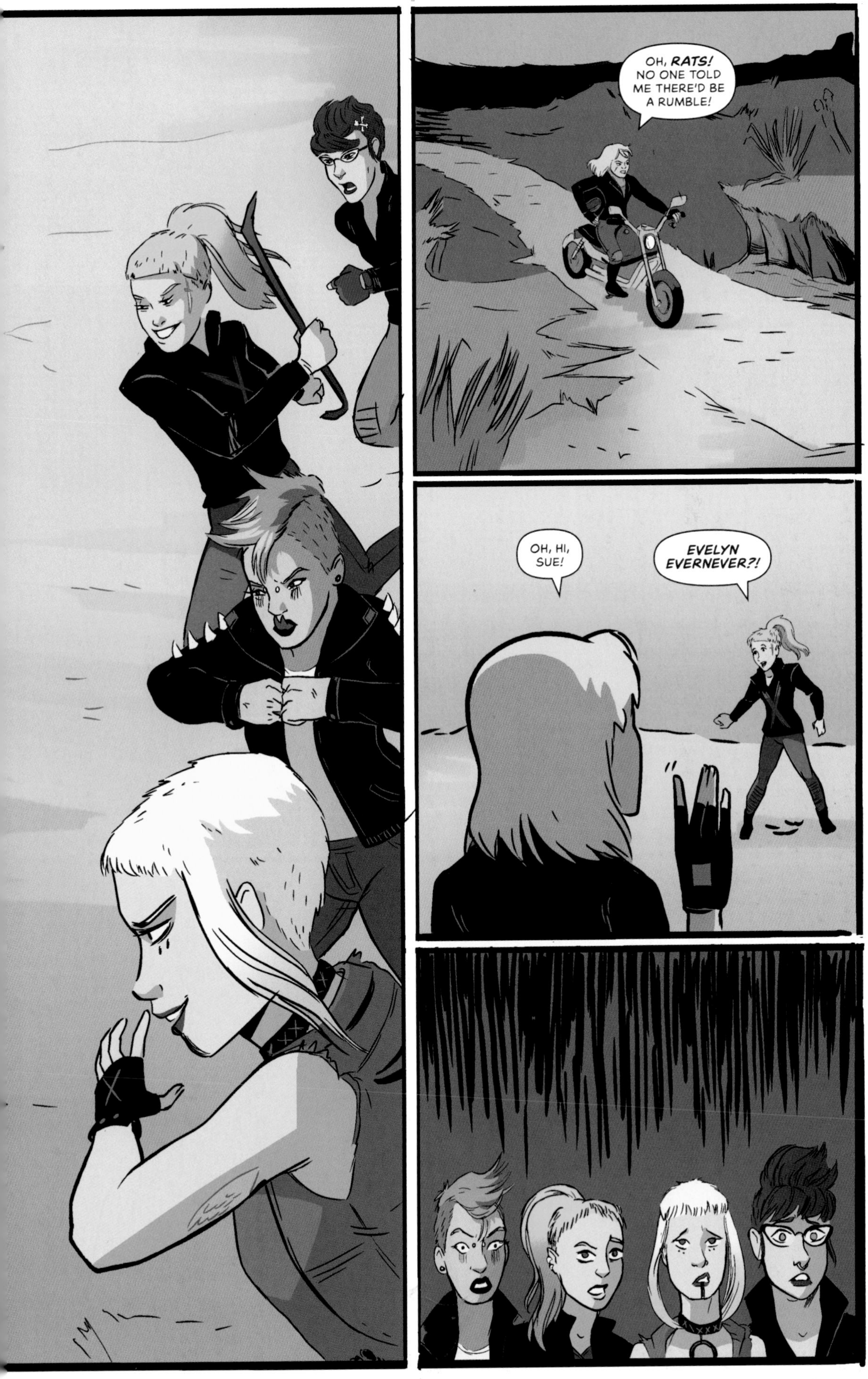
OH, RATS! NO ONE TOLD ME THERE'D BE A RUMBLE!
OH, HI, SUE!
EVELYN EVERNEVER?!

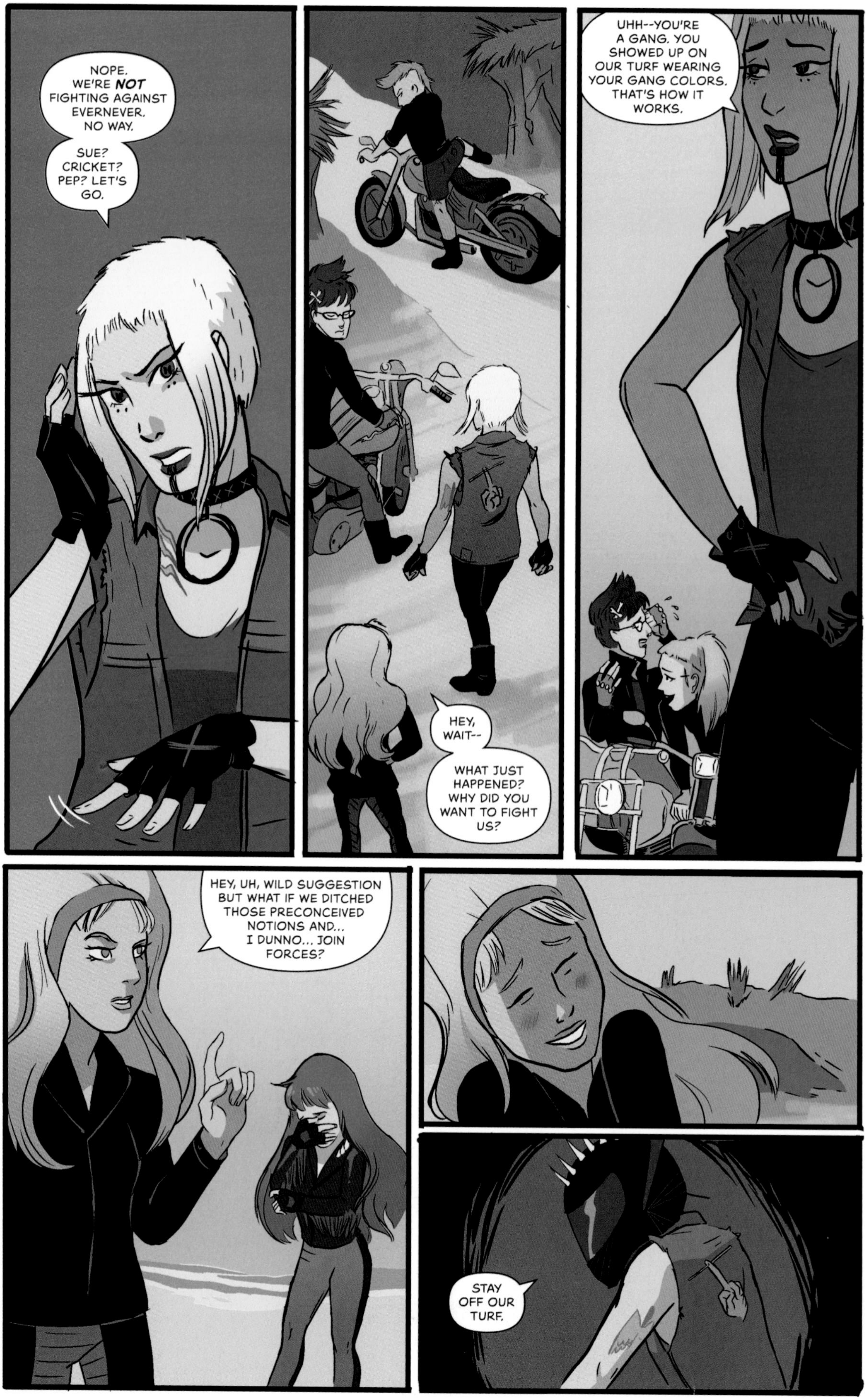
NOPE. WE'RE **NOT** FIGHTING AGAINST EVERNEVER. NO WAY.
SUE? CRICKET? PEP? LET'S GO.
HEY, WAIT--
WHAT JUST HAPPENED? WHY DID YOU WANT TO FIGHT US?
UHH--YOU'RE A GANG. YOU SHOWED UP ON OUR TURF WEARING YOUR GANG COLORS. THAT'S HOW IT WORKS.
HEY, UH, WILD SUGGESTION BUT WHAT IF WE DITCHED THOSE PRECONCEIVED NOTIONS AND... I DUNNO... JOIN FORCES?
STAY OFF OUR TURF.

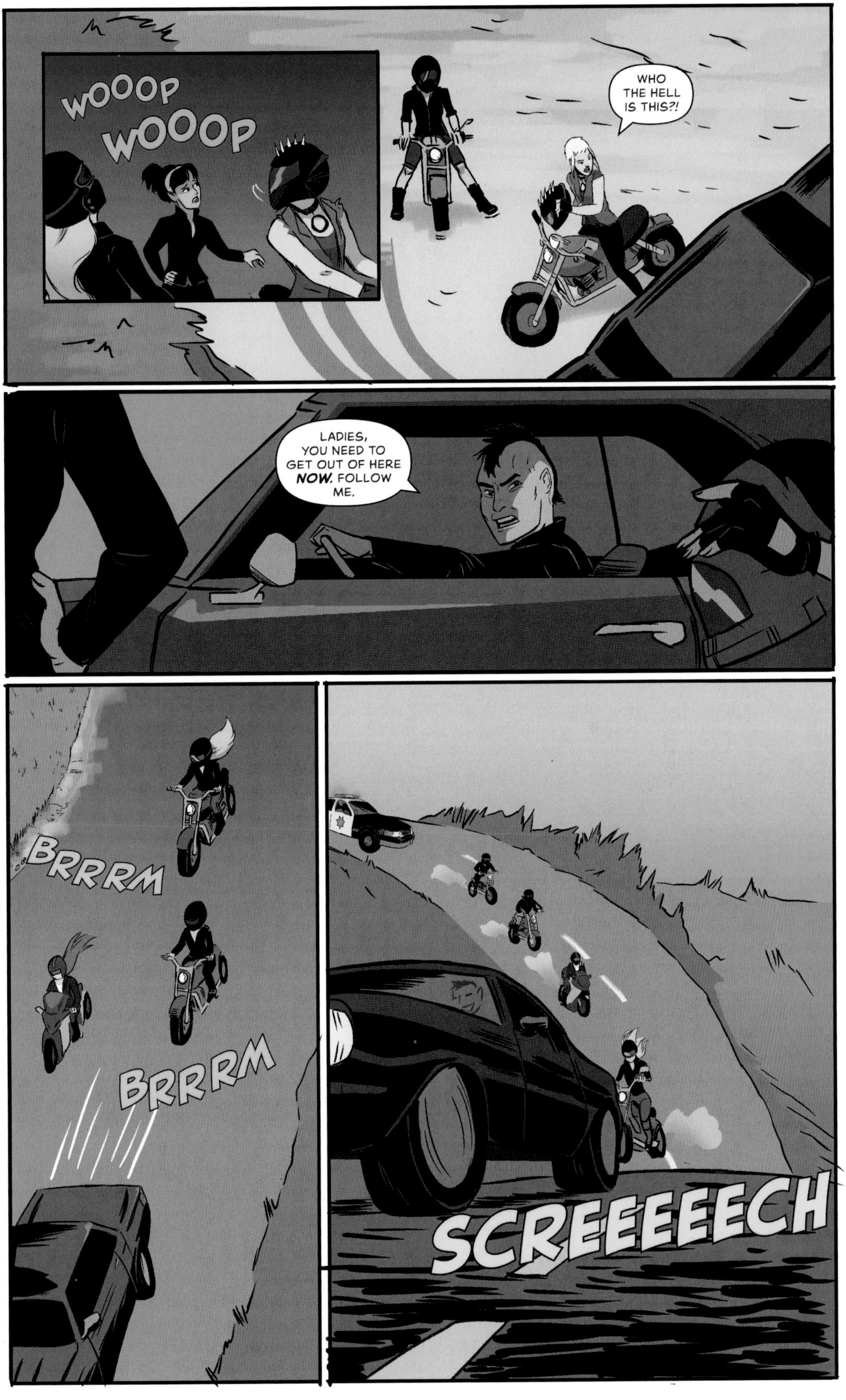
WOOOP
WOOOP
WHO THE HELL IS THIS?!
LADIES, YOU NEED TO GET OUT OF HERE NOW. FOLLOW ME.
BRRRM
BRRRM
SCREEEEECH

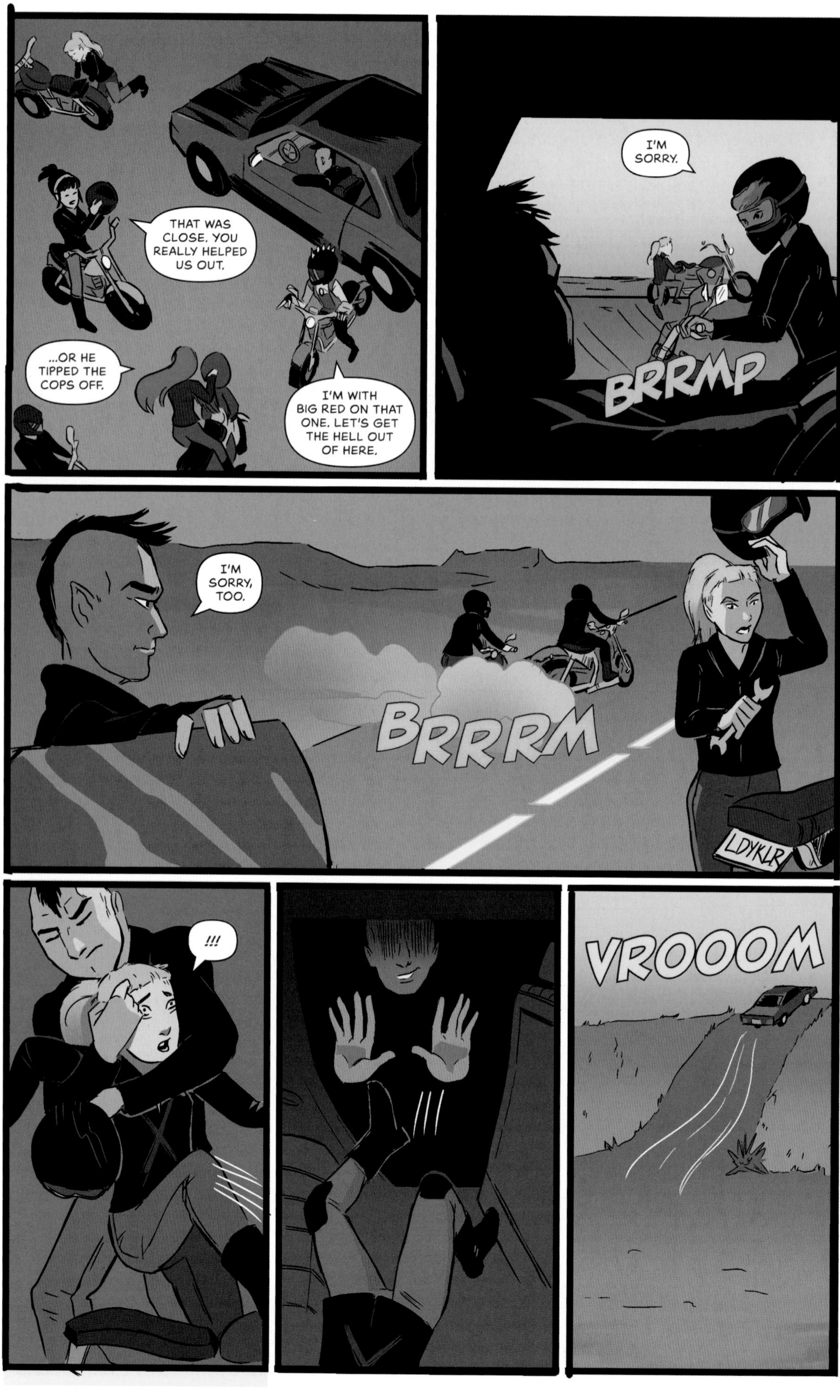
THAT WAS CLOSE. YOU REALLY HELPED US OUT.
...OR HE TIPPED THE COPS OFF.
I'M WITH BIG RED ON THAT ONE. LET'S GET THE HELL OUT OF HERE.
I'M SORRY.
BRRMP
I'M SORRY, TOO.
BRRRM
LDYKLR
!!!
VROOOM

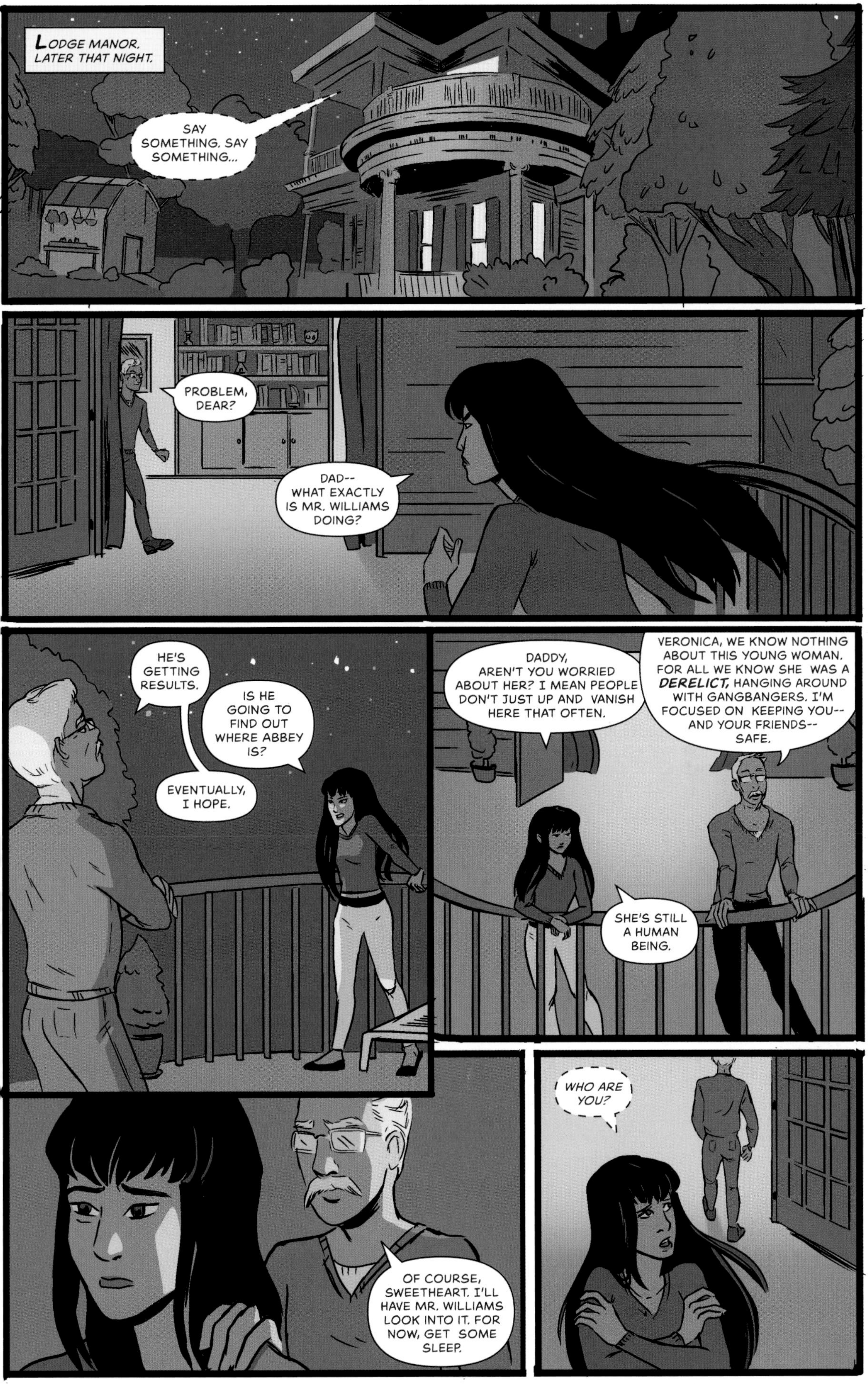
LODGE MANOR, LATER THAT NIGHT.
SAY SOMETHING, SAY SOMETHING...
PROBLEM, DEAR?
DAD-- WHAT EXACTLY IS MR. WILLIAMS DOING?
HE'S GETTING RESULTS.
IS HE GOING TO FIND OUT WHERE ABBEY IS?
EVENTUALLY, I HOPE.
DADDY, AREN'T YOU WORRIED ABOUT HER? I MEAN PEOPLE DON'T JUST UP AND VANISH HERE THAT OFTEN.
VERONICA, WE KNOW NOTHING ABOUT THIS YOUNG WOMAN. FOR ALL WE KNOW SHE WAS A DERELICT, HANGING AROUND WITH GANGBANGERS. I'M FOCUSED ON KEEPING YOU-- AND YOUR FRIENDS-- SAFE.
SHE'S STILL A HUMAN BEING.
OF COURSE, SWEETHEART. I'LL HAVE MR. WILLIAMS LOOK INTO IT. FOR NOW, GET SOME SLEEP.
WHO ARE YOU?

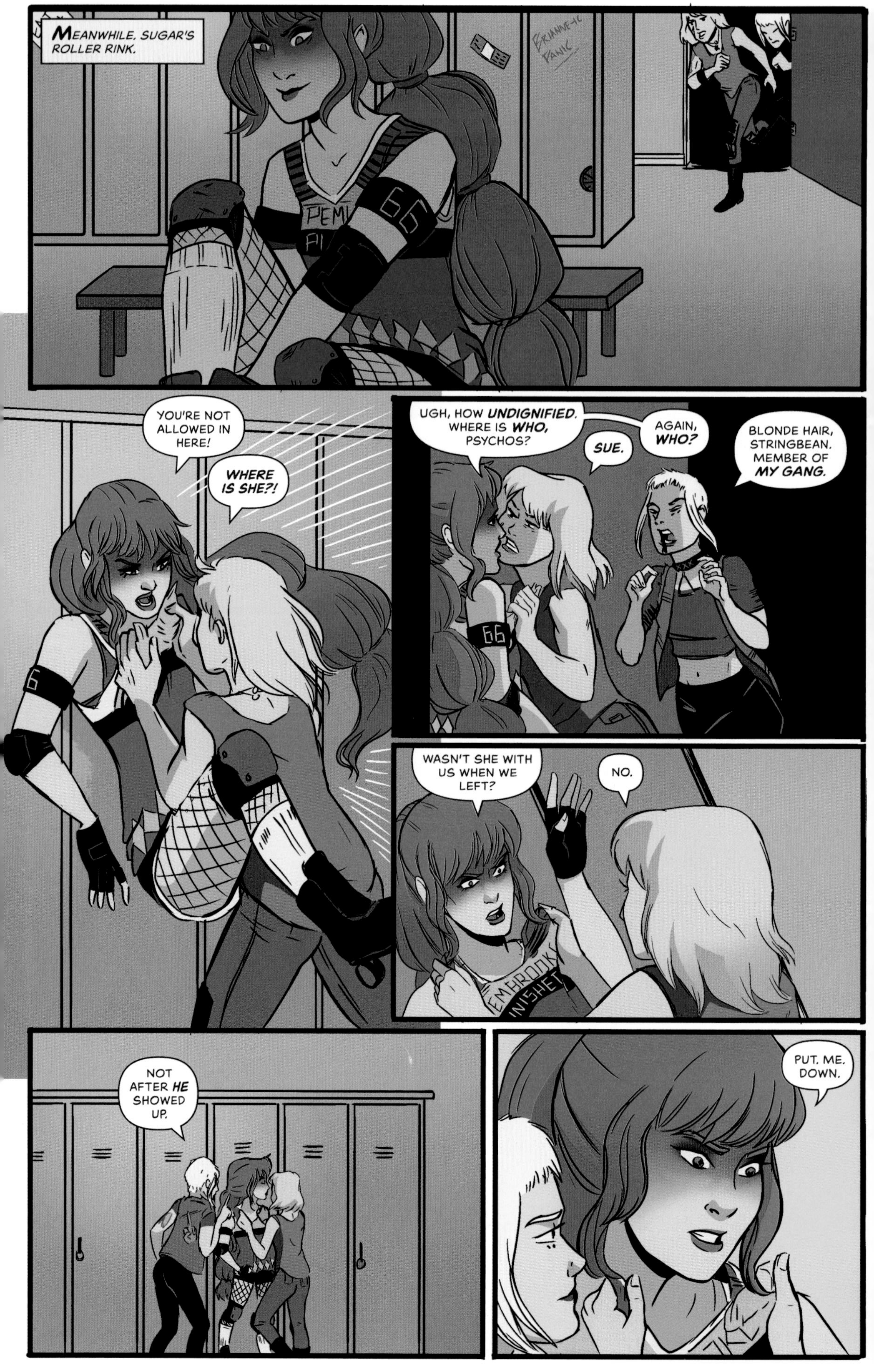
MEANWHILE, SUGAR'S ROLLER RINK.
YOU'RE NOT ALLOWED IN HERE!
WHERE IS SHE?!
UGH, HOW UNDIGNIFIED. WHERE IS WHO, PSYCHOS?
SUE.
AGAIN, WHO?
BLONDE HAIR, STRINGBEAN. MEMBER OF MY GANG.
WASN'T SHE WITH US WHEN WE LEFT?
NO.
NOT AFTER HE SHOWED UP.
PUT. ME. DOWN.

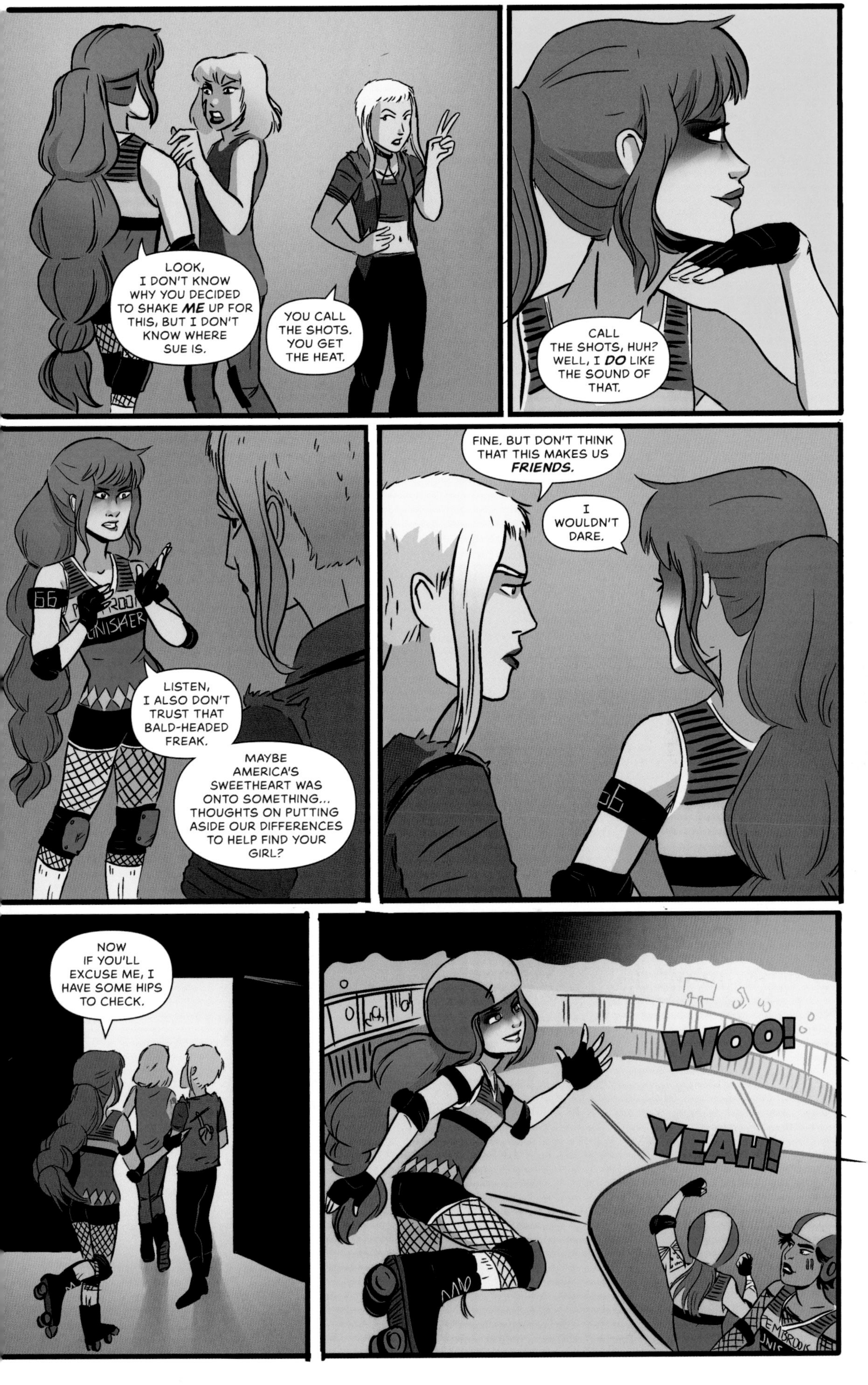
LOOK, I DON'T KNOW WHY YOU DECIDED TO SHAKE ME UP FOR THIS, BUT I DON'T KNOW WHERE SUE IS.
YOU CALL THE SHOTS. YOU GET THE HEAT.
CALL THE SHOTS, HUH? WELL, I DO LIKE THE SOUND OF THAT.
LISTEN, I ALSO DON'T TRUST THAT BALD-HEADED FREAK.
MAYBE AMERICA'S SWEETHEART WAS ONTO SOMETHING... THOUGHTS ON PUTTING ASIDE OUR DIFFERENCES TO HELP FIND YOUR GIRL?
FINE, BUT DON'T THINK THAT THIS MAKES US FRIENDS.
I WOULDN'T DARE.
NOW IF YOU'LL EXCUSE ME, I HAVE SOME HIPS TO CHECK.
WOO!
YEAH!

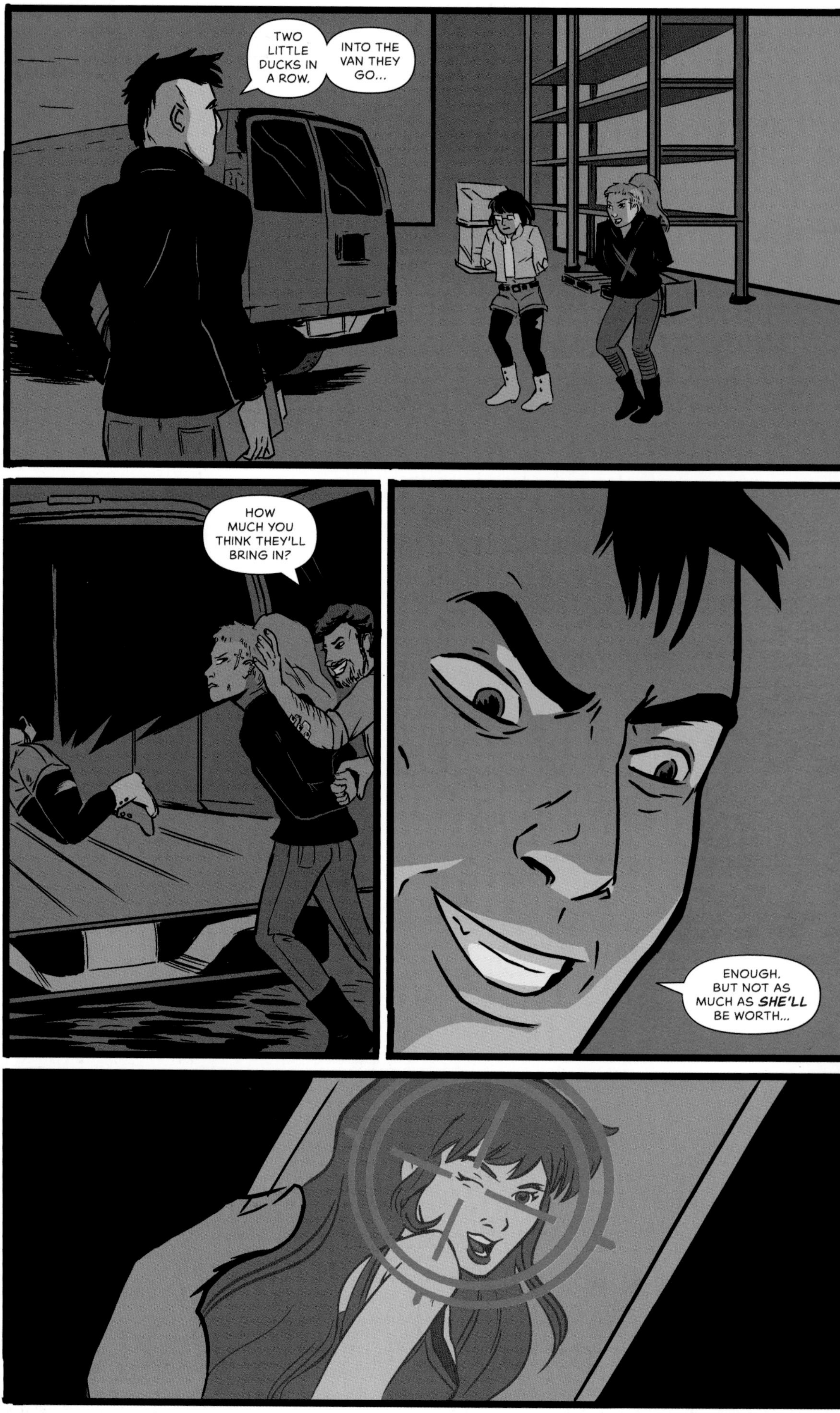
TWO LITTLE DUCKS IN A ROW.
INTO THE VAN THEY GO...
HOW MUCH YOU THINK THEY'LL BRING IN?
ENOUGH. BUT NOT AS MUCH AS ***SHE'LL*** BE WORTH...

to be continued...

Chapter Eight

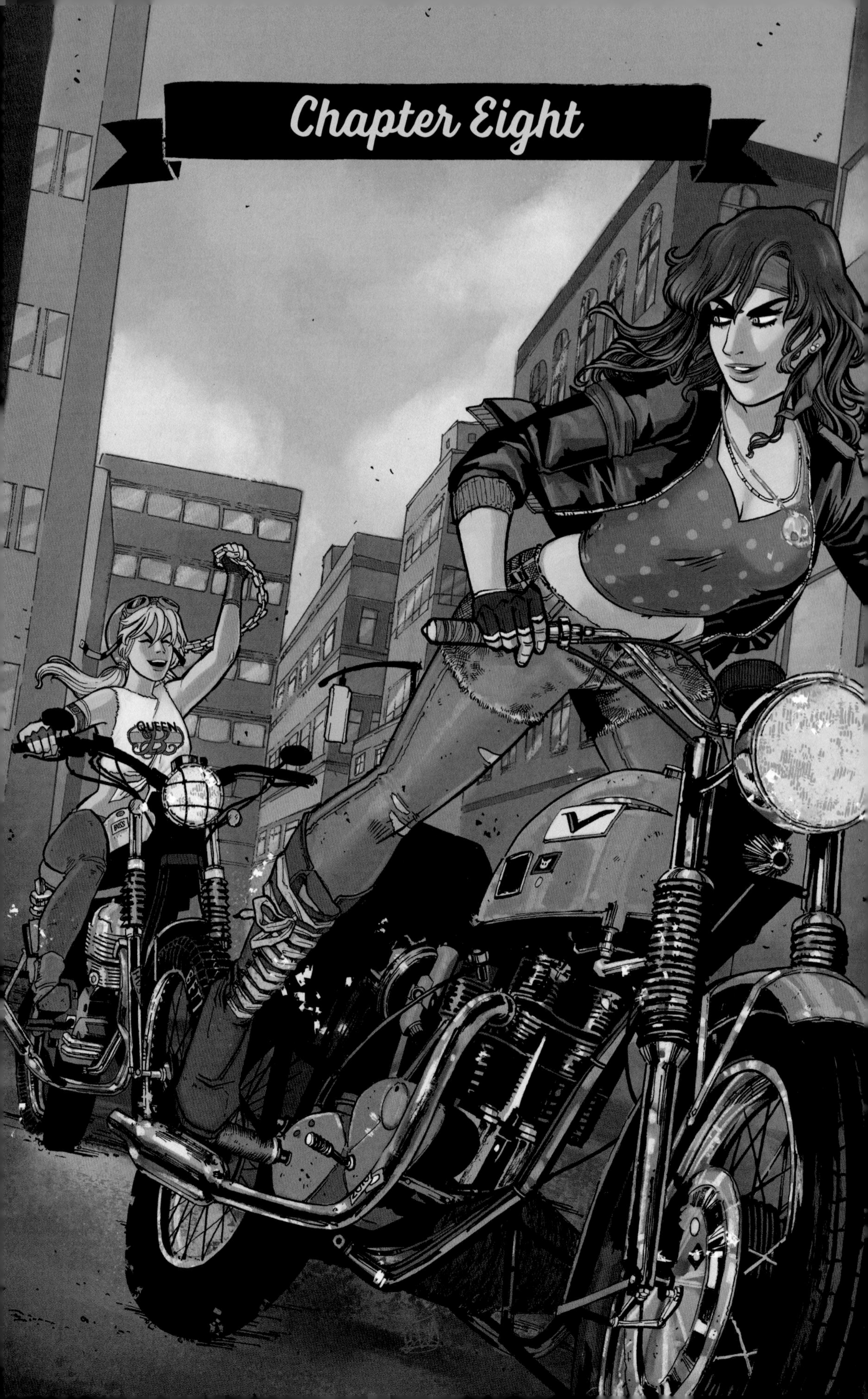
QUEEN

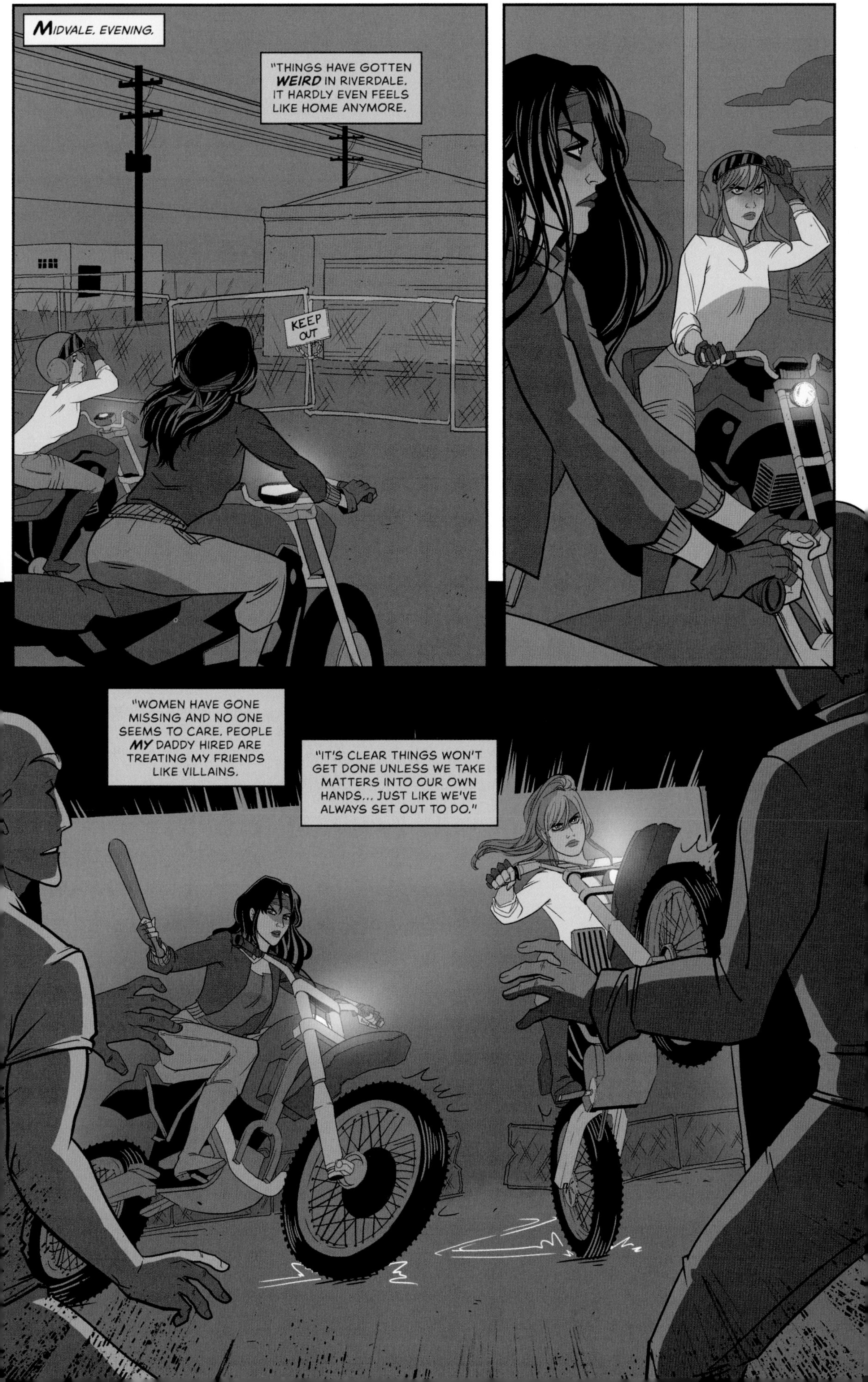
MIDVALE, EVENING.
"THINGS HAVE GOTTEN WEIRD IN RIVERDALE. IT HARDLY EVEN FEELS LIKE HOME ANYMORE.
KEEP OUT
"WOMEN HAVE GONE MISSING AND NO ONE SEEMS TO CARE. PEOPLE MY DADDY HIRED ARE TREATING MY FRIENDS LIKE VILLAINS.
"IT'S CLEAR THINGS WON'T GET DONE UNLESS WE TAKE MATTERS INTO OUR OWN HANDS... JUST LIKE WE'VE ALWAYS SET OUT TO DO."

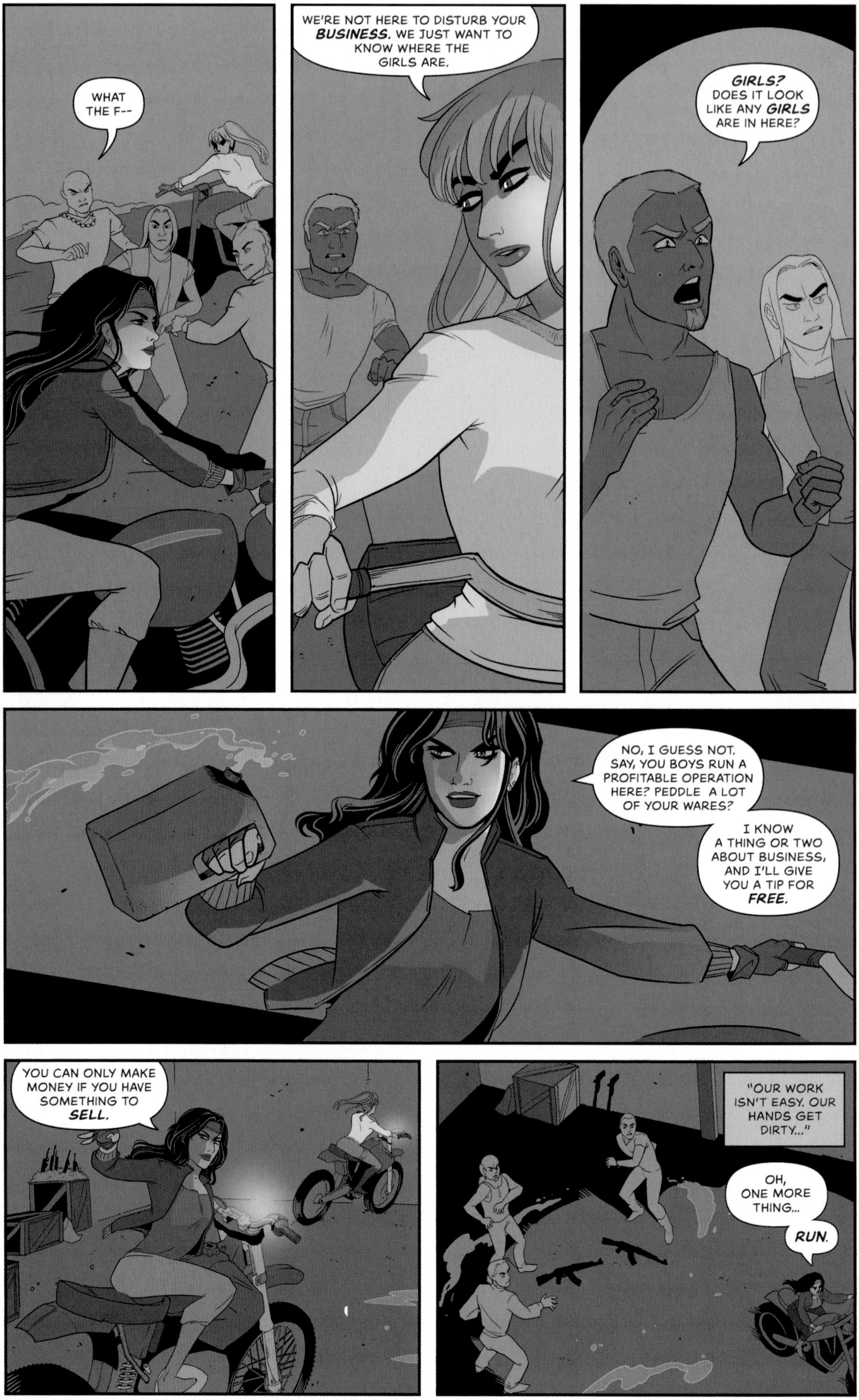
WHAT THE F--
WE'RE NOT HERE TO DISTURB YOUR **BUSINESS.** WE JUST WANT TO KNOW WHERE THE GIRLS ARE.
GIRLS? DOES IT LOOK LIKE ANY **GIRLS** ARE IN HERE?
NO, I GUESS NOT. SAY, YOU BOYS RUN A PROFITABLE OPERATION HERE? PEDDLE A LOT OF YOUR WARES?
I KNOW A THING OR TWO ABOUT BUSINESS, AND I'LL GIVE YOU A TIP FOR **FREE.**
YOU CAN ONLY MAKE MONEY IF YOU HAVE SOMETHING TO **SELL.**
"OUR WORK ISN'T EASY. OUR HANDS GET DIRTY..."
OH, ONE MORE THING...
RUN.

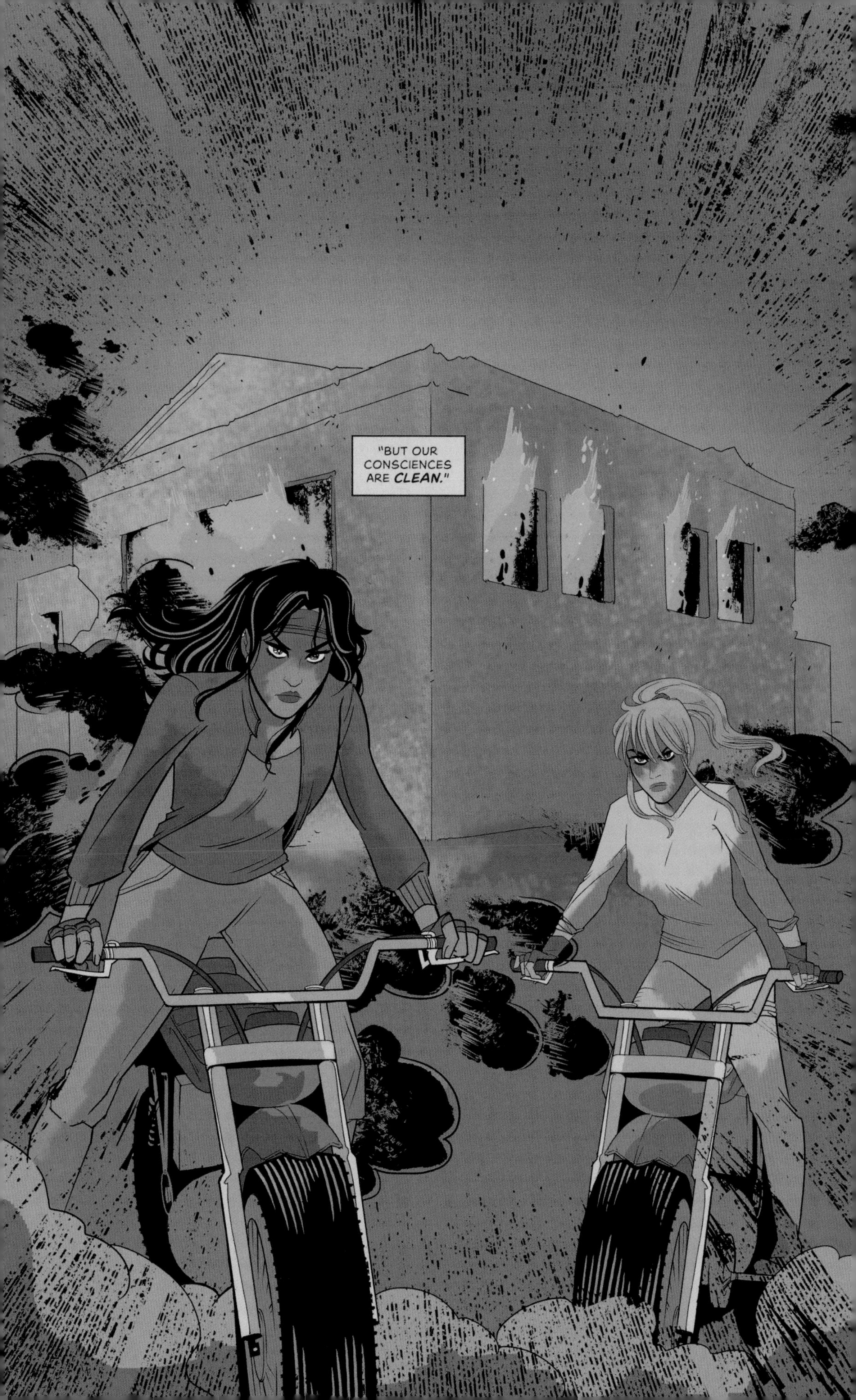
"BUT OUR CONSCIENCES ARE CLEAN."

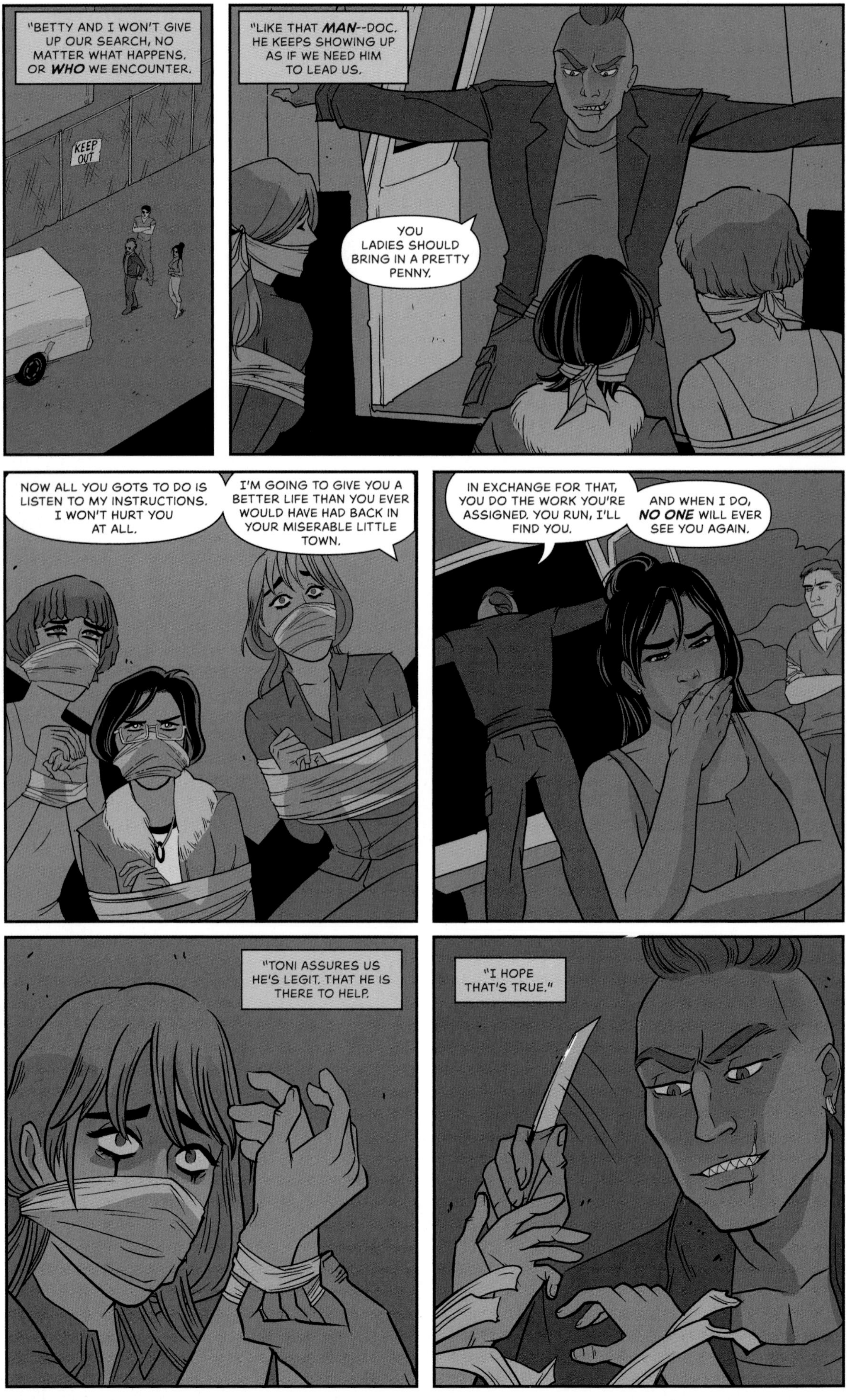
"BETTY AND I WON'T GIVE UP OUR SEARCH, NO MATTER WHAT HAPPENS, OR WHO WE ENCOUNTER.
KEEP OUT
"LIKE THAT MAN--DOC. HE KEEPS SHOWING UP AS IF WE NEED HIM TO LEAD US.
YOU LADIES SHOULD BRING IN A PRETTY PENNY.
NOW ALL YOU GOTS TO DO IS LISTEN TO MY INSTRUCTIONS. I WON'T HURT YOU AT ALL.
I'M GOING TO GIVE YOU A BETTER LIFE THAN YOU EVER WOULD HAVE HAD BACK IN YOUR MISERABLE LITTLE TOWN.
IN EXCHANGE FOR THAT, YOU DO THE WORK YOU'RE ASSIGNED. YOU RUN, I'LL FIND YOU.
AND WHEN I DO, NO ONE WILL EVER SEE YOU AGAIN.
"TONI ASSURES US HE'S LEGIT, THAT HE IS THERE TO HELP.
"I HOPE THAT'S TRUE."

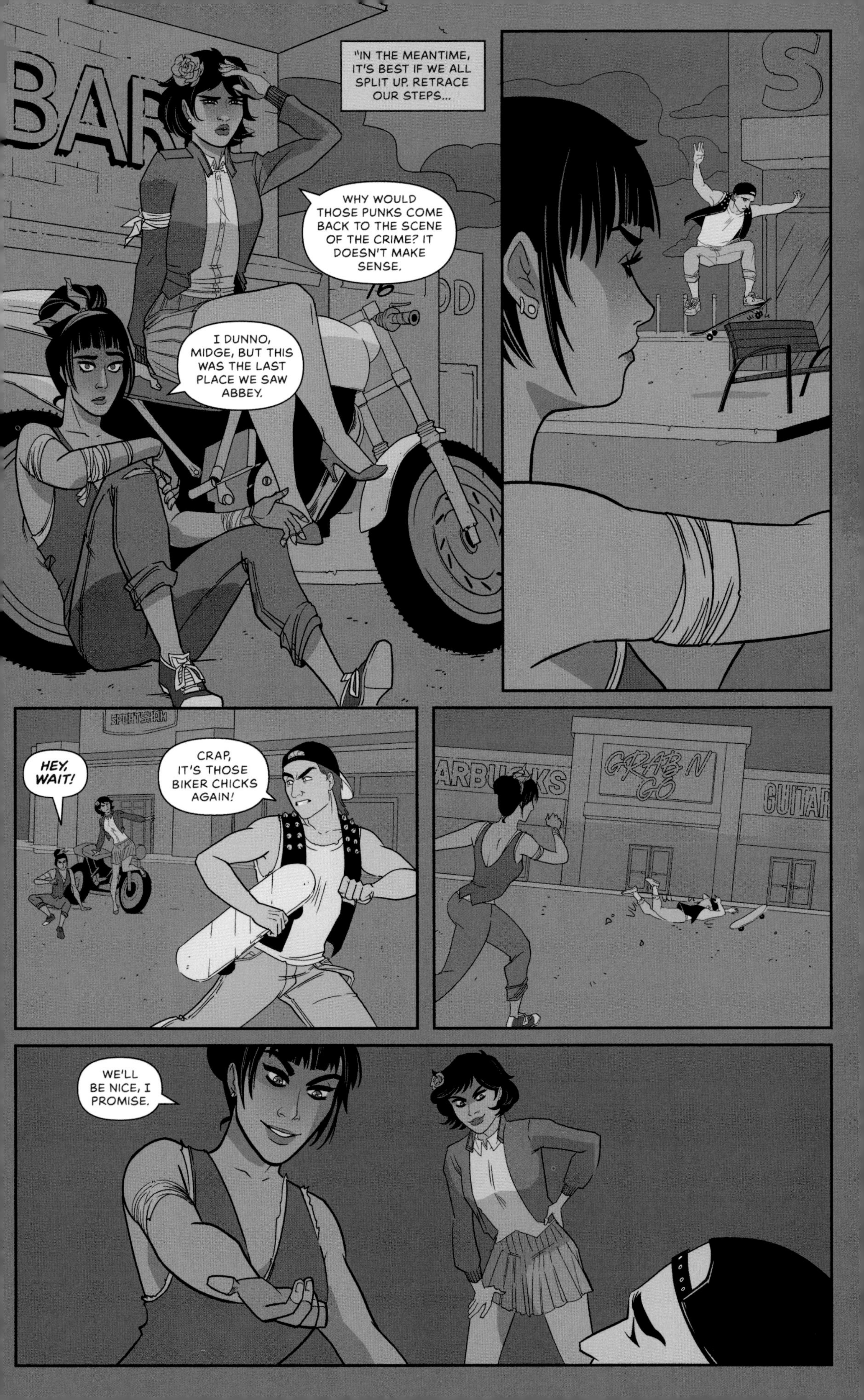
"IN THE MEANTIME, IT'S BEST IF WE ALL SPLIT UP. RETRACE OUR STEPS...
BAR
WHY WOULD THOSE PUNKS COME BACK TO THE SCENE OF THE CRIME? IT DOESN'T MAKE SENSE.
I DUNNO, MIDGE, BUT THIS WAS THE LAST PLACE WE SAW ABBEY.
SPORTSHAK
HEY, WAIT!
CRAP, IT'S THOSE BIKER CHICKS AGAIN!
GRAB N GO
GUITAR
WE'LL BE NICE, I PROMISE.

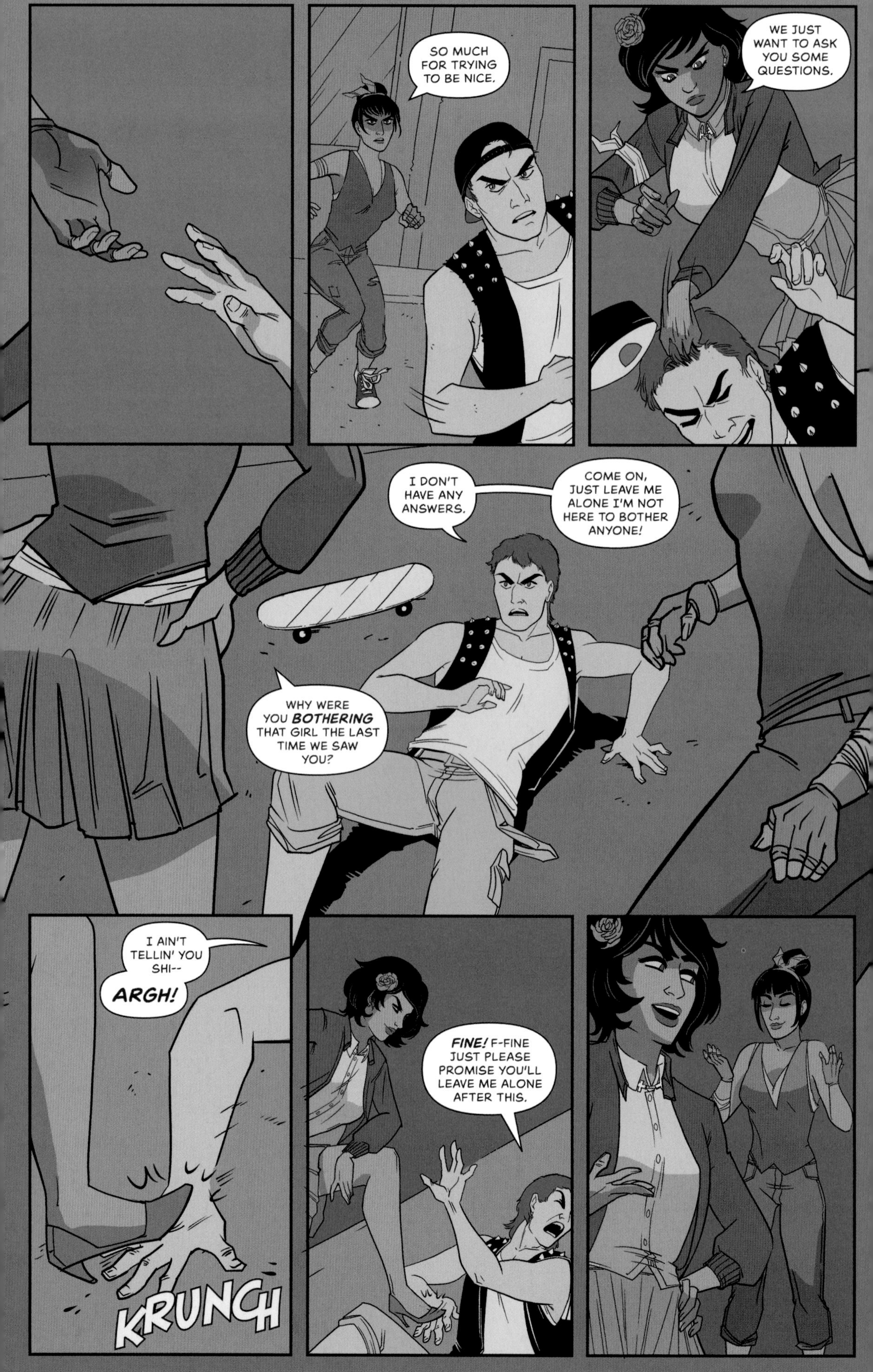
SO MUCH FOR TRYING TO BE NICE.
WE JUST WANT TO ASK YOU SOME QUESTIONS.
I DON'T HAVE ANY ANSWERS.
COME ON, JUST LEAVE ME ALONE I'M NOT HERE TO BOTHER ANYONE!
WHY WERE YOU BOTHERING THAT GIRL THE LAST TIME WE SAW YOU?
I AIN'T TELLIN' YOU SHI--
ARGH!
KRUNCH
FINE! F-FINE JUST PLEASE PROMISE YOU'LL LEAVE ME ALONE AFTER THIS.

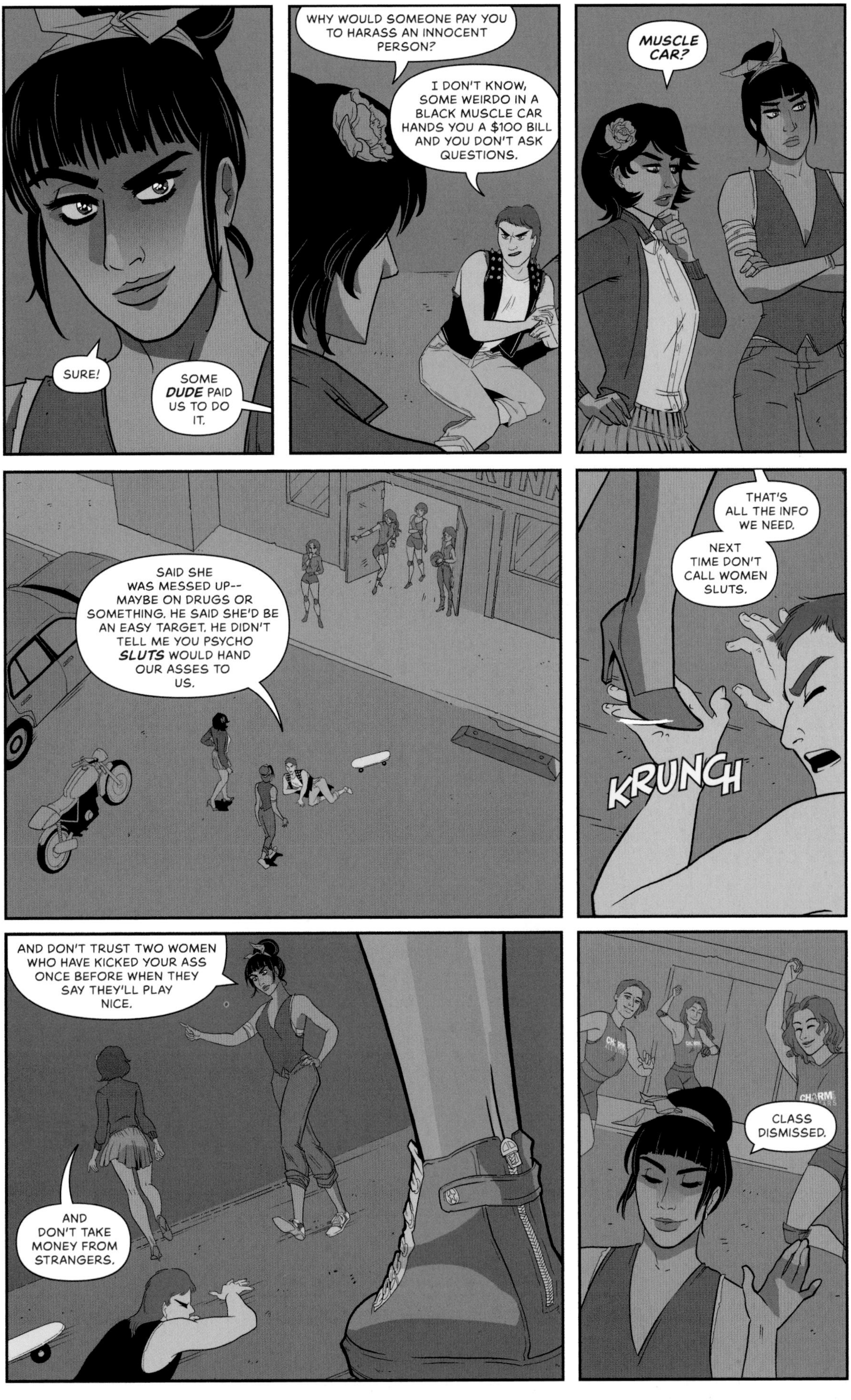
SURE!
SOME DUDE PAID US TO DO IT.
WHY WOULD SOMEONE PAY YOU TO HARASS AN INNOCENT PERSON?
I DON'T KNOW, SOME WEIRDO IN A BLACK MUSCLE CAR HANDS YOU A $100 BILL AND YOU DON'T ASK QUESTIONS.
MUSCLE CAR?
SAID SHE WAS MESSED UP-- MAYBE ON DRUGS OR SOMETHING. HE SAID SHE'D BE AN EASY TARGET. HE DIDN'T TELL ME YOU PSYCHO SLUTS WOULD HAND OUR ASSES TO US.
THAT'S ALL THE INFO WE NEED.
NEXT TIME DON'T CALL WOMEN SLUTS.
KRUNCH
AND DON'T TRUST TWO WOMEN WHO HAVE KICKED YOUR ASS ONCE BEFORE WHEN THEY SAY THEY'LL PLAY NICE.
AND DON'T TAKE MONEY FROM STRANGERS.
CLASS DISMISSED.

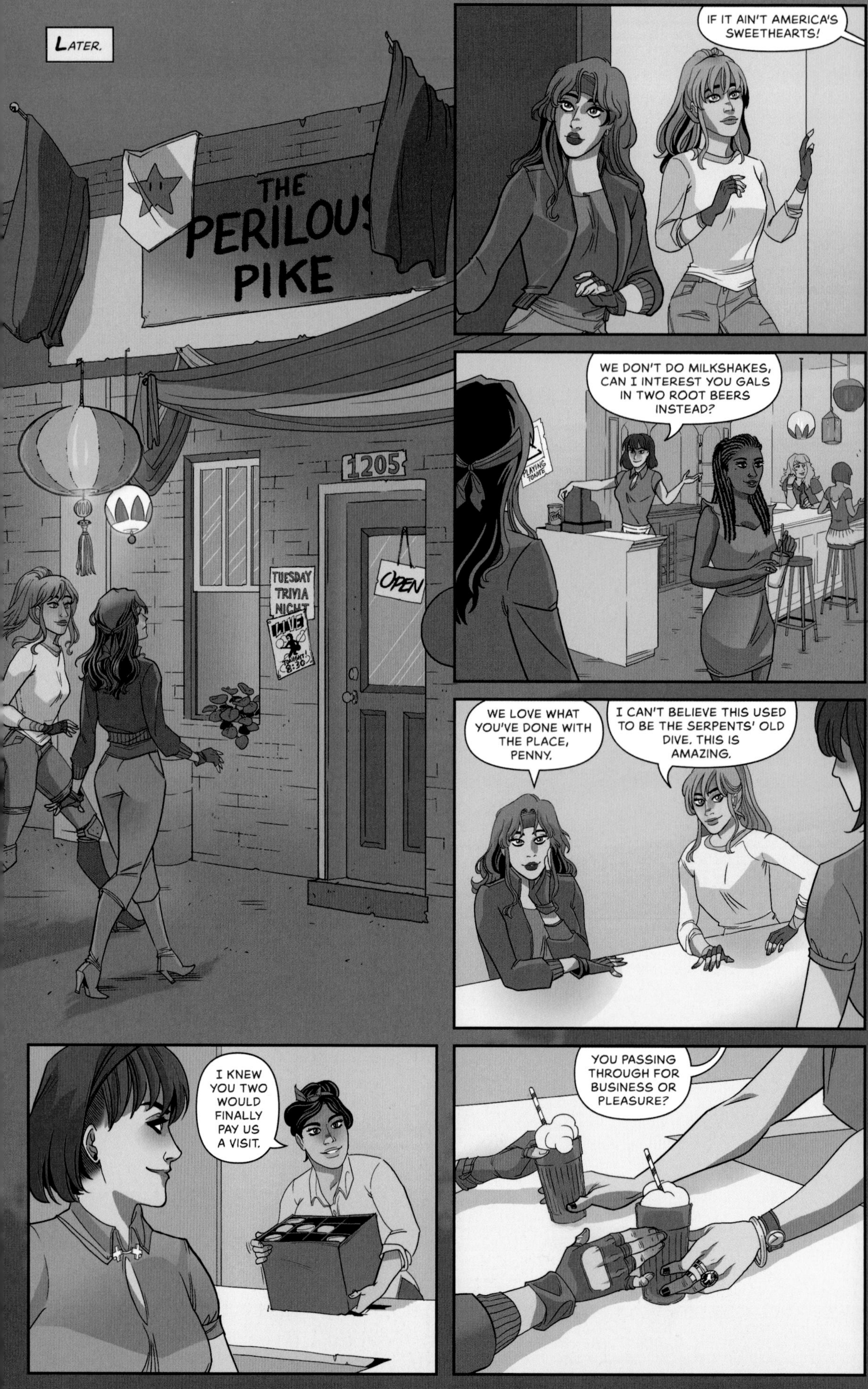
LATER.
THE PERILOUS PIKE
1205
TUESDAY TRIVIA NIGHT
LIVE TONIGHT! 8:30
OPEN
IF IT AIN'T AMERICA'S SWEETHEARTS!
WE DON'T DO MILKSHAKES, CAN I INTEREST YOU GALS IN TWO ROOT BEERS INSTEAD?
PLAYING TONITE
WE LOVE WHAT YOU'VE DONE WITH THE PLACE, PENNY.
I CAN'T BELIEVE THIS USED TO BE THE SERPENTS' OLD DIVE. THIS IS AMAZING.
I KNEW YOU TWO WOULD FINALLY PAY US A VISIT.
YOU PASSING THROUGH FOR BUSINESS OR PLEASURE?

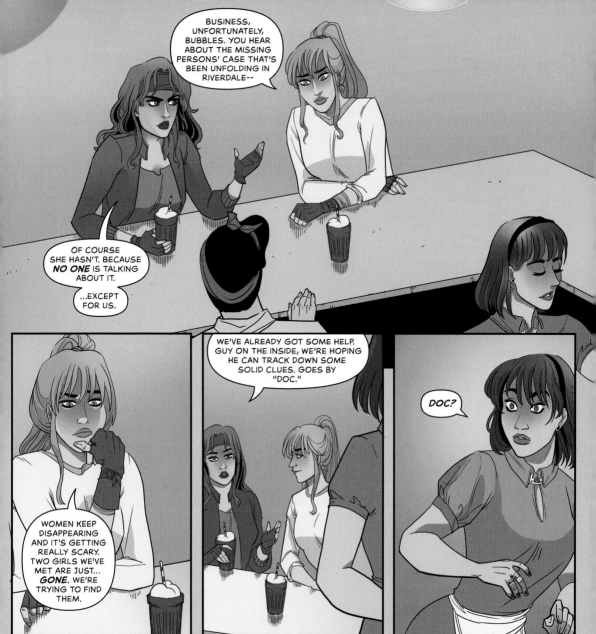

BUSINESS, UNFORTUNATELY, BUBBLES. YOU HEAR ABOUT THE MISSING PERSONS' CASE THAT'S BEEN UNFOLDING IN RIVERDALE--

OF COURSE SHE HASN'T, BECAUSE *NO ONE* IS TALKING ABOUT IT.

...EXCEPT FOR US.

WE'VE ALREADY GOT SOME HELP. GUY ON THE INSIDE, WE'RE HOPING HE CAN TRACK DOWN SOME SOLID CLUES. GOES BY "DOC."

DOC?

WOMEN KEEP DISAPPEARING AND IT'S GETTING REALLY SCARY. TWO GIRLS WE'VE MET ARE JUST... *GONE.* WE'RE TRYING TO FIND THEM.

DID YOU SAY "DOC"? BIG DUDE, MOHAWK?

YES! DO YOU KNOW HIM?

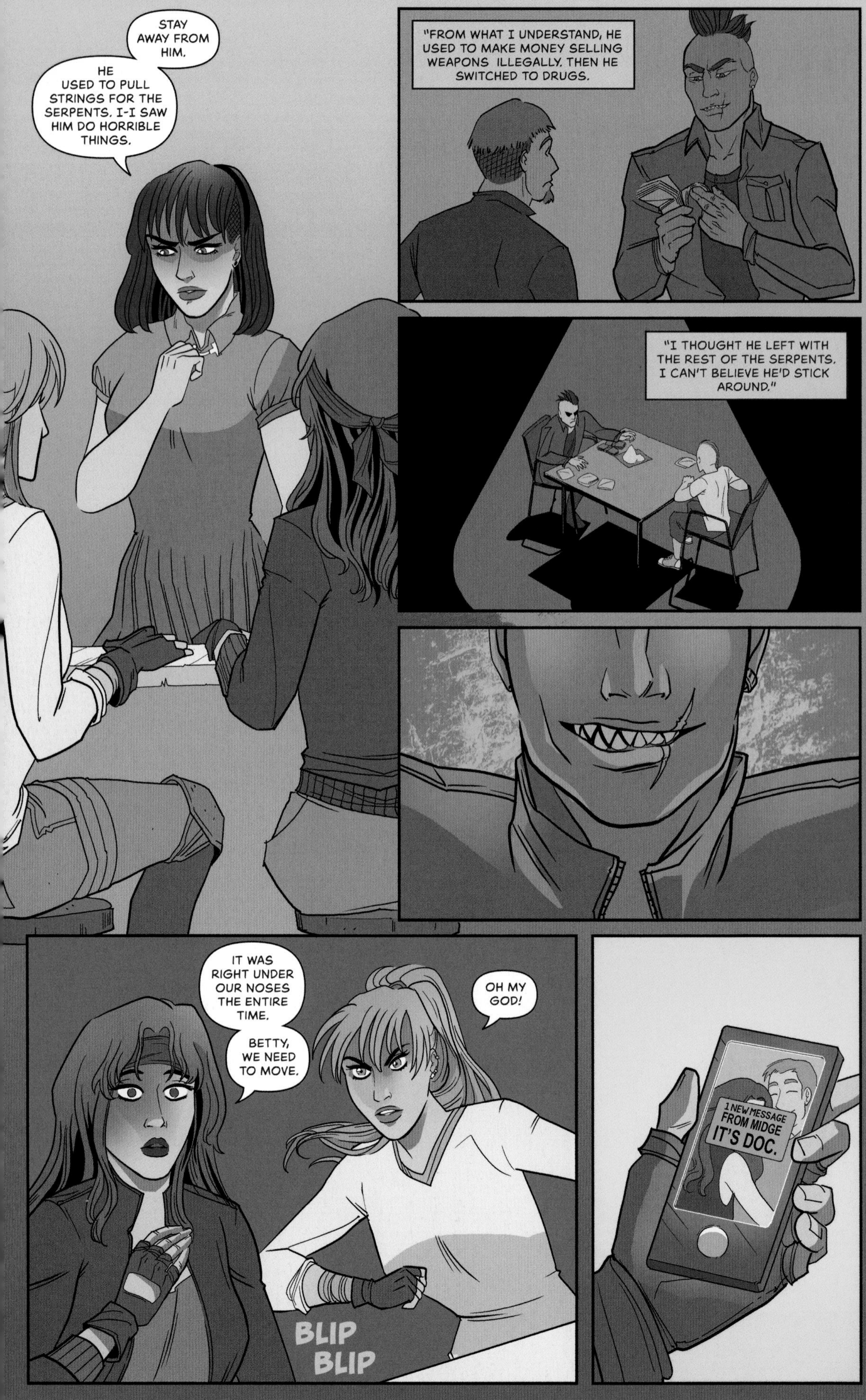
STAY AWAY FROM HIM.
HE USED TO PULL STRINGS FOR THE SERPENTS. I-I SAW HIM DO HORRIBLE THINGS.
"FROM WHAT I UNDERSTAND, HE USED TO MAKE MONEY SELLING WEAPONS ILLEGALLY. THEN HE SWITCHED TO DRUGS.
"I THOUGHT HE LEFT WITH THE REST OF THE SERPENTS. I CAN'T BELIEVE HE'D STICK AROUND."
IT WAS RIGHT UNDER OUR NOSES THE ENTIRE TIME.
OH MY GOD!
BETTY, WE NEED TO MOVE.
BLIP
BLIP
1 NEW MESSAGE FROM MIDGE
IT'S DOC.

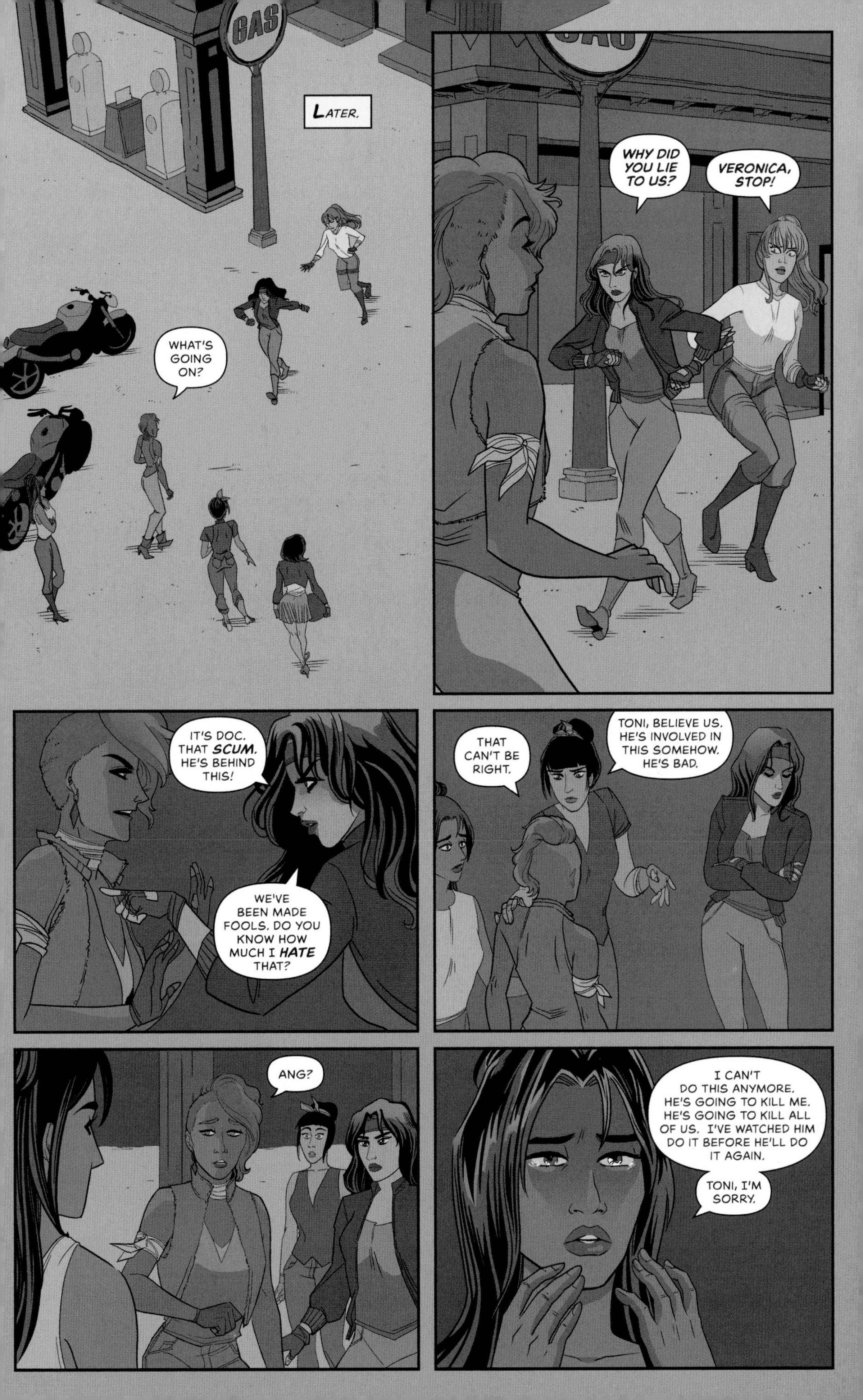
GAS
LATER.
WHAT'S GOING ON?
WHY DID YOU LIE TO US?
VERONICA, STOP!
IT'S DOC. THAT SCUM. HE'S BEHIND THIS!
WE'VE BEEN MADE FOOLS. DO YOU KNOW HOW MUCH I HATE THAT?
THAT CAN'T BE RIGHT.
TONI, BELIEVE US. HE'S INVOLVED IN THIS SOMEHOW. HE'S BAD.
ANG?
I CAN'T DO THIS ANYMORE. HE'S GOING TO KILL ME. HE'S GOING TO KILL ALL OF US. I'VE WATCHED HIM DO IT BEFORE HE'LL DO IT AGAIN.
TONI, I'M SORRY.

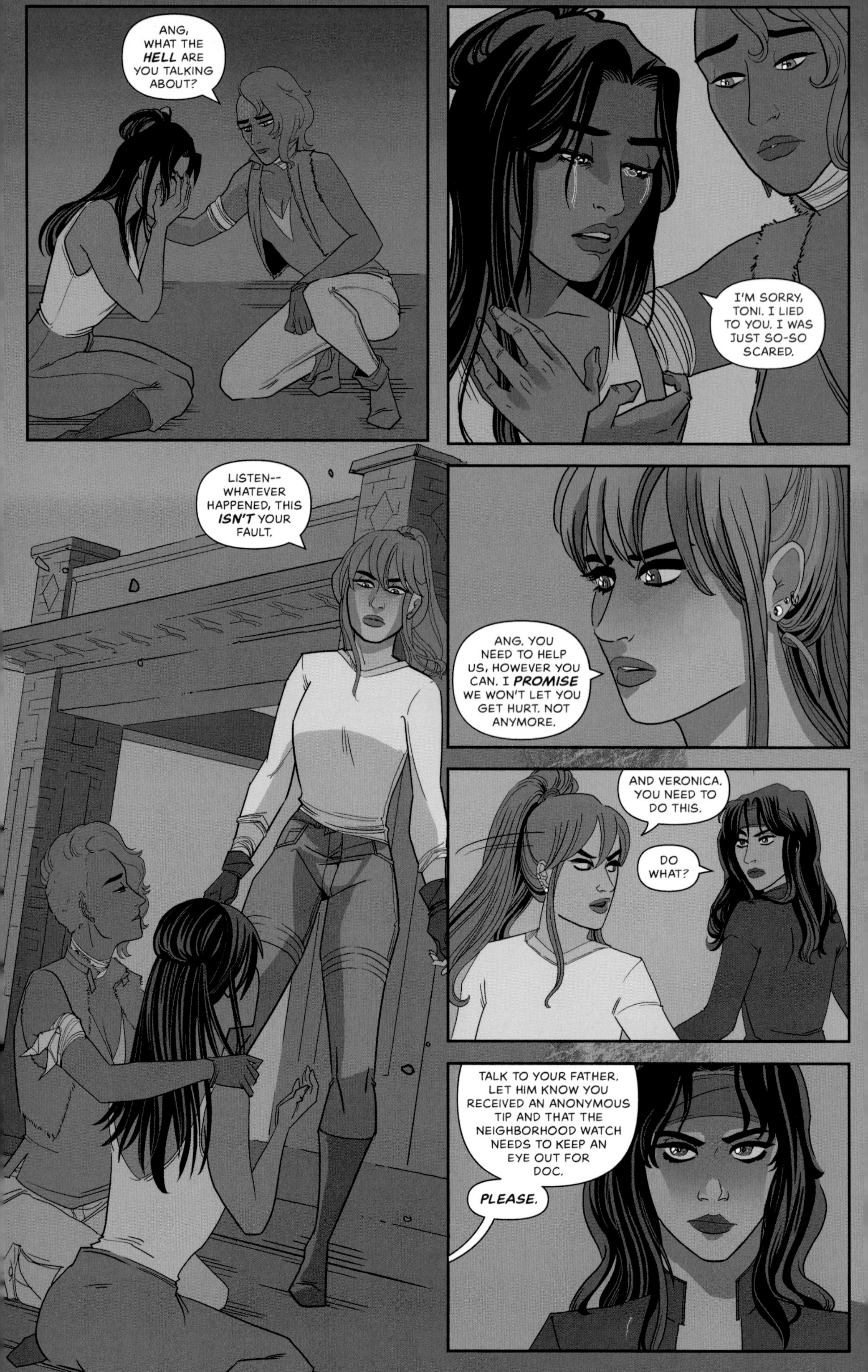
ANG, WHAT THE **HELL** ARE YOU TALKING ABOUT?
I'M SORRY, TONI. I LIED TO YOU. I WAS JUST SO-SO SCARED.
LISTEN-- WHATEVER HAPPENED, THIS **ISN'T** YOUR FAULT.
ANG, YOU NEED TO HELP US, HOWEVER YOU CAN. I **PROMISE** WE WON'T LET YOU GET HURT. NOT ANYMORE.
AND VERONICA, YOU NEED TO DO THIS.
DO WHAT?
TALK TO YOUR FATHER. LET HIM KNOW YOU RECEIVED AN ANONYMOUS TIP AND THAT THE NEIGHBORHOOD WATCH NEEDS TO KEEP AN EYE OUT FOR DOC.
PLEASE.

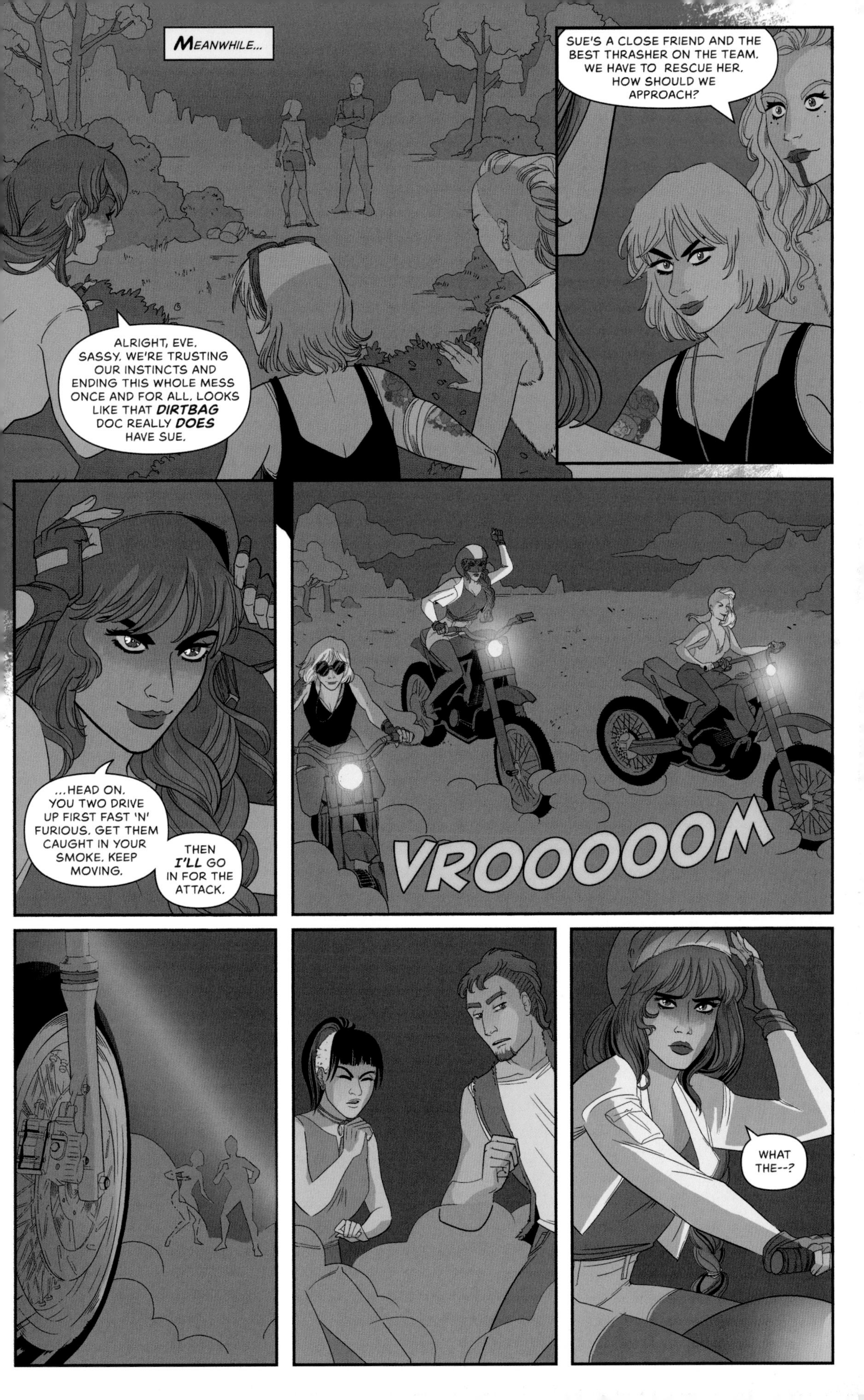
MEANWHILE...
ALRIGHT, EVE. SASSY. WE'RE TRUSTING OUR INSTINCTS AND ENDING THIS WHOLE MESS ONCE AND FOR ALL. LOOKS LIKE THAT DIRTBAG DOC REALLY DOES HAVE SUE.
SUE'S A CLOSE FRIEND AND THE BEST THRASHER ON THE TEAM. WE HAVE TO RESCUE HER. HOW SHOULD WE APPROACH?
...HEAD ON. YOU TWO DRIVE UP FIRST FAST 'N' FURIOUS. GET THEM CAUGHT IN YOUR SMOKE. KEEP MOVING.
THEN I'LL GO IN FOR THE ATTACK.
VROOOOOM
WHAT THE--?

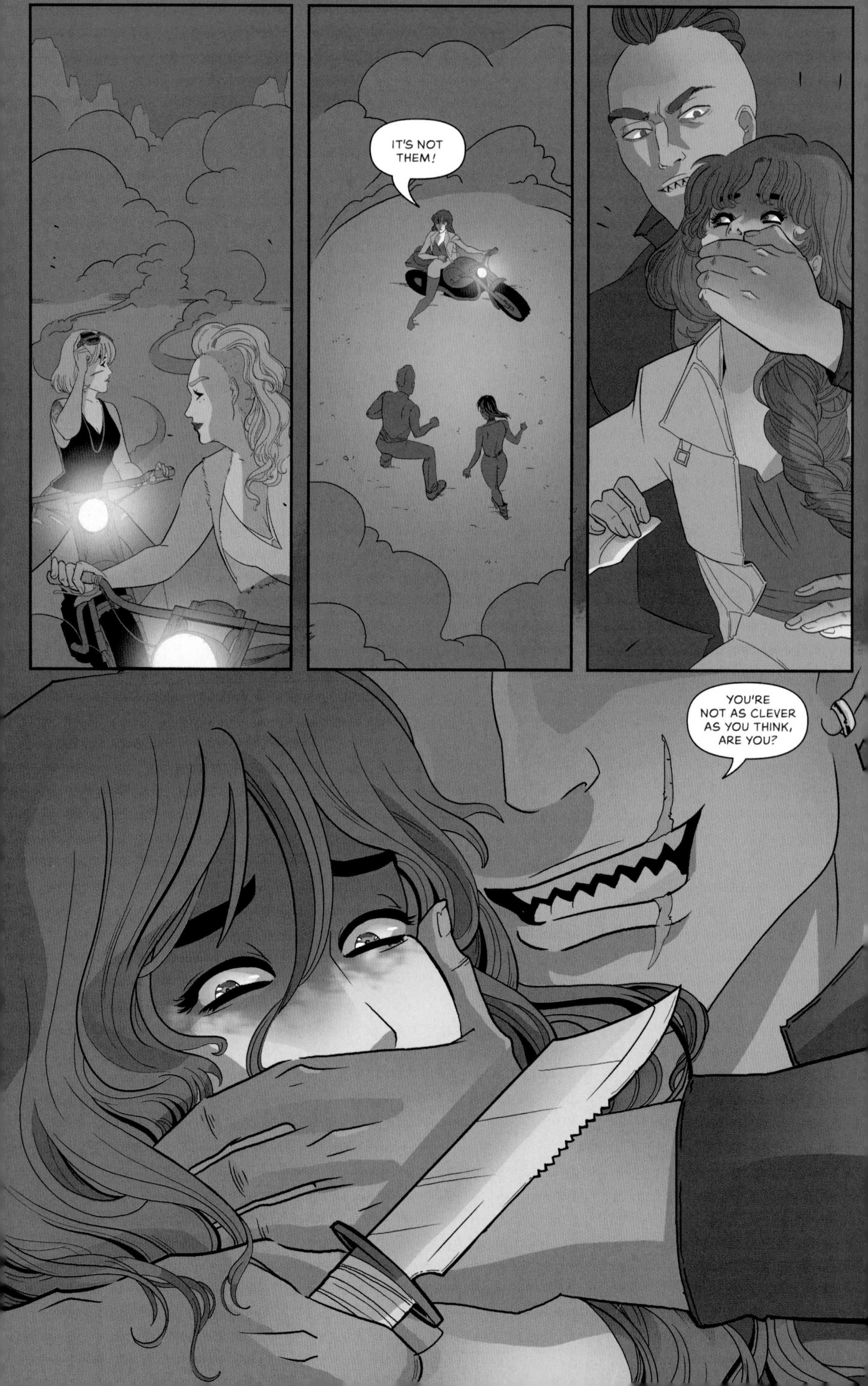
IT'S NOT THEM!
YOU'RE NOT AS CLEVER AS YOU THINK, ARE YOU?

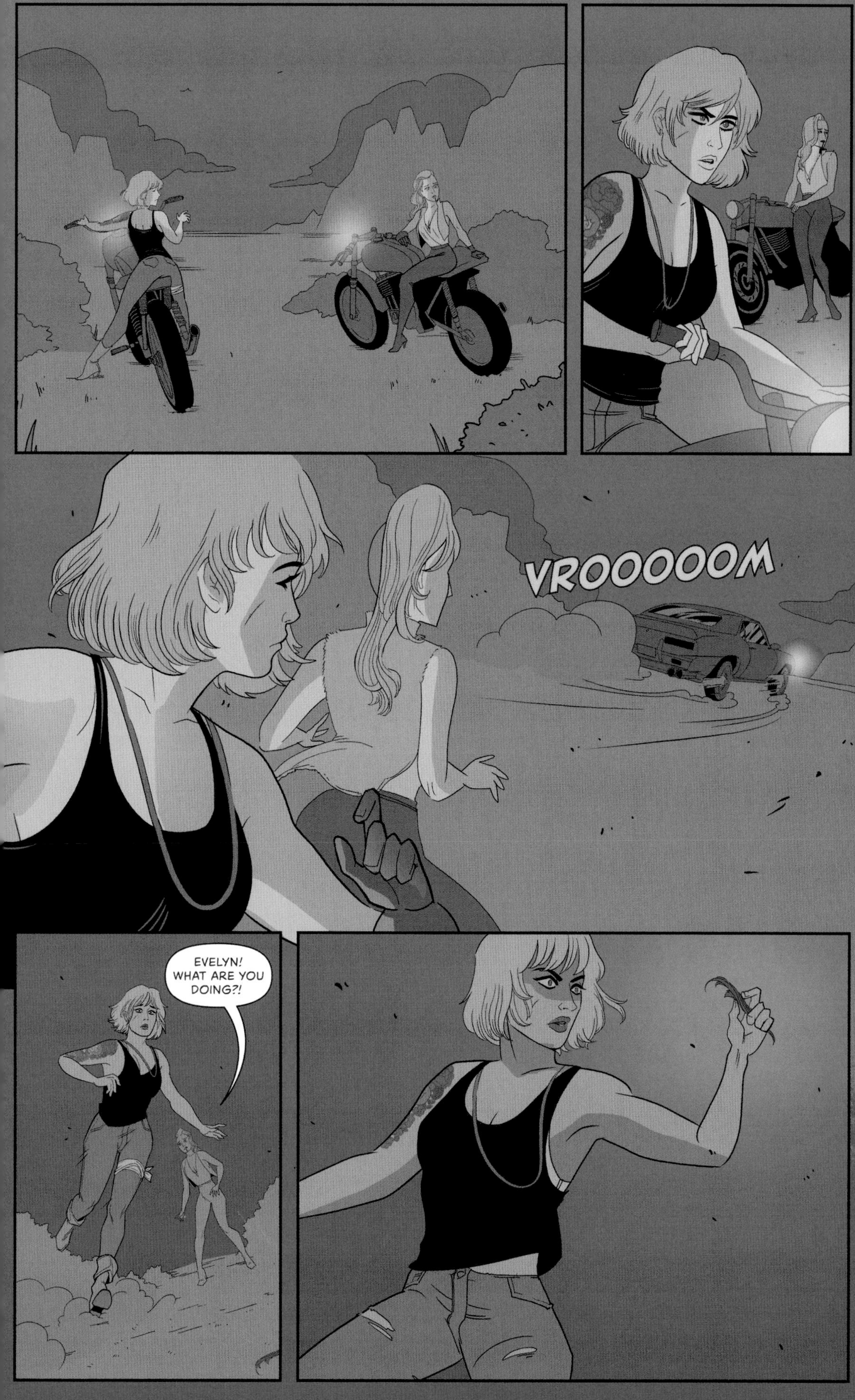
VROOOOOM
EVELYN! WHAT ARE YOU DOING?!

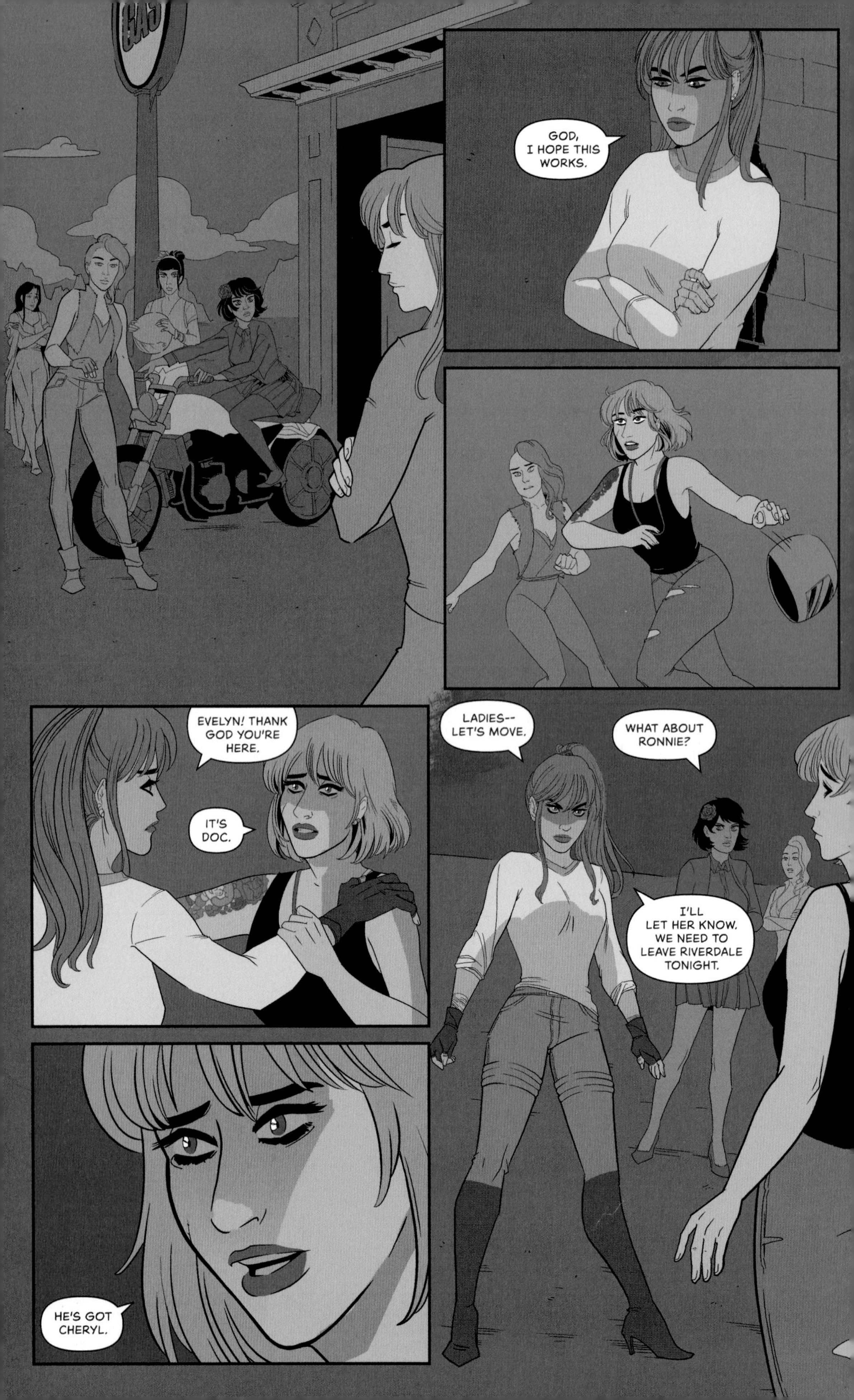

GAS
GOD, I HOPE THIS WORKS.
EVELYN! THANK GOD YOU'RE HERE.
IT'S DOC.
HE'S GOT CHERYL.
LADIES-- LET'S MOVE.
WHAT ABOUT RONNIE?
I'LL LET HER KNOW. WE NEED TO LEAVE RIVERDALE TONIGHT.

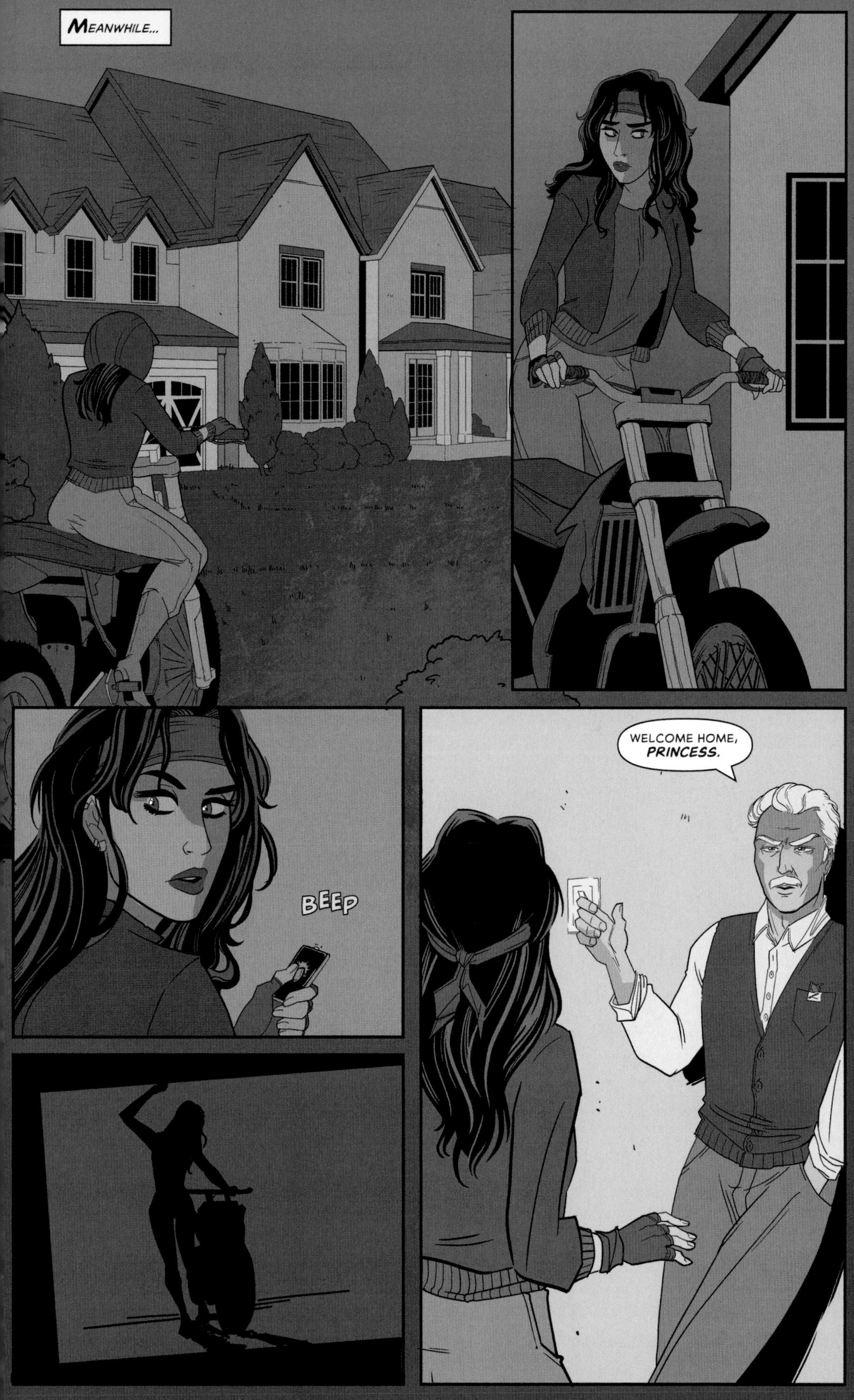
MEANWHILE...
BEEP
WELCOME HOME, PRINCESS.

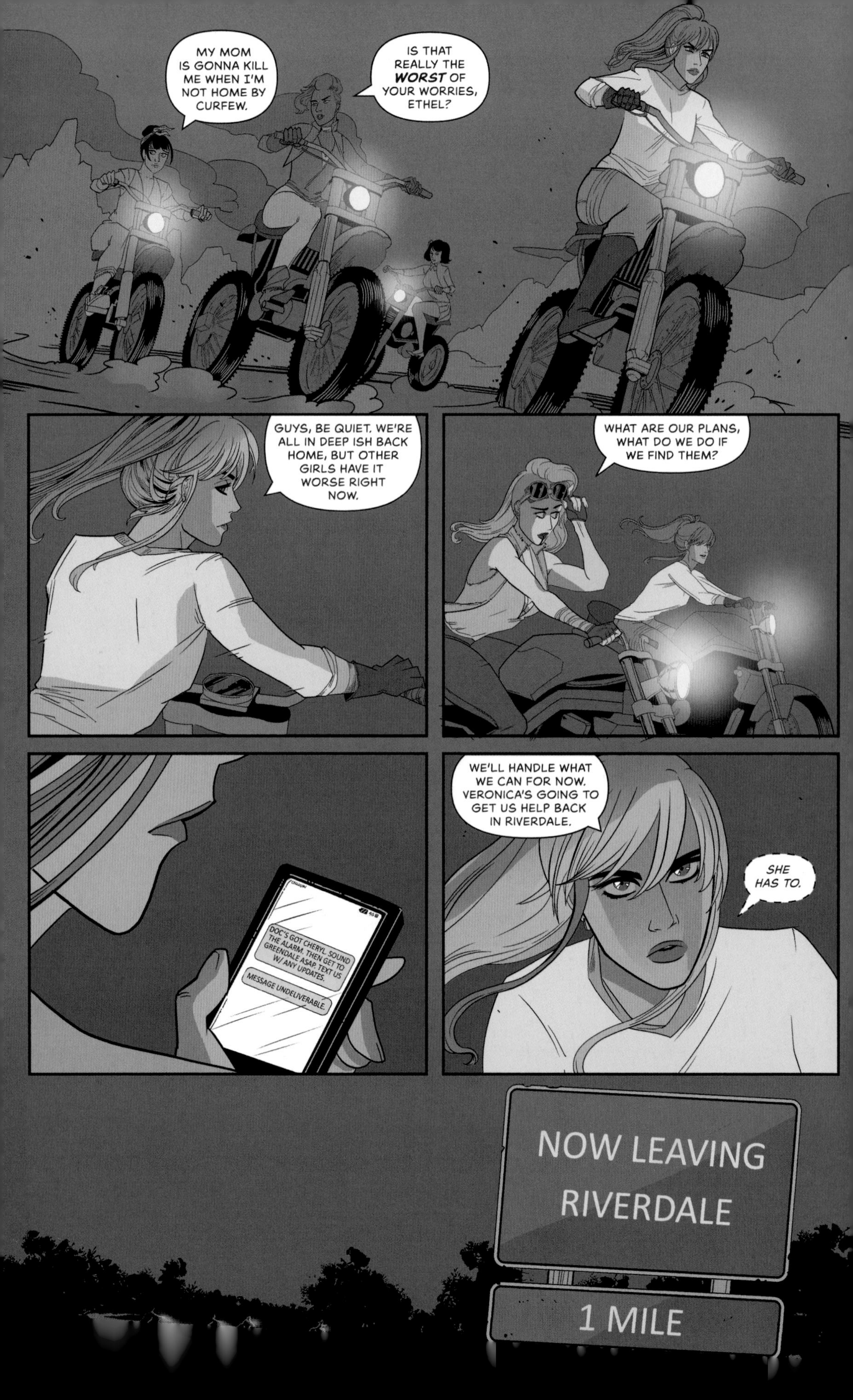
MY MOM IS GONNA KILL ME WHEN I'M NOT HOME BY CURFEW.
IS THAT REALLY THE **WORST** OF YOUR WORRIES, ETHEL?
GUYS, BE QUIET. WE'RE ALL IN DEEP ISH BACK HOME, BUT OTHER GIRLS HAVE IT WORSE RIGHT NOW.
WHAT ARE OUR PLANS, WHAT DO WE DO IF WE FIND THEM?
4G
DOC'S GOT CHERYL. SOUND THE ALARM. THEN GET TO GREENDALE ASAP. TEXT US W/ ANY UPDATES.
MESSAGE UNDELIVERABLE.
WE'LL HANDLE WHAT WE CAN FOR NOW. VERONICA'S GOING TO GET US HELP BACK IN RIVERDALE.
SHE HAS TO.
NOW LEAVING RIVERDALE
1 MILE

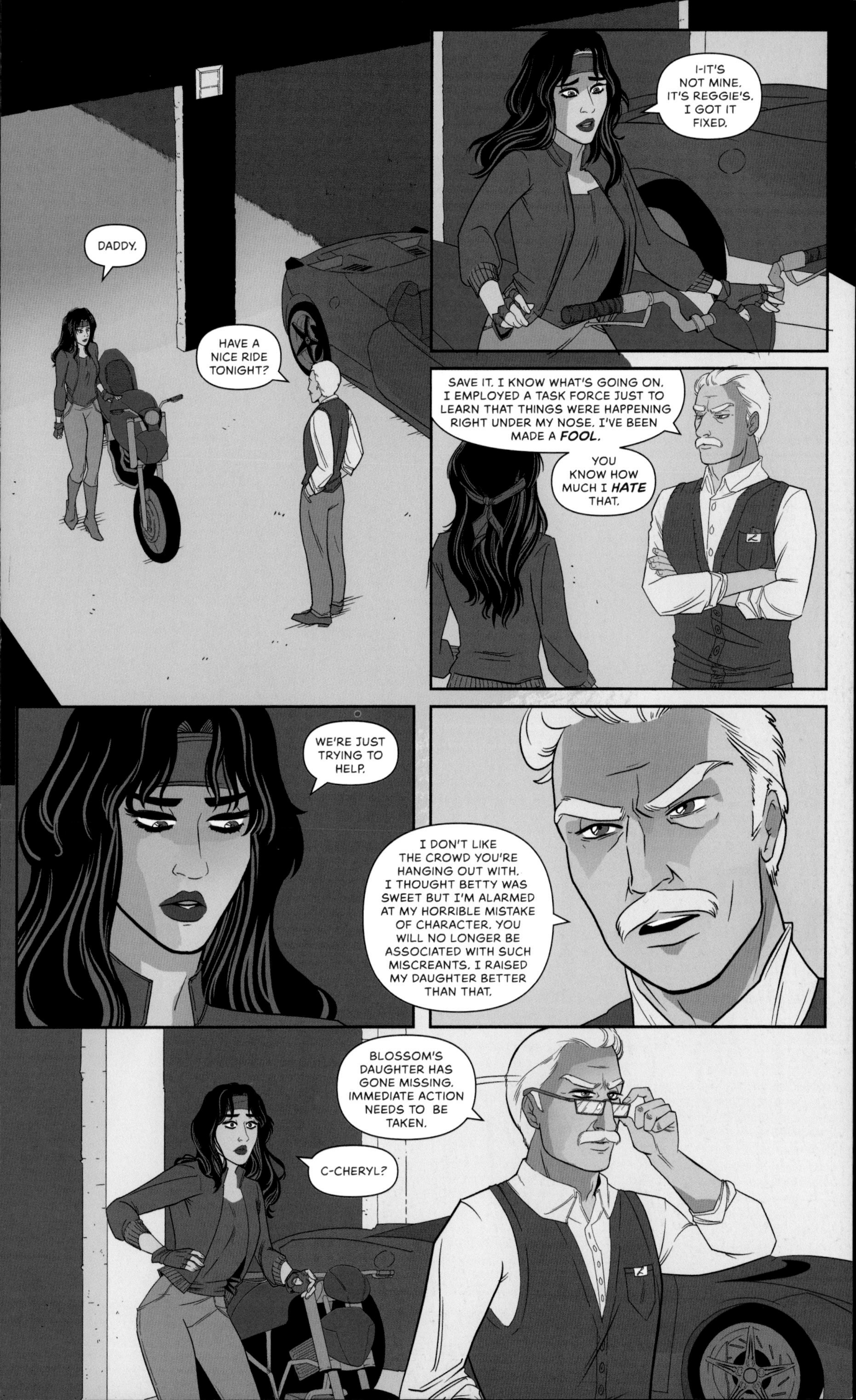
DADDY.
HAVE A NICE RIDE TONIGHT?
I-IT'S NOT MINE. IT'S REGGIE'S. I GOT IT FIXED.
SAVE IT. I KNOW WHAT'S GOING ON. I EMPLOYED A TASK FORCE JUST TO LEARN THAT THINGS WERE HAPPENING RIGHT UNDER MY NOSE. I'VE BEEN MADE A ***FOOL.***
YOU KNOW HOW MUCH I ***HATE*** THAT.
WE'RE JUST TRYING TO HELP.
I DON'T LIKE THE CROWD YOU'RE HANGING OUT WITH. I THOUGHT BETTY WAS SWEET BUT I'M ALARMED AT MY HORRIBLE MISTAKE OF CHARACTER. YOU WILL NO LONGER BE ASSOCIATED WITH SUCH MISCREANTS. I RAISED MY DAUGHTER BETTER THAN THAT.
BLOSSOM'S DAUGHTER HAS GONE MISSING. IMMEDIATE ACTION NEEDS TO BE TAKEN.
C-CHERYL?

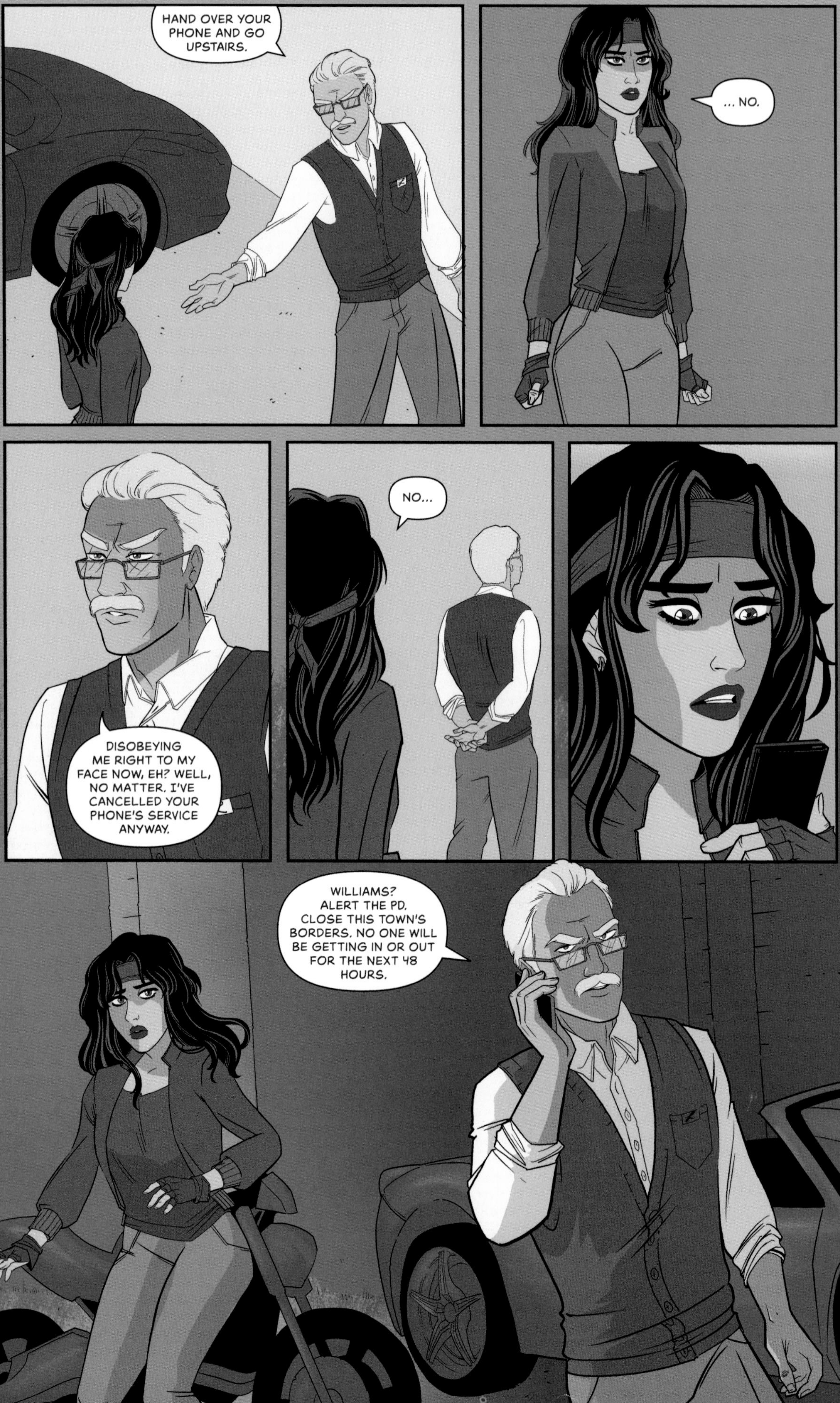
HAND OVER YOUR PHONE AND GO UPSTAIRS.
... NO.
DISOBEYING ME RIGHT TO MY FACE NOW, EH? WELL, NO MATTER. I'VE CANCELLED YOUR PHONE'S SERVICE ANYWAY.
NO...
WILLIAMS? ALERT THE PD. CLOSE THIS TOWN'S BORDERS. NO ONE WILL BE GETTING IN OR OUT FOR THE NEXT 48 HOURS.

to be continued...

Chapter Nine

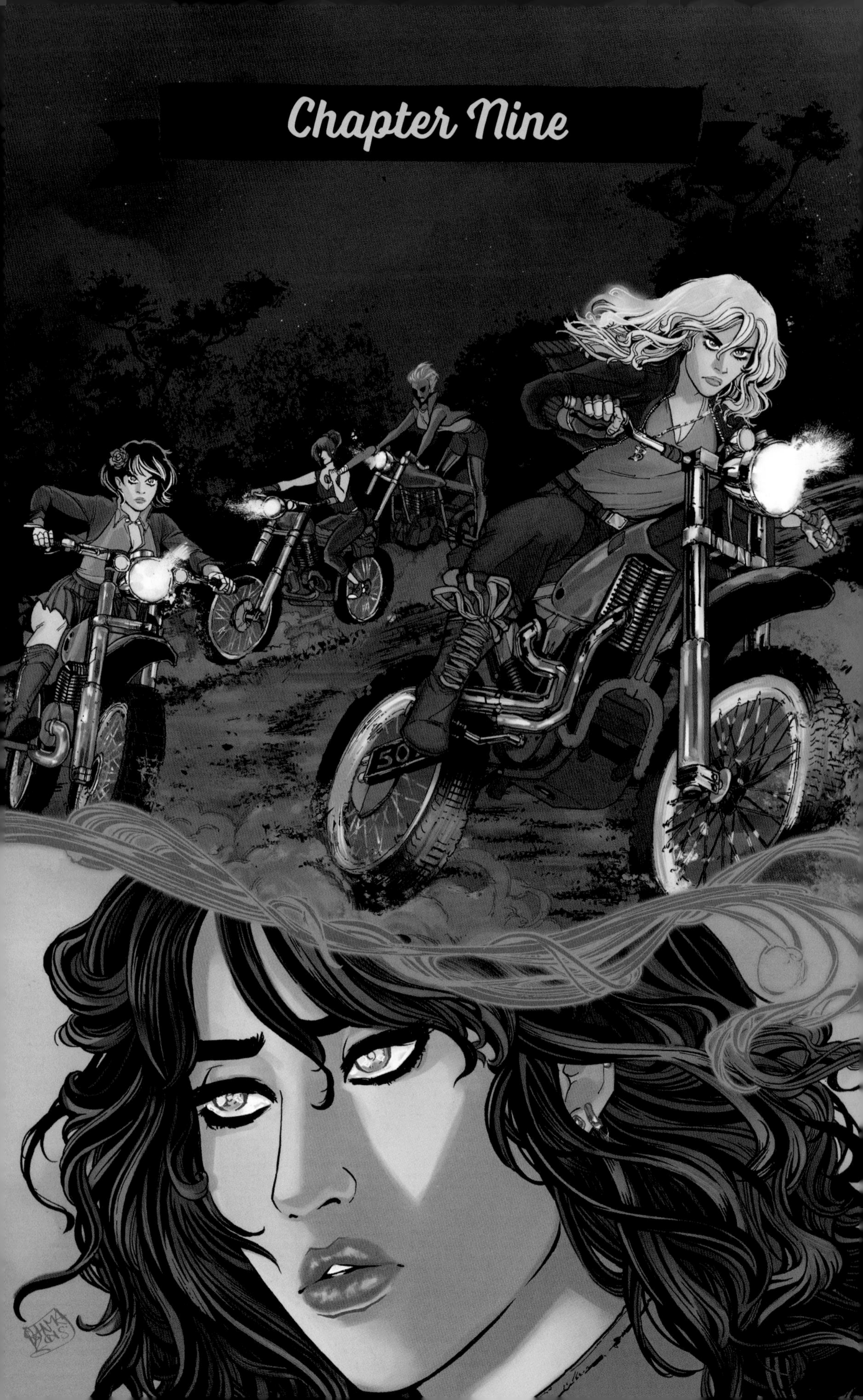

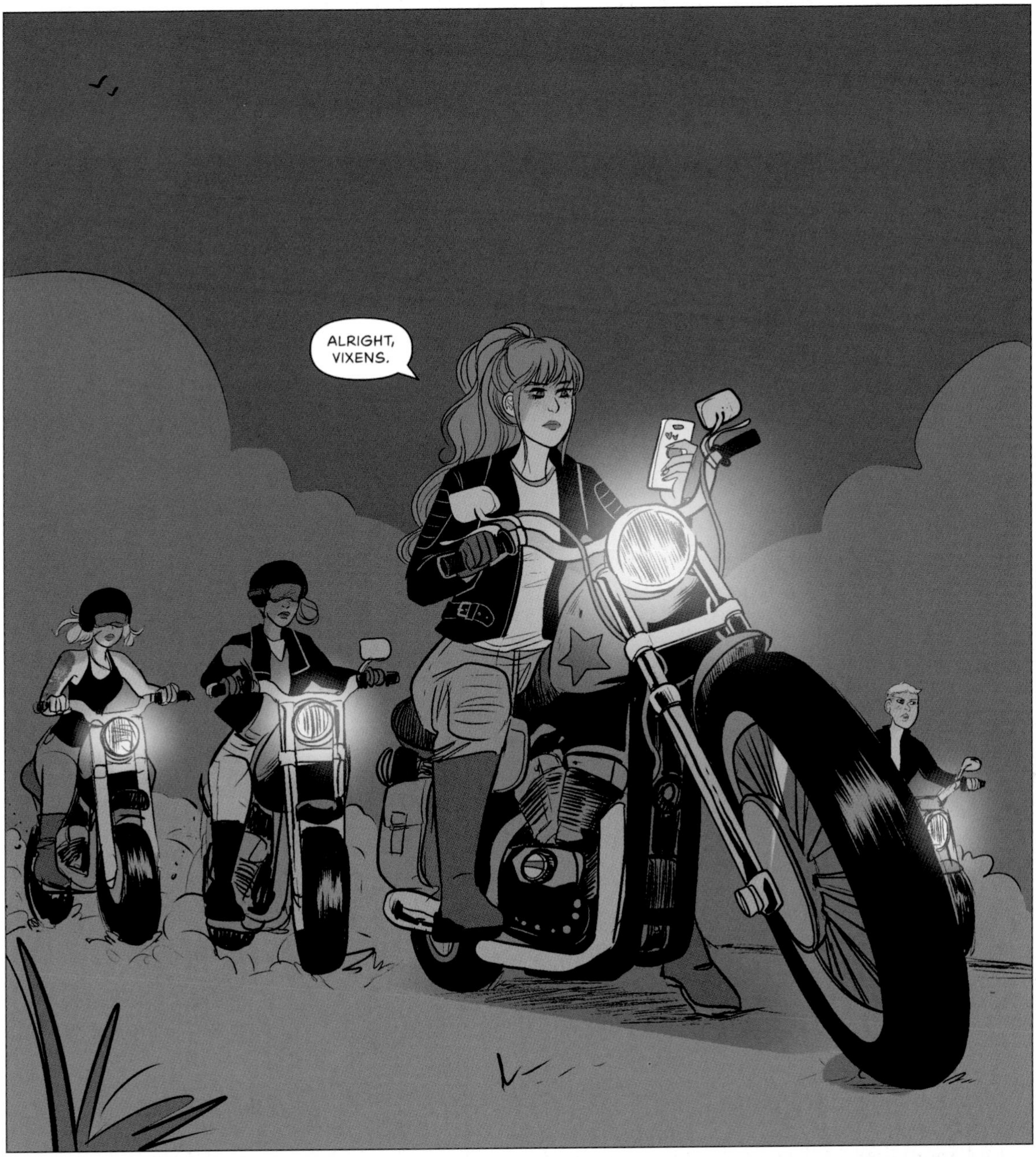
ALRIGHT, VIXENS.

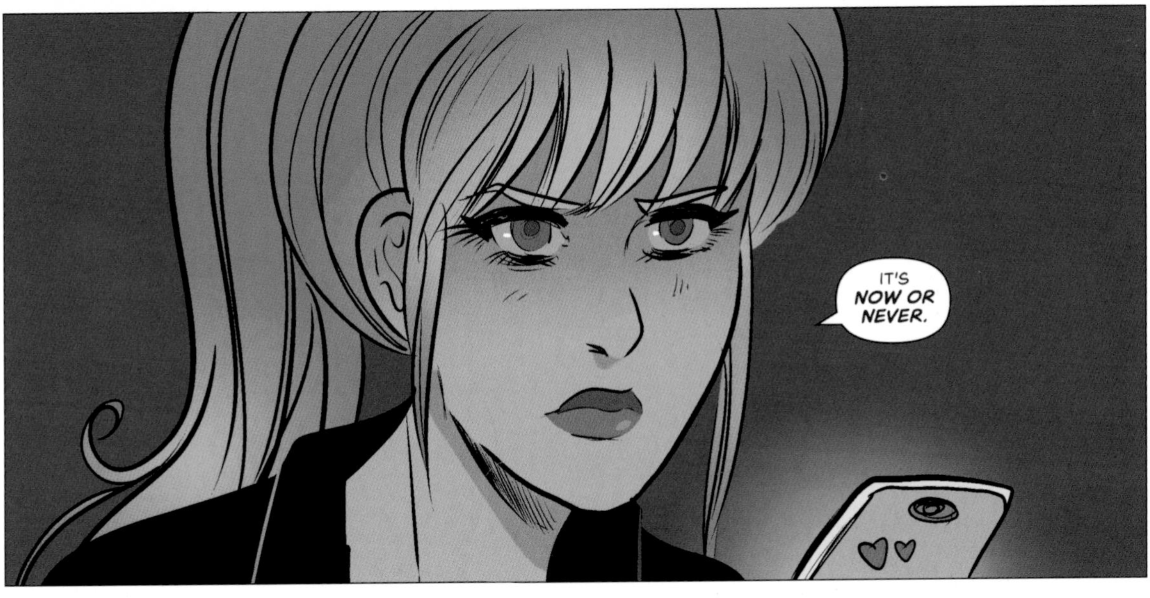
IT'S *NOW OR NEVER.*

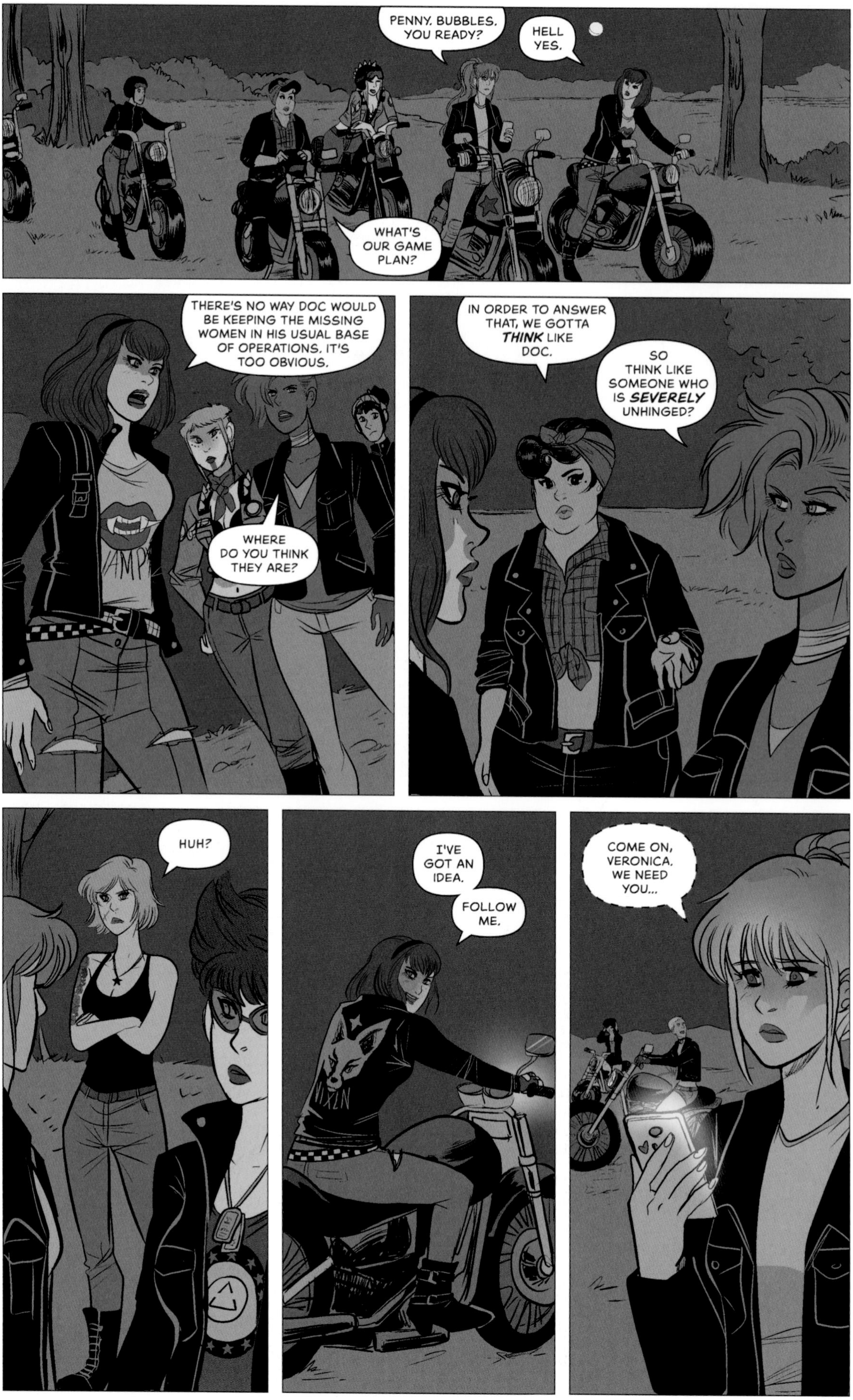
PENNY. BUBBLES. YOU READY?
HELL YES.
WHAT'S OUR GAME PLAN?
THERE'S NO WAY DOC WOULD BE KEEPING THE MISSING WOMEN IN HIS USUAL BASE OF OPERATIONS. IT'S TOO OBVIOUS.
WHERE DO YOU THINK THEY ARE?
IN ORDER TO ANSWER THAT, WE GOTTA **THINK** LIKE DOC.
SO THINK LIKE SOMEONE WHO IS **SEVERELY** UNHINGED?
HUH?
I'VE GOT AN IDEA.
FOLLOW ME.
COME ON, VERONICA, WE NEED YOU...

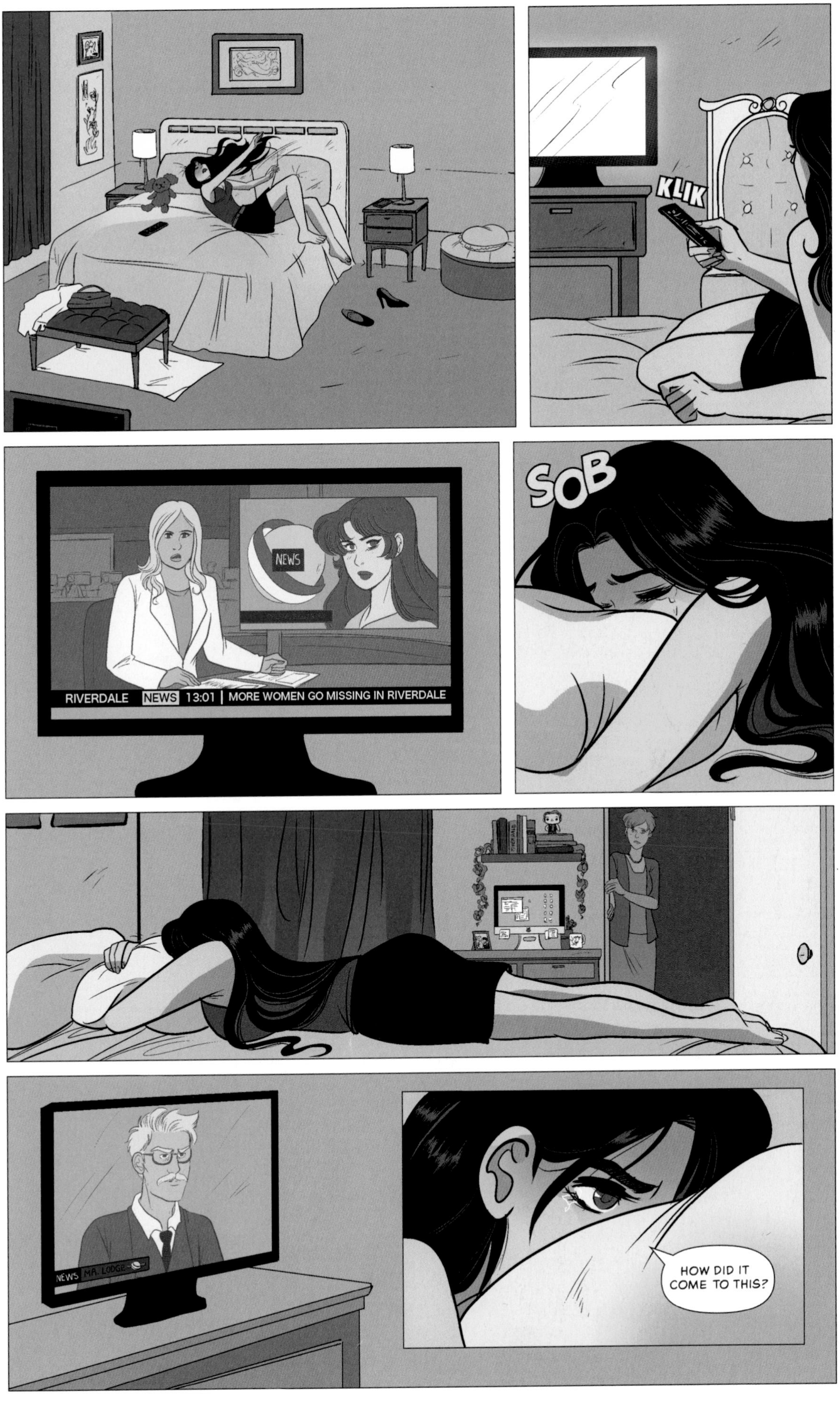
KLIK
RIVERDALE NEWS 13:01 | MORE WOMEN GO MISSING IN RIVERDALE
NEWS
SOB
NEWS MA. LODGE
HOW DID IT COME TO THIS?

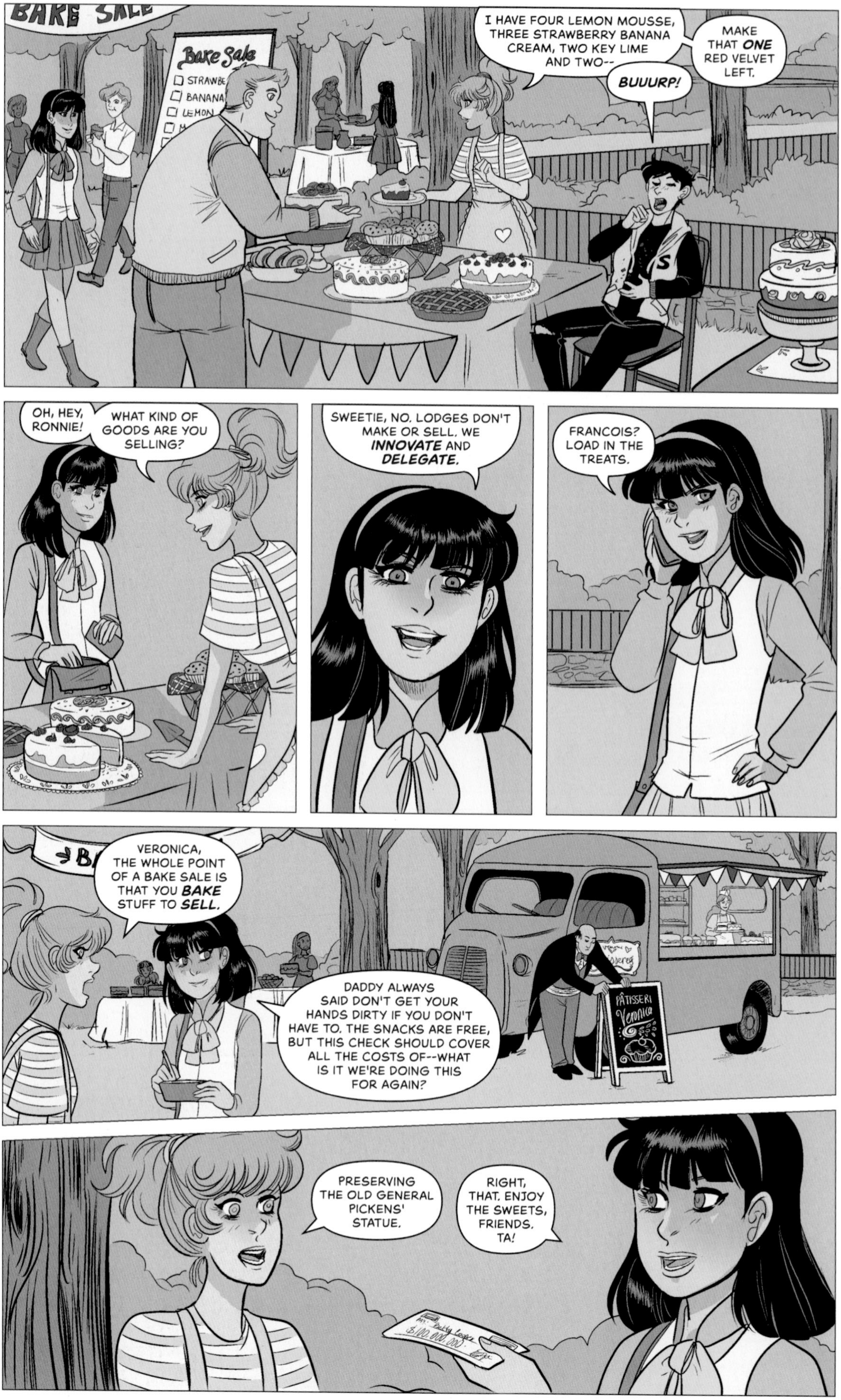
BAKE SALE
Bake Sale
STRAWBE
BANANA
LEMON
I HAVE FOUR LEMON MOUSSE, THREE STRAWBERRY BANANA CREAM, TWO KEY LIME AND TWO--
BUUURP!
MAKE THAT ONE RED VELVET LEFT.
OH, HEY, RONNIE!
WHAT KIND OF GOODS ARE YOU SELLING?
SWEETIE, NO. LODGES DON'T MAKE OR SELL. WE INNOVATE AND DELEGATE.
FRANCOIS? LOAD IN THE TREATS.
VERONICA, THE WHOLE POINT OF A BAKE SALE IS THAT YOU BAKE STUFF TO SELL.
DADDY ALWAYS SAID DON'T GET YOUR HANDS DIRTY IF YOU DON'T HAVE TO. THE SNACKS ARE FREE, BUT THIS CHECK SHOULD COVER ALL THE COSTS OF--WHAT IS IT WE'RE DOING THIS FOR AGAIN?
PÂTISSERI
Veronica
PRESERVING THE OLD GENERAL PICKENS' STATUE.
RIGHT, THAT. ENJOY THE SWEETS, FRIENDS. TA!
$100,000.00

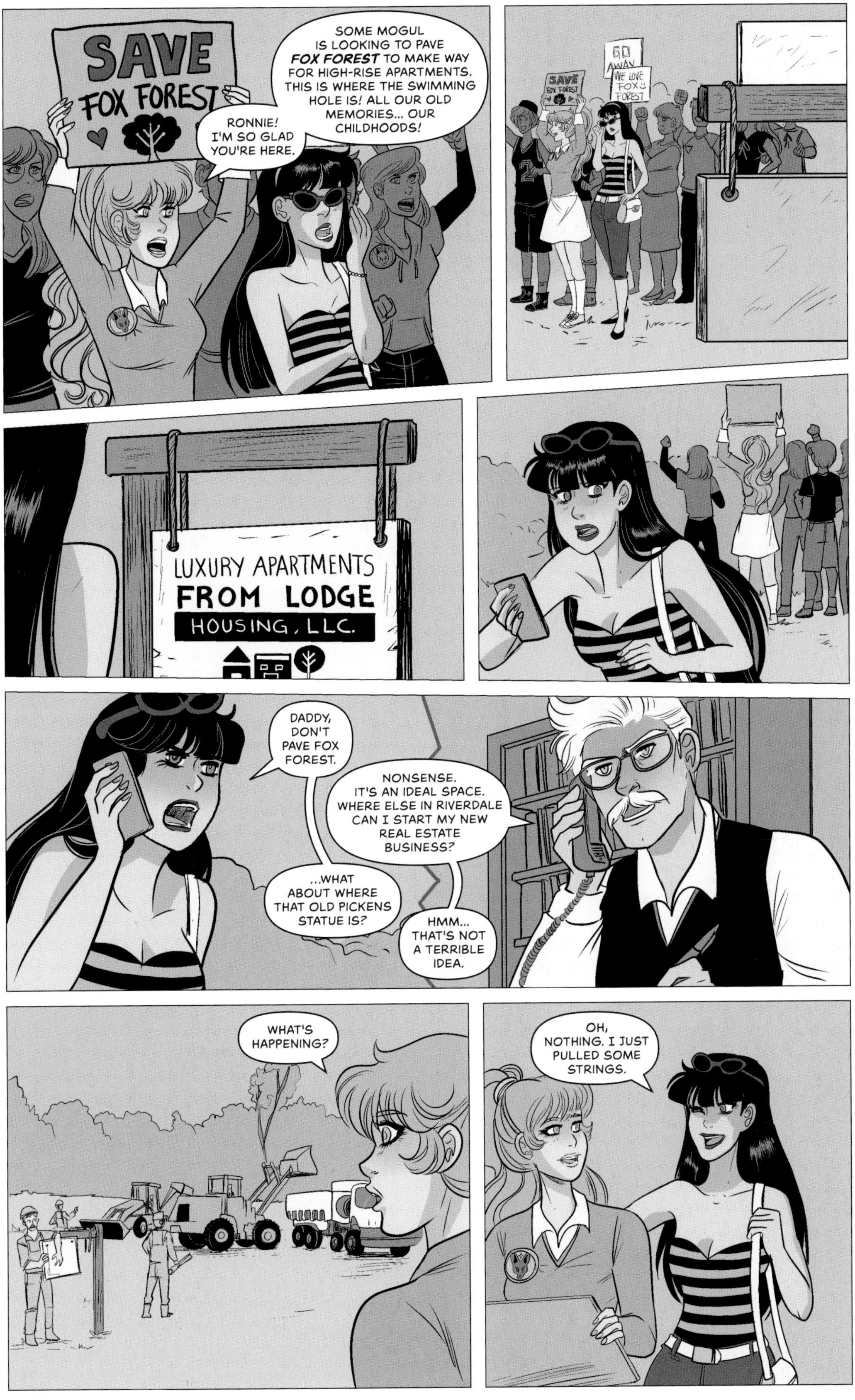
SAVE FOX FOREST
RONNIE! I'M SO GLAD YOU'RE HERE.
SOME MOGUL IS LOOKING TO PAVE **FOX FOREST** TO MAKE WAY FOR HIGH-RISE APARTMENTS. THIS IS WHERE THE SWIMMING HOLE IS! ALL OUR OLD MEMORIES... OUR CHILDHOODS!
GO AWAY
SAVE FOX FOREST
WE LOVE FOX FOREST
LUXURY APARTMENTS FROM LODGE HOUSING, LLC.
DADDY, DON'T PAVE FOX FOREST.
NONSENSE. IT'S AN IDEAL SPACE. WHERE ELSE IN RIVERDALE CAN I START MY NEW REAL ESTATE BUSINESS?
...WHAT ABOUT WHERE THAT OLD PICKENS STATUE IS?
HMM... THAT'S NOT A TERRIBLE IDEA.
WHAT'S HAPPENING?
OH, NOTHING. I JUST PULLED SOME STRINGS.

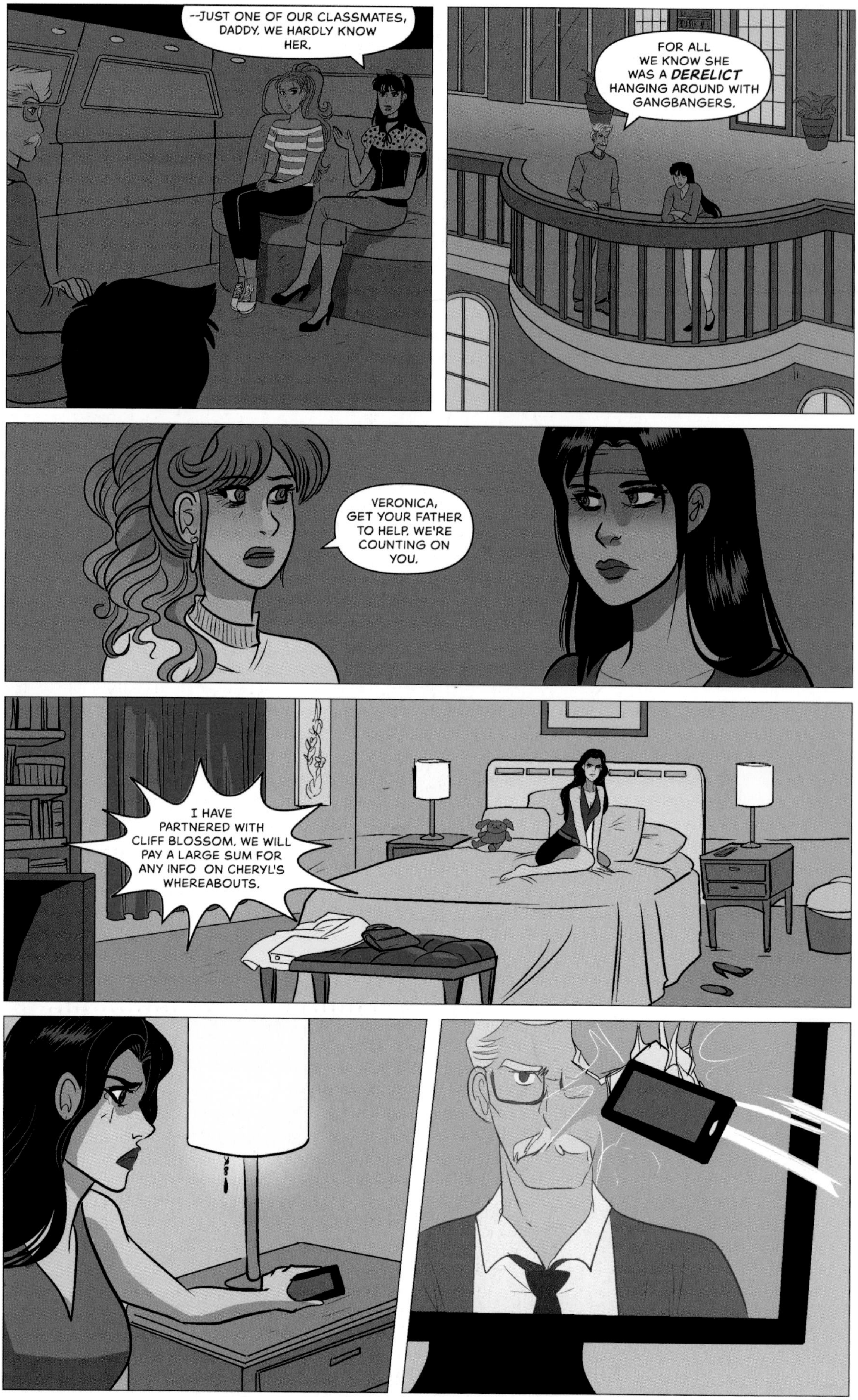
--JUST ONE OF OUR CLASSMATES, DADDY. WE HARDLY KNOW HER.
FOR ALL WE KNOW SHE WAS A *DERELICT* HANGING AROUND WITH GANGBANGERS.
VERONICA, GET YOUR FATHER TO HELP. WE'RE COUNTING ON YOU.
I HAVE PARTNERED WITH CLIFF BLOSSOM. WE WILL PAY A LARGE SUM FOR ANY INFO ON CHERYL'S WHEREABOUTS.

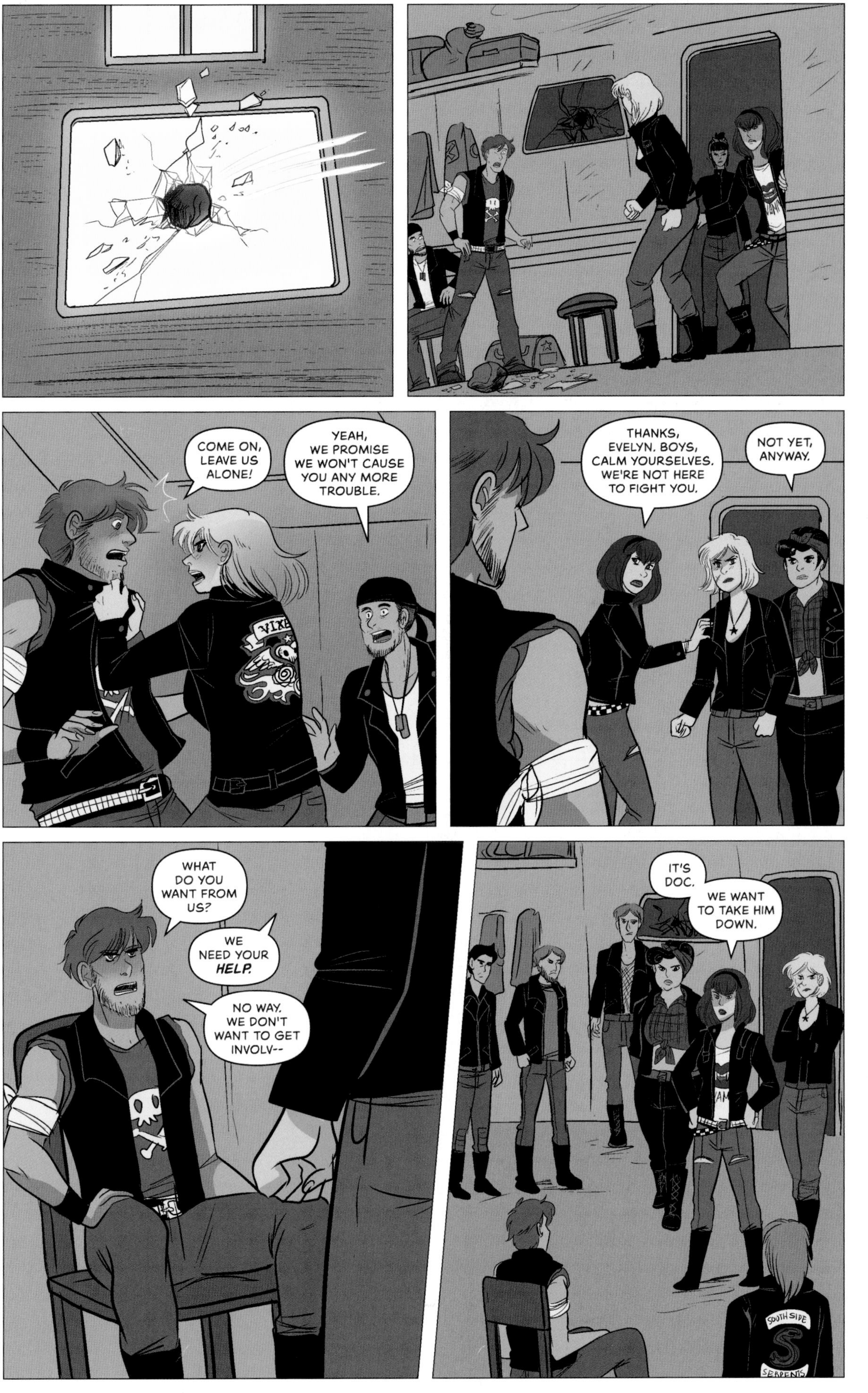
COME ON, LEAVE US ALONE!
YEAH, WE PROMISE WE WON'T CAUSE YOU ANY MORE TROUBLE.
THANKS, EVELYN. BOYS, CALM YOURSELVES. WE'RE NOT HERE TO FIGHT YOU.
NOT YET, ANYWAY.
WHAT DO YOU WANT FROM US?
WE NEED YOUR *HELP.*
NO WAY. WE DON'T WANT TO GET INVOLV--
IT'S DOC.
WE WANT TO TAKE HIM DOWN.
SOUTH SIDE SERPENTS

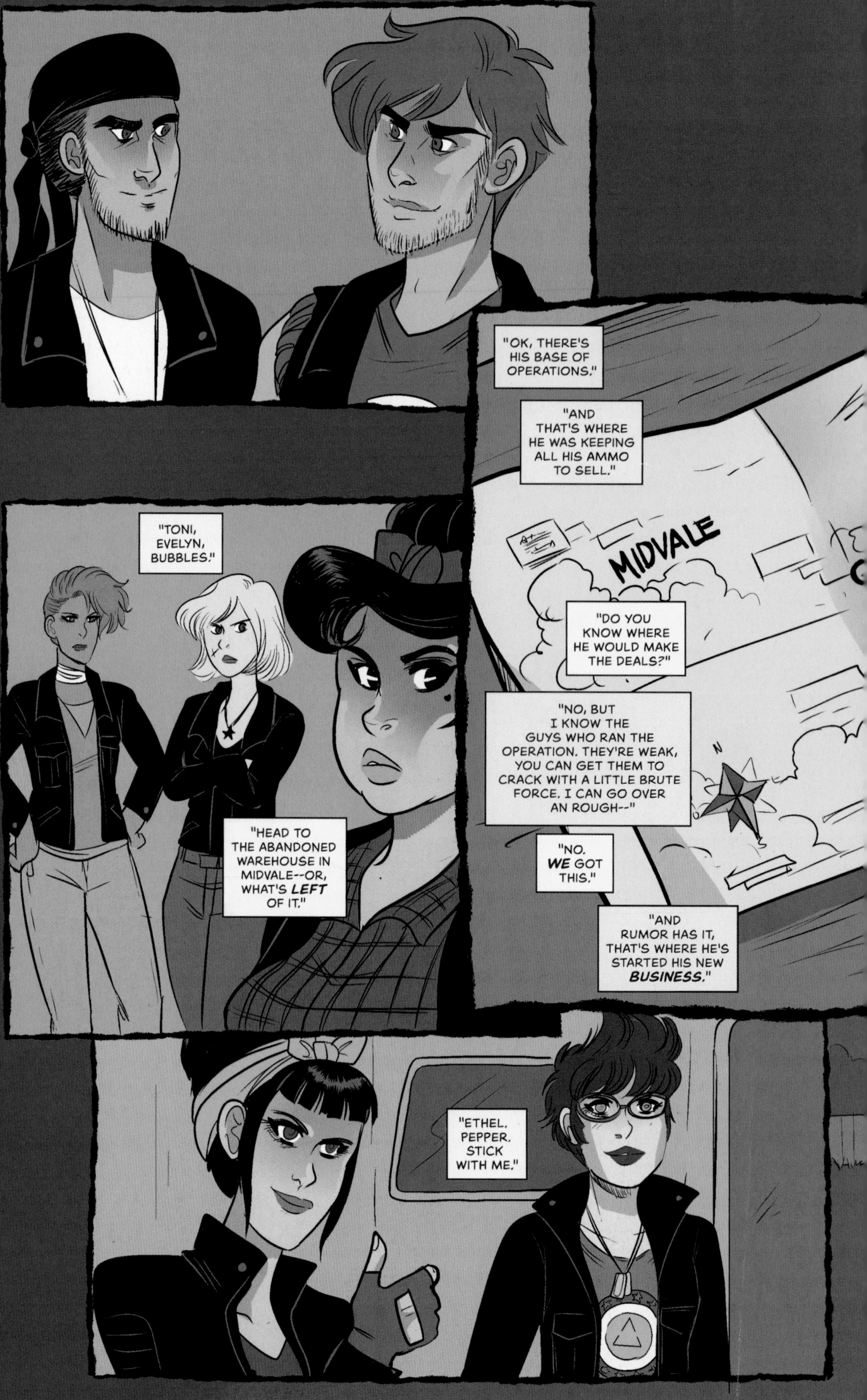
"OK, THERE'S HIS BASE OF OPERATIONS."
"AND THAT'S WHERE HE WAS KEEPING ALL HIS AMMO TO SELL."
MIDVALE
"DO YOU KNOW WHERE HE WOULD MAKE THE DEALS?"
"NO, BUT I KNOW THE GUYS WHO RAN THE OPERATION. THEY'RE WEAK, YOU CAN GET THEM TO CRACK WITH A LITTLE BRUTE FORCE. I CAN GO OVER AN ROUGH--"
"NO. WE GOT THIS."
"AND RUMOR HAS IT, THAT'S WHERE HE'S STARTED HIS NEW BUSINESS."
"TONI, EVELYN, BUBBLES."
"HEAD TO THE ABANDONED WAREHOUSE IN MIDVALE--OR, WHAT'S LEFT OF IT."
"ETHEL. PEPPER. STICK WITH ME."

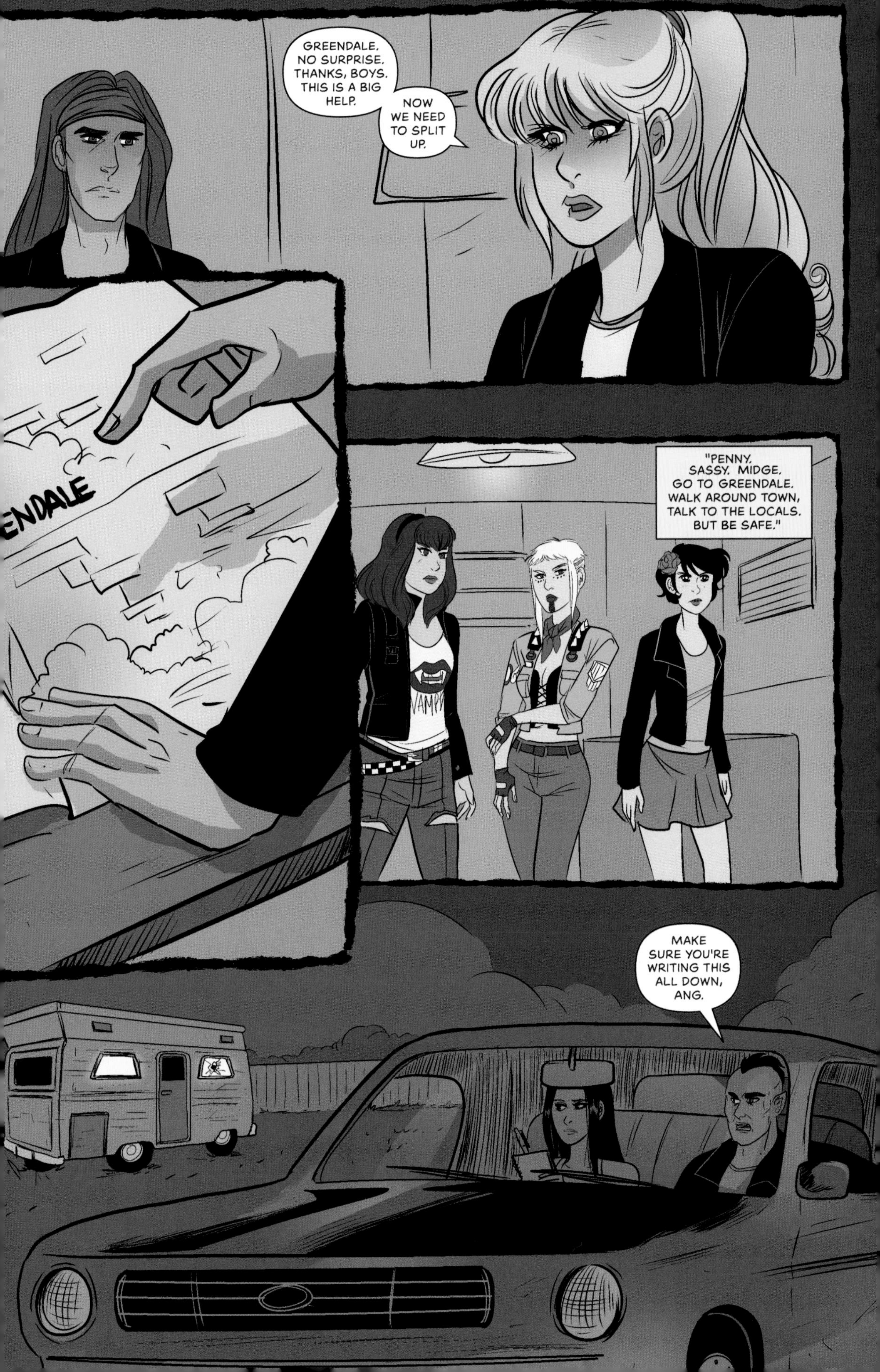
GREENDALE. NO SURPRISE. THANKS, BOYS. THIS IS A BIG HELP.
NOW WE NEED TO SPLIT UP.
ENDALE
"PENNY. SASSY. MIDGE. GO TO GREENDALE. WALK AROUND TOWN, TALK TO THE LOCALS. BUT BE SAFE."
MAKE SURE YOU'RE WRITING THIS ALL DOWN, ANG.

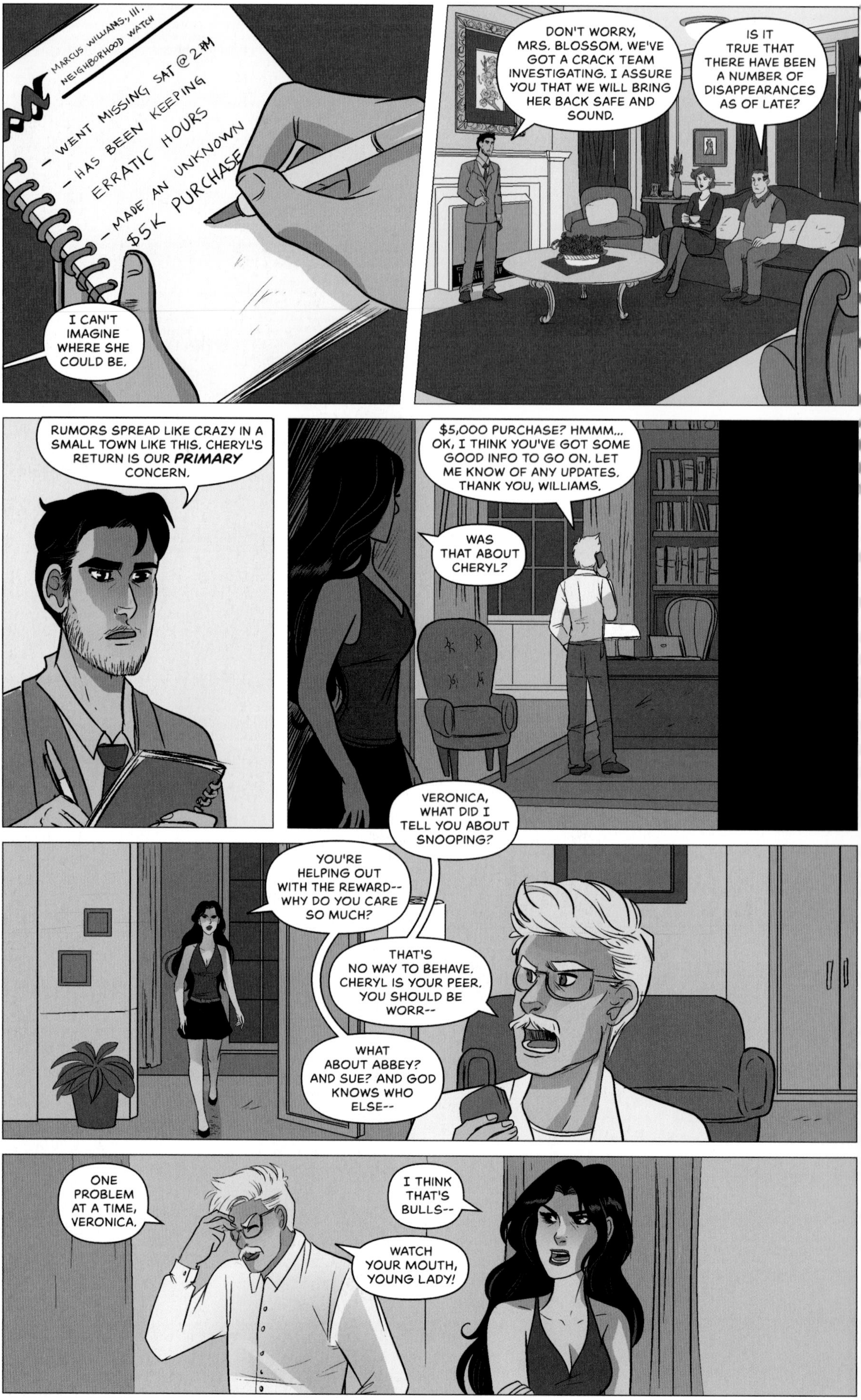
MARCUS WILLIAMS, III.
NEIGHBORHOOD WATCH
- WENT MISSING SAT @ 2PM
- HAS BEEN KEEPING ERRATIC HOURS
- MADE AN UNKNOWN $5K PURCHASE
I CAN'T IMAGINE WHERE SHE COULD BE.
DON'T WORRY, MRS. BLOSSOM. WE'VE GOT A CRACK TEAM INVESTIGATING. I ASSURE YOU THAT WE WILL BRING HER BACK SAFE AND SOUND.
IS IT TRUE THAT THERE HAVE BEEN A NUMBER OF DISAPPEARANCES AS OF LATE?
RUMORS SPREAD LIKE CRAZY IN A SMALL TOWN LIKE THIS. CHERYL'S RETURN IS OUR PRIMARY CONCERN.
$5,000 PURCHASE? HMMM... OK, I THINK YOU'VE GOT SOME GOOD INFO TO GO ON. LET ME KNOW OF ANY UPDATES. THANK YOU, WILLIAMS.
WAS THAT ABOUT CHERYL?
VERONICA, WHAT DID I TELL YOU ABOUT SNOOPING?
YOU'RE HELPING OUT WITH THE REWARD--WHY DO YOU CARE SO MUCH?
THAT'S NO WAY TO BEHAVE. CHERYL IS YOUR PEER. YOU SHOULD BE WORR--
WHAT ABOUT ABBEY? AND SUE? AND GOD KNOWS WHO ELSE--
ONE PROBLEM AT A TIME, VERONICA.
I THINK THAT'S BULLS--
WATCH YOUR MOUTH, YOUNG LADY!

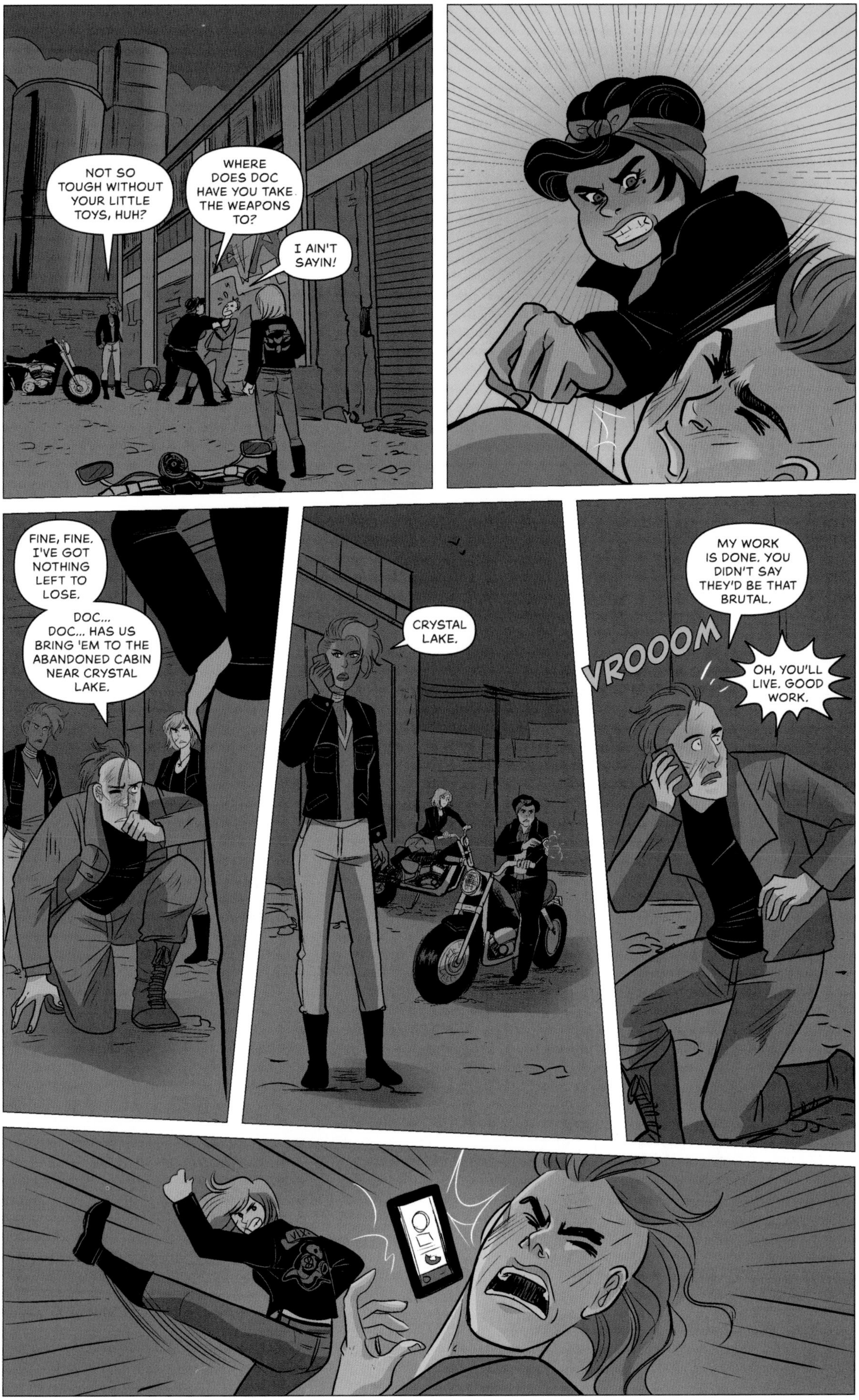
NOT SO TOUGH WITHOUT YOUR LITTLE TOYS, HUH?
WHERE DOES DOC HAVE YOU TAKE THE WEAPONS TO?
I AIN'T SAYIN!
FINE, FINE. I'VE GOT NOTHING LEFT TO LOSE.
DOC... DOC... HAS US BRING 'EM TO THE ABANDONED CABIN NEAR CRYSTAL LAKE.
CRYSTAL LAKE.
MY WORK IS DONE. YOU DIDN'T SAY THEY'D BE THAT BRUTAL.
VROOOM
OH, YOU'LL LIVE. GOOD WORK.
VIX

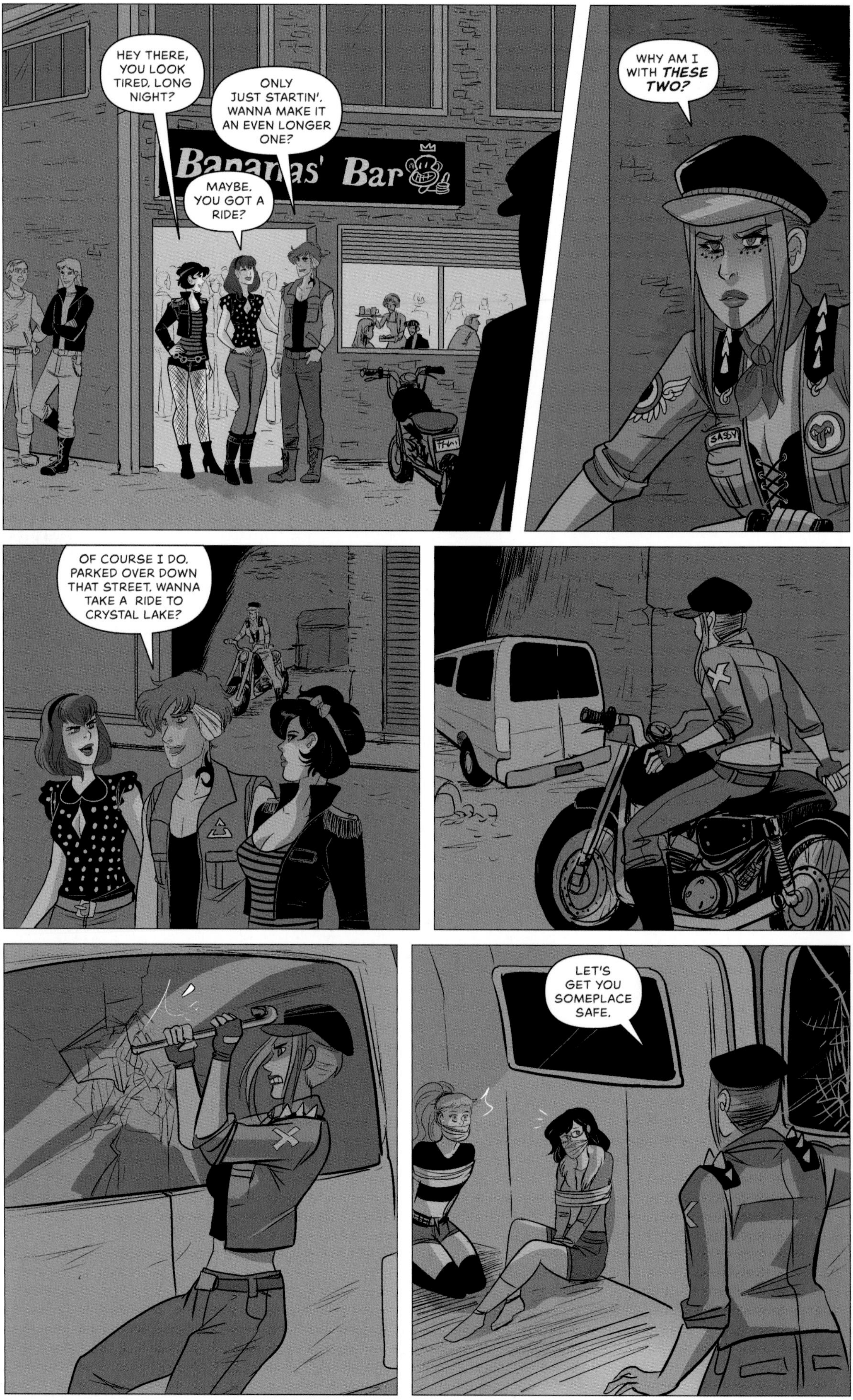
HEY THERE, YOU LOOK TIRED, LONG NIGHT?
ONLY JUST STARTIN', WANNA MAKE IT AN EVEN LONGER ONE?
MAYBE, YOU GOT A RIDE?
Bananas' Bar
WHY AM I WITH THESE TWO?
SASSY
OF COURSE I DO, PARKED OVER DOWN THAT STREET, WANNA TAKE A RIDE TO CRYSTAL LAKE?
LET'S GET YOU SOMEPLACE SAFE.

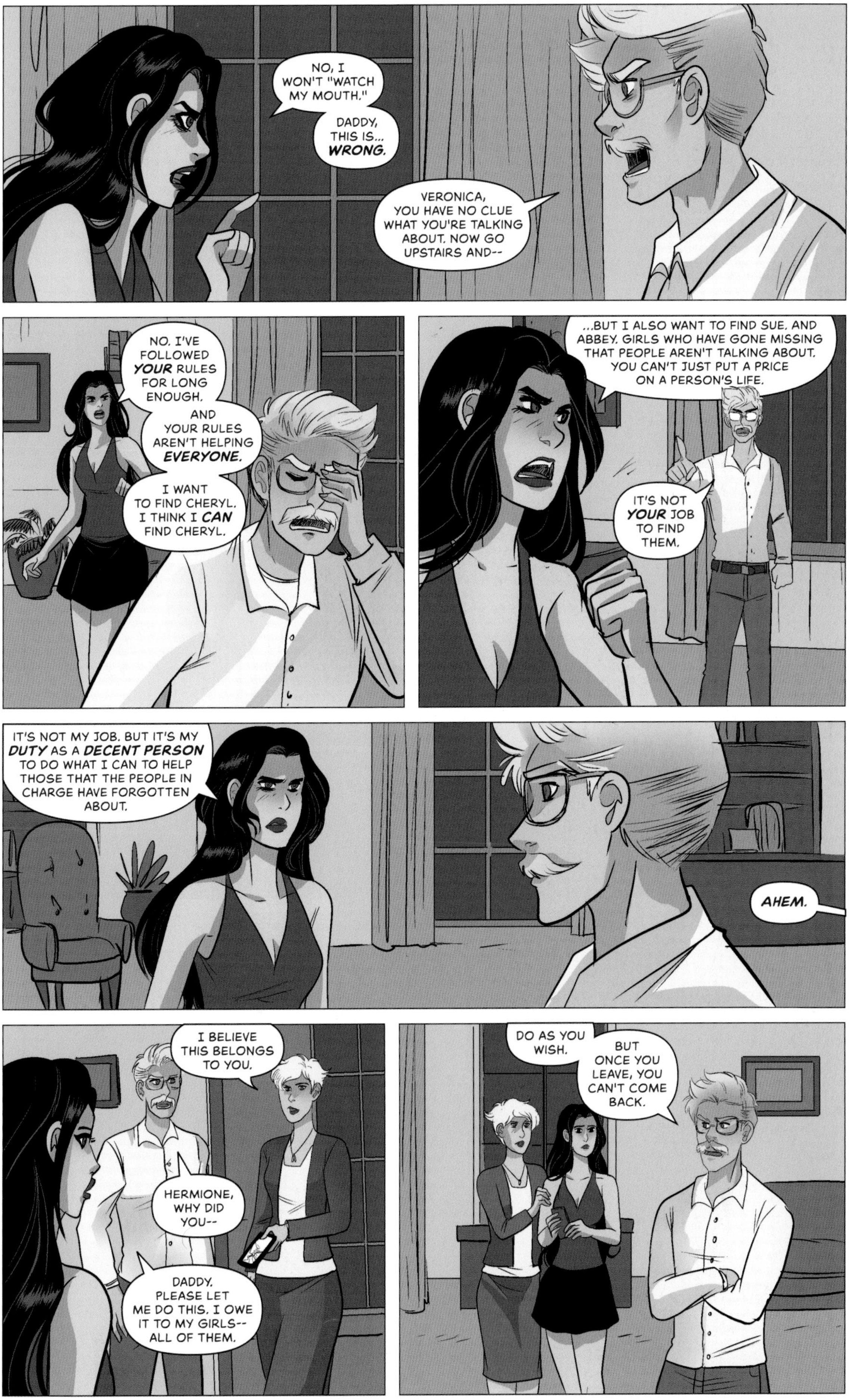
NO, I WON'T "WATCH MY MOUTH."
DADDY, THIS IS... WRONG.
VERONICA, YOU HAVE NO CLUE WHAT YOU'RE TALKING ABOUT. NOW GO UPSTAIRS AND--
NO. I'VE FOLLOWED YOUR RULES FOR LONG ENOUGH.
AND YOUR RULES AREN'T HELPING EVERYONE.
I WANT TO FIND CHERYL. I THINK I CAN FIND CHERYL.
...BUT I ALSO WANT TO FIND SUE. AND ABBEY. GIRLS WHO HAVE GONE MISSING THAT PEOPLE AREN'T TALKING ABOUT. YOU CAN'T JUST PUT A PRICE ON A PERSON'S LIFE.
IT'S NOT YOUR JOB TO FIND THEM.
IT'S NOT MY JOB. BUT IT'S MY DUTY AS A DECENT PERSON TO DO WHAT I CAN TO HELP THOSE THAT THE PEOPLE IN CHARGE HAVE FORGOTTEN ABOUT.
AHEM.
I BELIEVE THIS BELONGS TO YOU.
HERMIONE, WHY DID YOU--
DADDY. PLEASE LET ME DO THIS. I OWE IT TO MY GIRLS-- ALL OF THEM.
DO AS YOU WISH.
BUT ONCE YOU LEAVE, YOU CAN'T COME BACK.

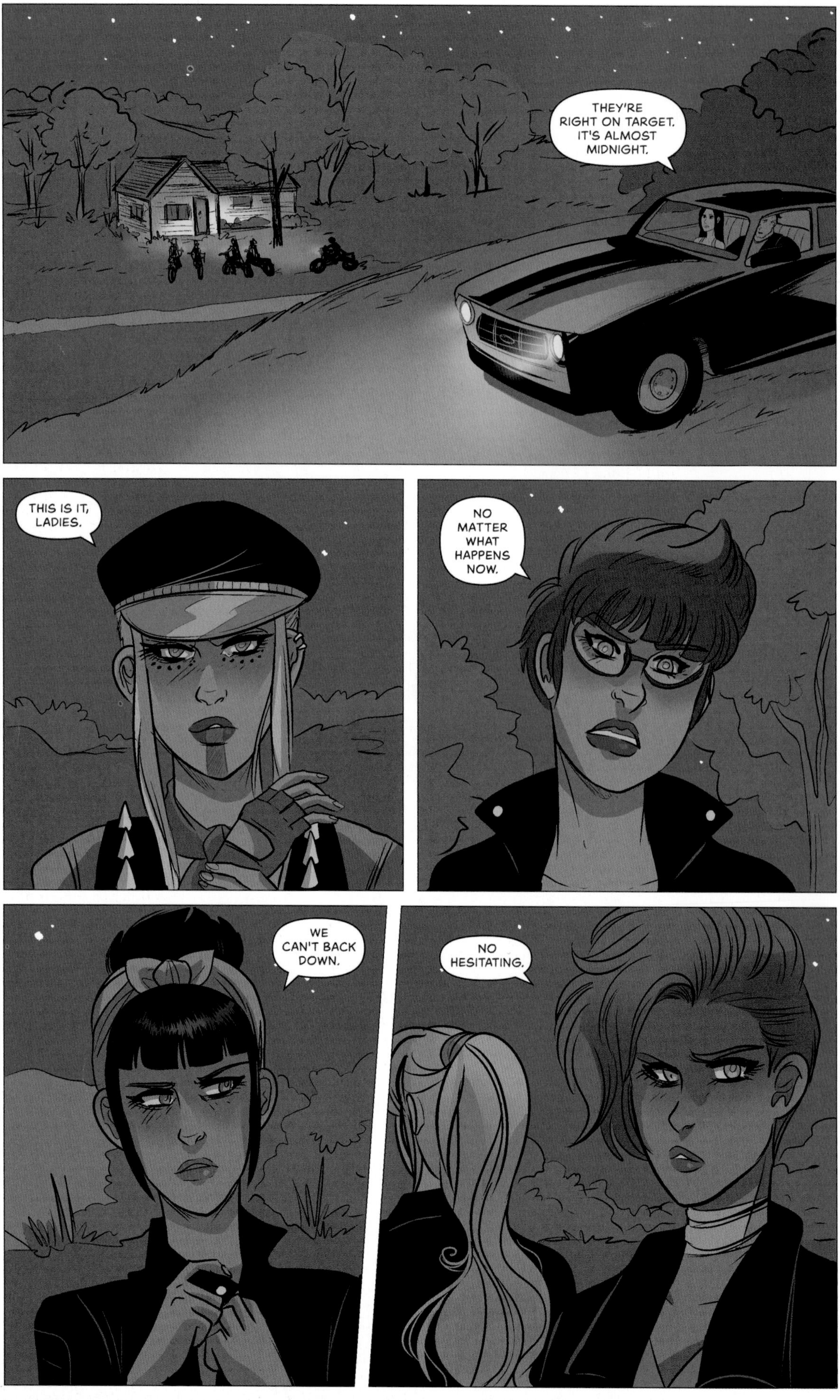

THEY'RE RIGHT ON TARGET. IT'S ALMOST MIDNIGHT.
THIS IS IT, LADIES.
NO MATTER WHAT HAPPENS NOW.
WE CAN'T BACK DOWN.
NO HESITATING.

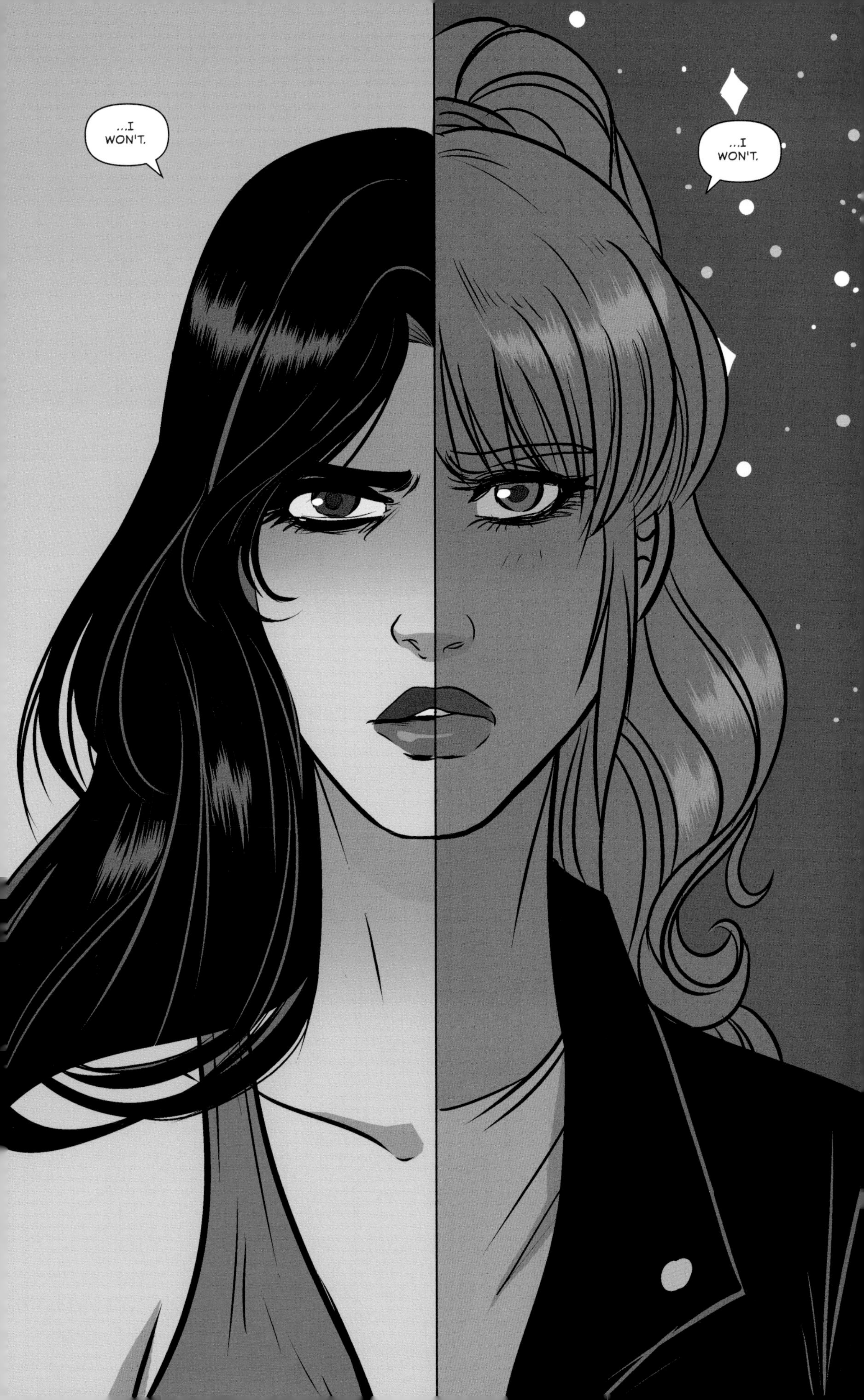
...I WON'T.
...I WON'T.

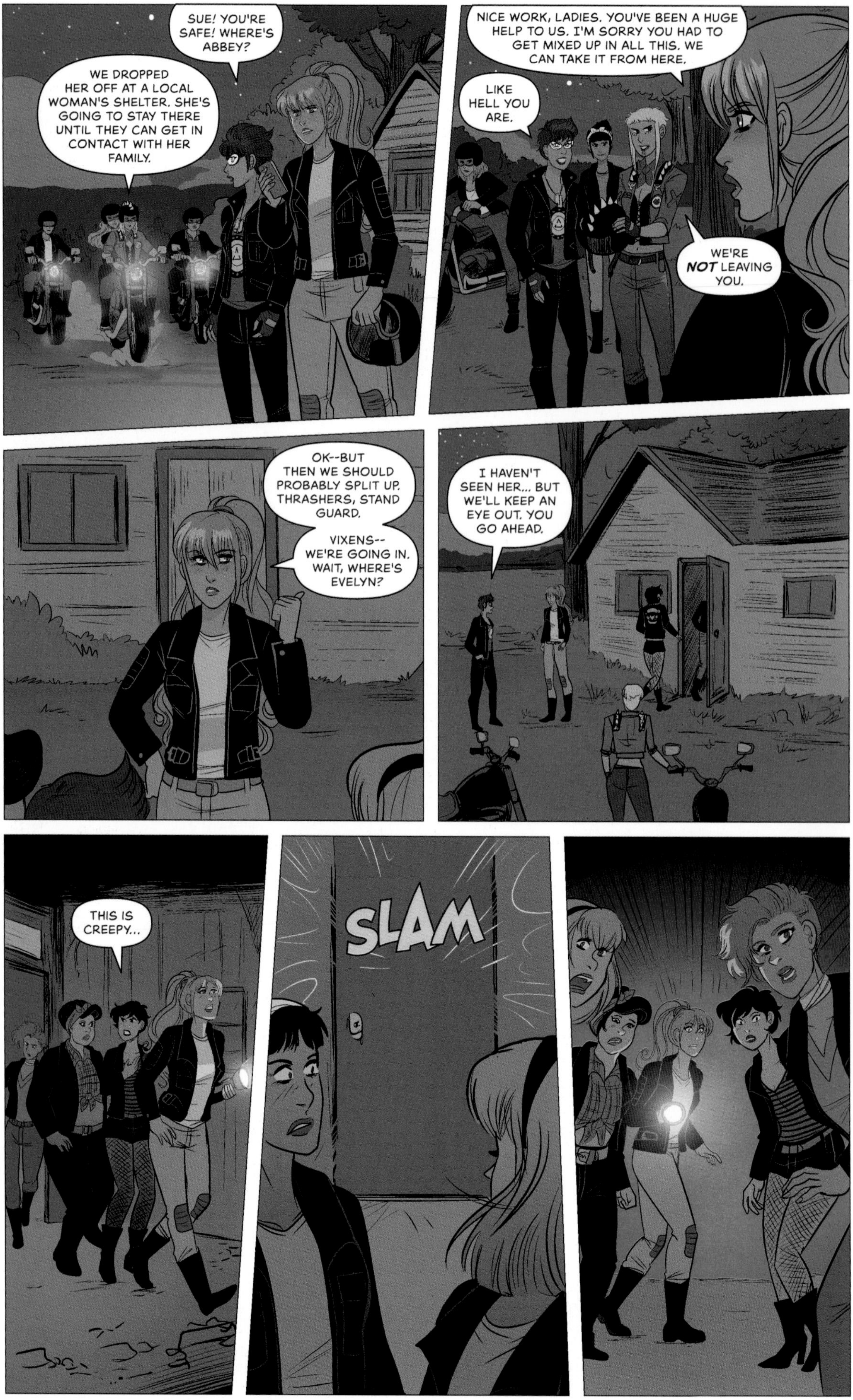
SUE! YOU'RE SAFE! WHERE'S ABBEY?
WE DROPPED HER OFF AT A LOCAL WOMAN'S SHELTER. SHE'S GOING TO STAY THERE UNTIL THEY CAN GET IN CONTACT WITH HER FAMILY.
NICE WORK, LADIES. YOU'VE BEEN A HUGE HELP TO US. I'M SORRY YOU HAD TO GET MIXED UP IN ALL THIS. WE CAN TAKE IT FROM HERE.
LIKE HELL YOU ARE.
WE'RE NOT LEAVING YOU.
OK--BUT THEN WE SHOULD PROBABLY SPLIT UP. THRASHERS, STAND GUARD.
VIXENS-- WE'RE GOING IN. WAIT, WHERE'S EVELYN?
I HAVEN'T SEEN HER... BUT WE'LL KEEP AN EYE OUT. YOU GO AHEAD.
THIS IS CREEPY...
SLAM

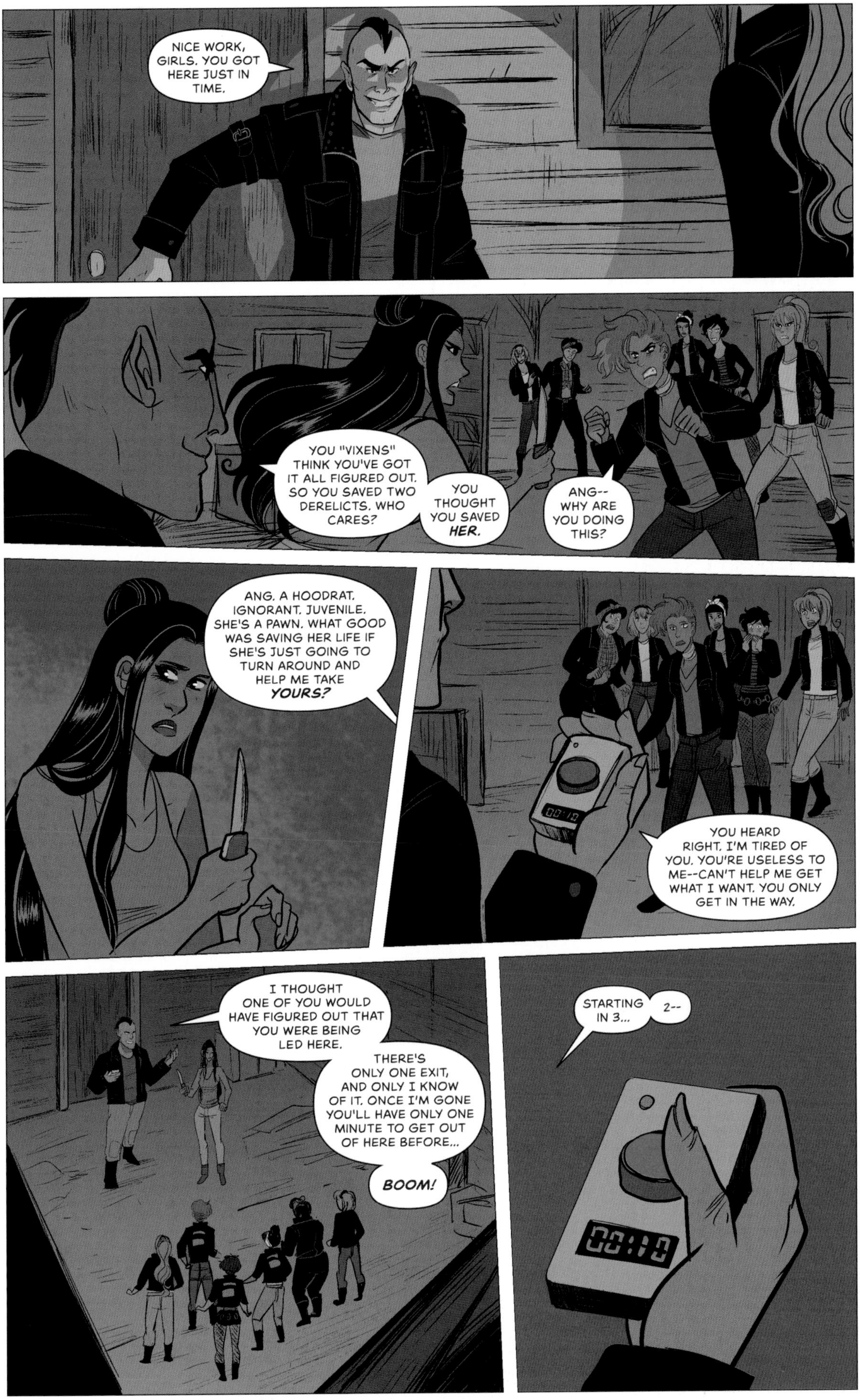
NICE WORK, GIRLS. YOU GOT HERE JUST IN TIME.
YOU "VIXENS" THINK YOU'VE GOT IT ALL FIGURED OUT. SO YOU SAVED TWO DERELICTS. WHO CARES?
YOU THOUGHT YOU SAVED HER.
ANG-- WHY ARE YOU DOING THIS?
ANG. A HOODRAT. IGNORANT. JUVENILE. SHE'S A PAWN. WHAT GOOD WAS SAVING HER LIFE IF SHE'S JUST GOING TO TURN AROUND AND HELP ME TAKE YOURS?
YOU HEARD RIGHT. I'M TIRED OF YOU. YOU'RE USELESS TO ME--CAN'T HELP ME GET WHAT I WANT. YOU ONLY GET IN THE WAY.
I THOUGHT ONE OF YOU WOULD HAVE FIGURED OUT THAT YOU WERE BEING LED HERE.
THERE'S ONLY ONE EXIT, AND ONLY I KNOW OF IT. ONCE I'M GONE YOU'LL HAVE ONLY ONE MINUTE TO GET OUT OF HERE BEFORE...
BOOM!
STARTING IN 3...
2--

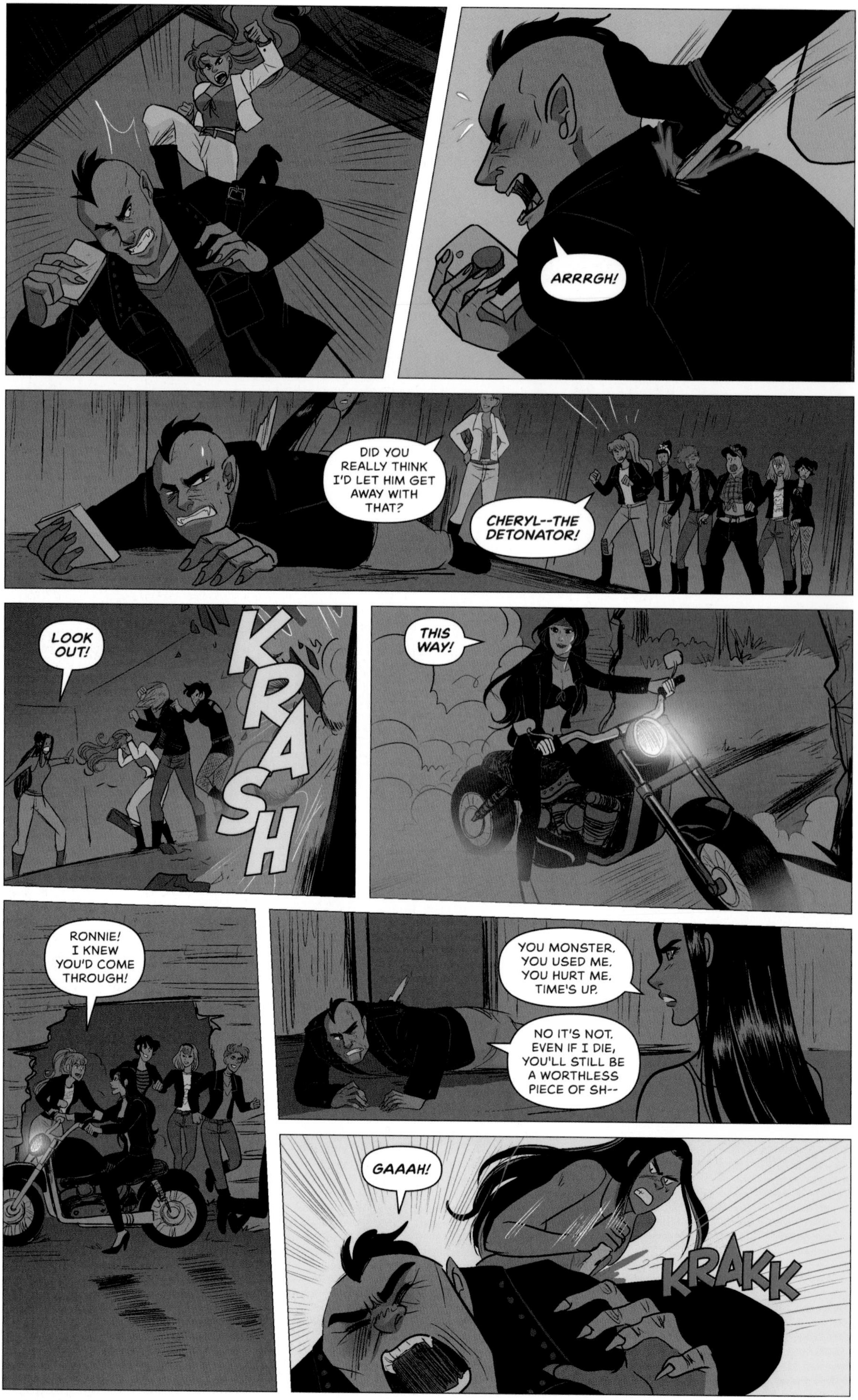
ARRRGH!
DID YOU REALLY THINK I'D LET HIM GET AWAY WITH THAT?
CHERYL--THE DETONATOR!
LOOK OUT!
KRASH
THIS WAY!
RONNIE! I KNEW YOU'D COME THROUGH!
YOU MONSTER. YOU USED ME. YOU HURT ME. TIME'S UP.
NO IT'S NOT. EVEN IF I DIE, YOU'LL STILL BE A WORTHLESS PIECE OF SH--
GAAAH!
KRAKK

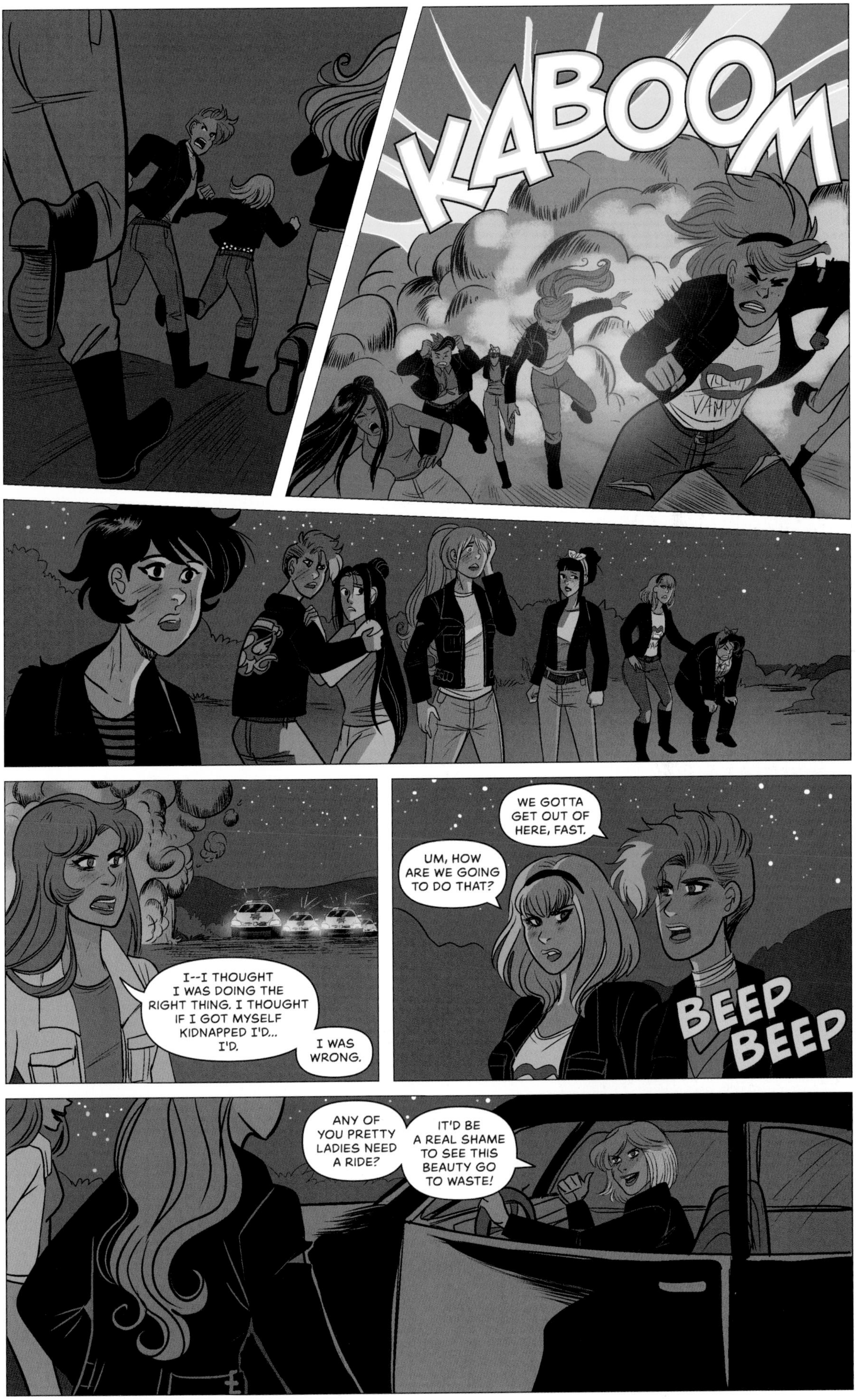
KABOOM
I--I THOUGHT I WAS DOING THE RIGHT THING. I THOUGHT IF I GOT MYSELF KIDNAPPED I'D... I'D.
I WAS WRONG.
WE GOTTA GET OUT OF HERE, FAST.
UM, HOW ARE WE GOING TO DO THAT?
BEEP BEEP
ANY OF YOU PRETTY LADIES NEED A RIDE?
IT'D BE A REAL SHAME TO SEE THIS BEAUTY GO TO WASTE!

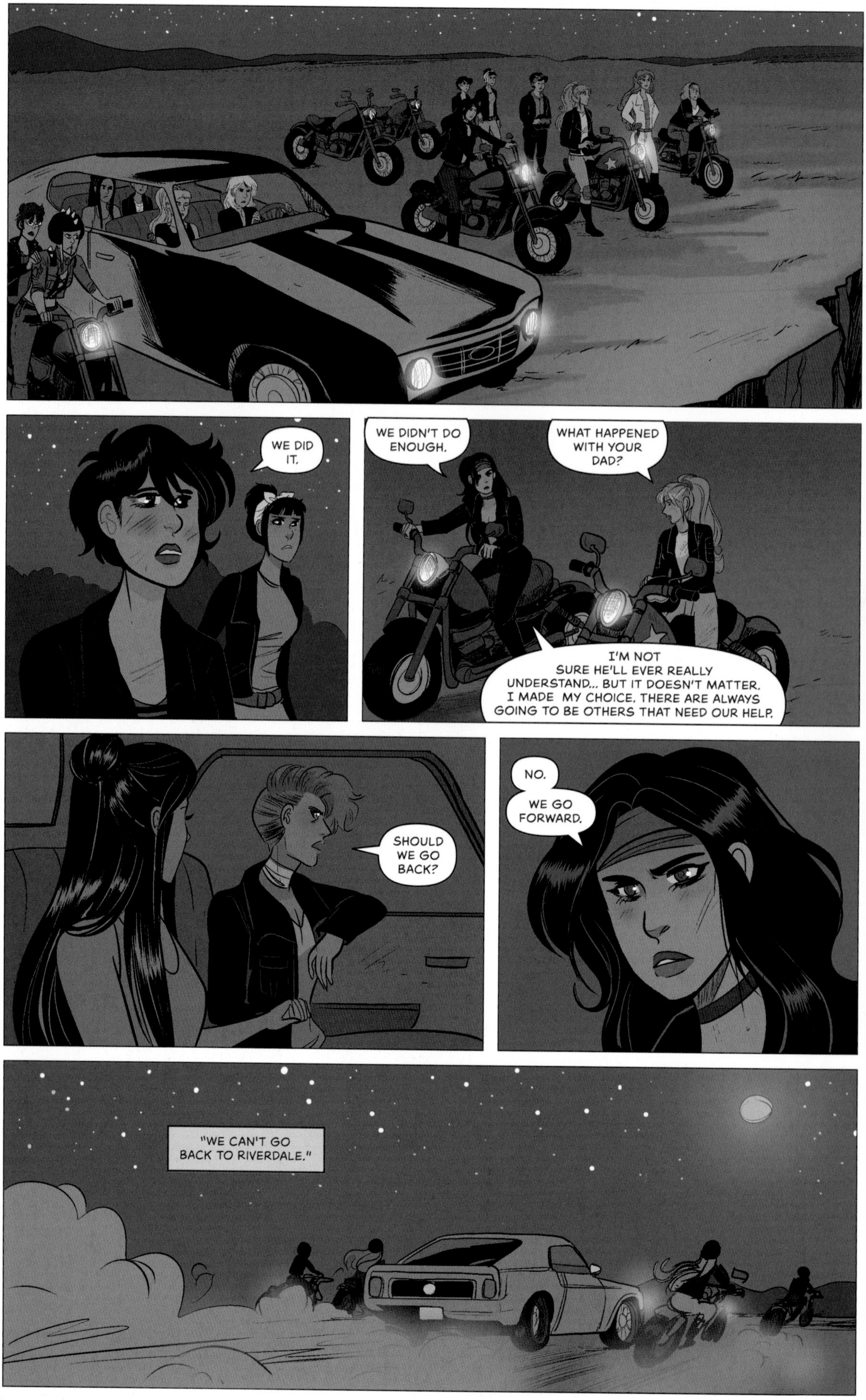
WE DID IT.
WE DIDN'T DO ENOUGH.
WHAT HAPPENED WITH YOUR DAD?
I'M NOT SURE HE'LL EVER REALLY UNDERSTAND... BUT IT DOESN'T MATTER. I MADE MY CHOICE. THERE ARE ALWAYS GOING TO BE OTHERS THAT NEED OUR HELP.
SHOULD WE GO BACK?
NO.
WE GO FORWARD.
"WE CAN'T GO BACK TO RIVERDALE."

to be continued...

Chapter Ten

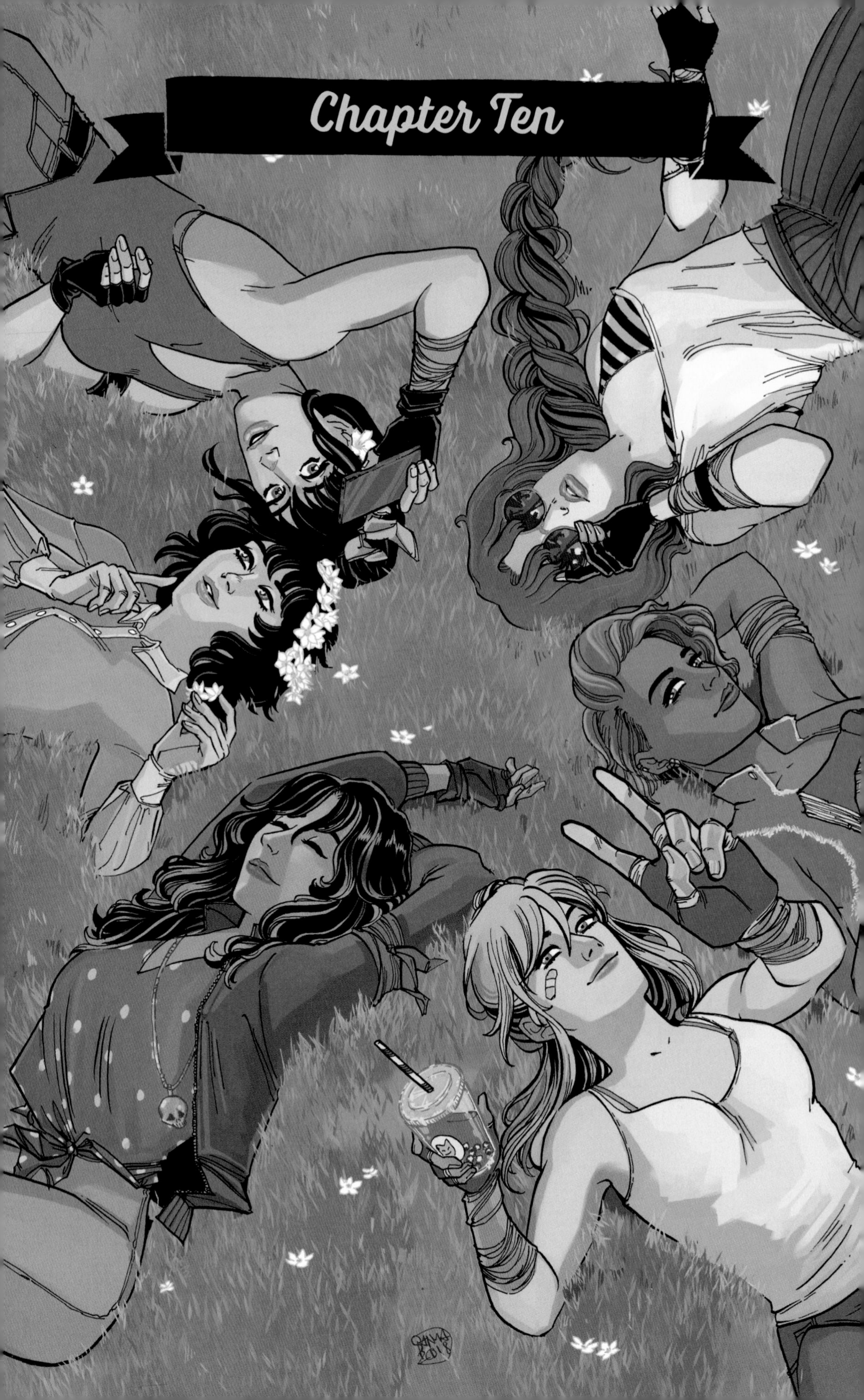

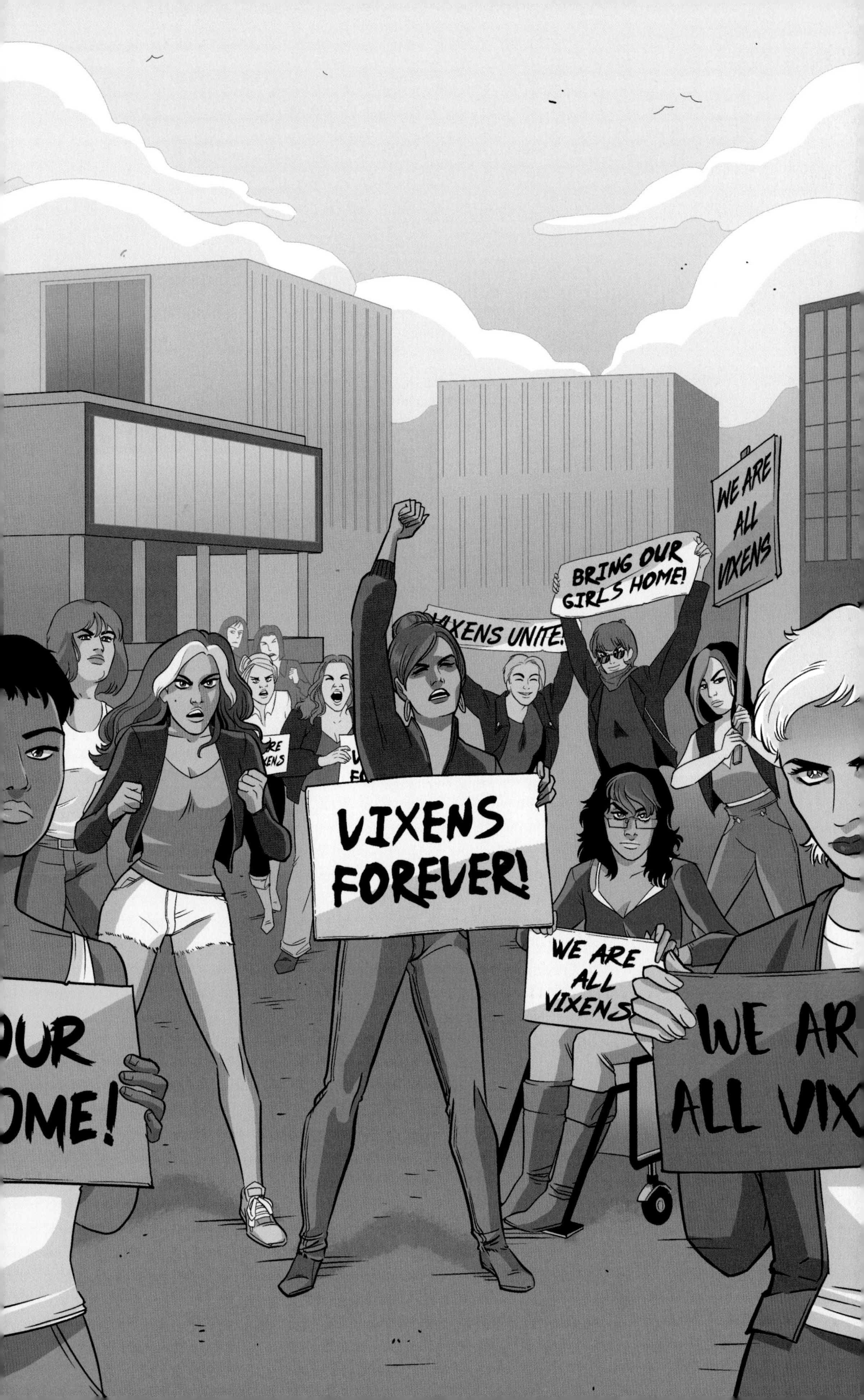

BRING OUR GIRLS HOME!
WE ARE ALL VIXENS
VIXENS UNITE!
VIXENS FOREVER!
WE ARE ALL VIXENS
OUR
OME!
WE AR
ALL VIX

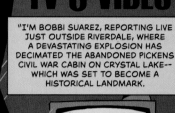

TV & VIDEO

"I'M BOBBI SUAREZ, REPORTING LIVE JUST OUTSIDE RIVERDALE, WHERE A DEVASTATING EXPLOSION HAS DECIMATED THE ABANDONED PICKENS CIVIL WAR CABIN ON CRYSTAL LAKE-- WHICH WAS SET TO BECOME A HISTORICAL LANDMARK.

$50⁰⁰ - OBO -

$599⁹⁹

LIVE | WORK OF THE "VIXENS" GANG?

TELECOLOR

"THERE APPEARS TO HAVE BEEN A SURVIVOR, IDENTIFIED ONLY AS "DOC." HE HAS BEEN ACCUSED OF HEADING UP THE RECENT TRAFFICKING RING THAT EXTENDED BEYOND RIVERDALE'S BORDERS. ALL OF THE CAPTURED WOMEN HAVE BEEN REPORTEDLY FOUND AND RETURNED TO SAFETY.

"WE HAVE LEARNED FROM AN ANONYMOUS SOURCE THAT A NUMBER OF TEENAGE GIRLS FROM RIVERDALE KNOWN AS THE "VIXENS" WERE ALSO A PART OF THE ACTION.

"THE TEENS IN QUESTION HAVE BEEN IDENTIFIED AS ELIZABETH COOPER, MIDGE KLUMP, ETHEL MUGGS, TONI TOPAZ AND AN UNKNOWN SIXTH MEMBER WHO HAS NOT YET BEEN IDENTIFIED.

"MOST SURPRISINGLY, THE LEADER OF THE GANG IS BELIEVED TO BE VERONICA LODGE, HEIRESS TO THE LODGE FORTUNE AND DAUGHTER OF HIRAM LODGE, WHO MOST RECENTLY ESTABLISHED A NEIGHBORHOOD WATCH COMMITTEE TO CUT DOWN ON GANG VIOLENCE RIGHT HERE IN RIVERDALE.

"IT IS ALSO BELIEVED THAT CHERYL BLOSSOM, THE MISSING DAUGHTER OF FORMER BLOSSOM-COMM BIGWIG CLIFF BLOSSOM, IS A PART OF THIS VIGILANTE GROUP."

Cheryl

THE WHEREABOUTS OF THESE YOUNG WOMEN ARE CURRENTLY UNKNOWN.

RTV

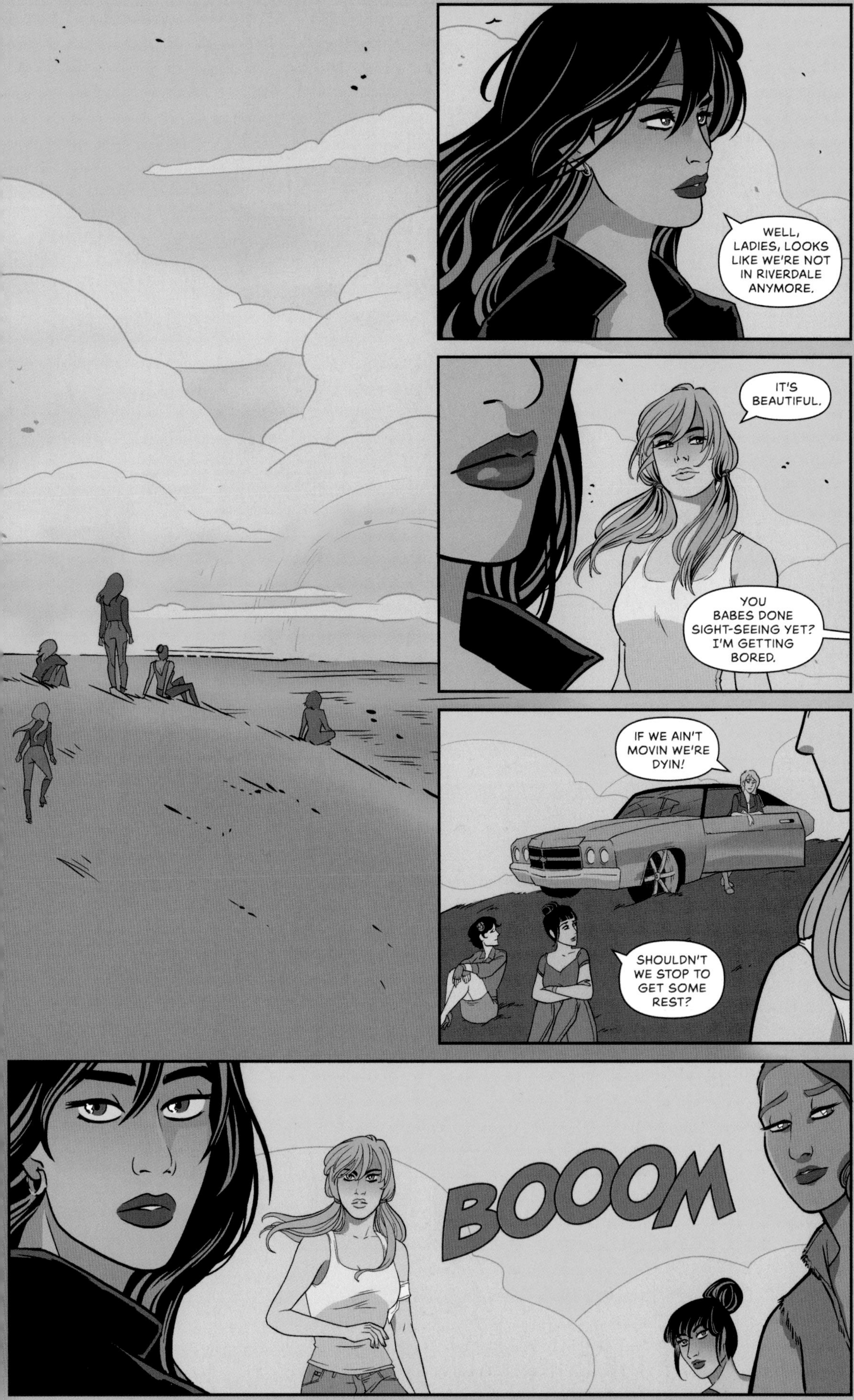
WELL, LADIES, LOOKS LIKE WE'RE NOT IN RIVERDALE ANYMORE.
IT'S BEAUTIFUL.
YOU BABES DONE SIGHT-SEEING YET? I'M GETTING BORED.
IF WE AIN'T MOVIN WE'RE DYIN!
SHOULDN'T WE STOP TO GET SOME REST?
BOOOM

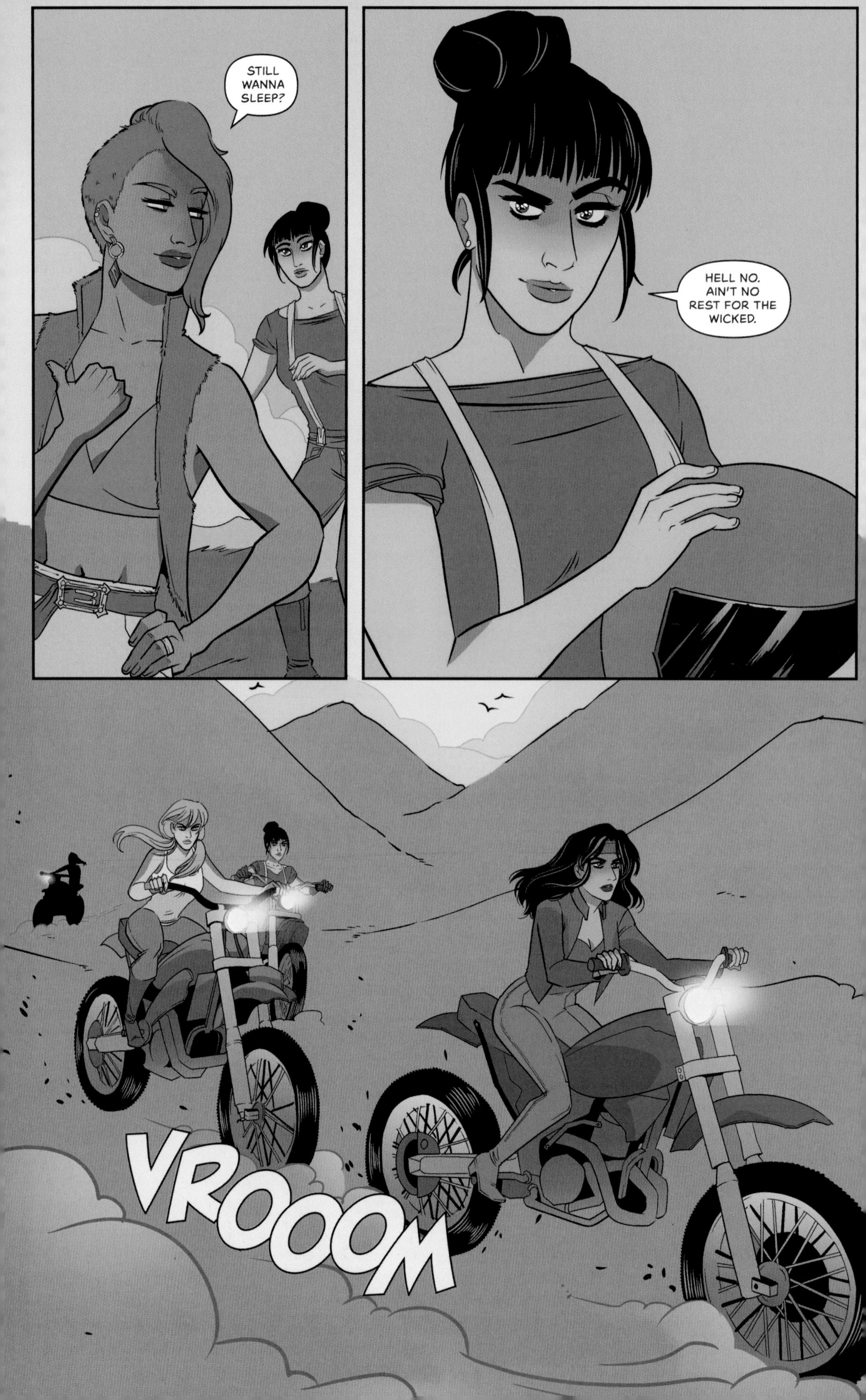
STILL WANNA SLEEP?
HELL NO. AIN'T NO REST FOR THE WICKED.
VROOOM

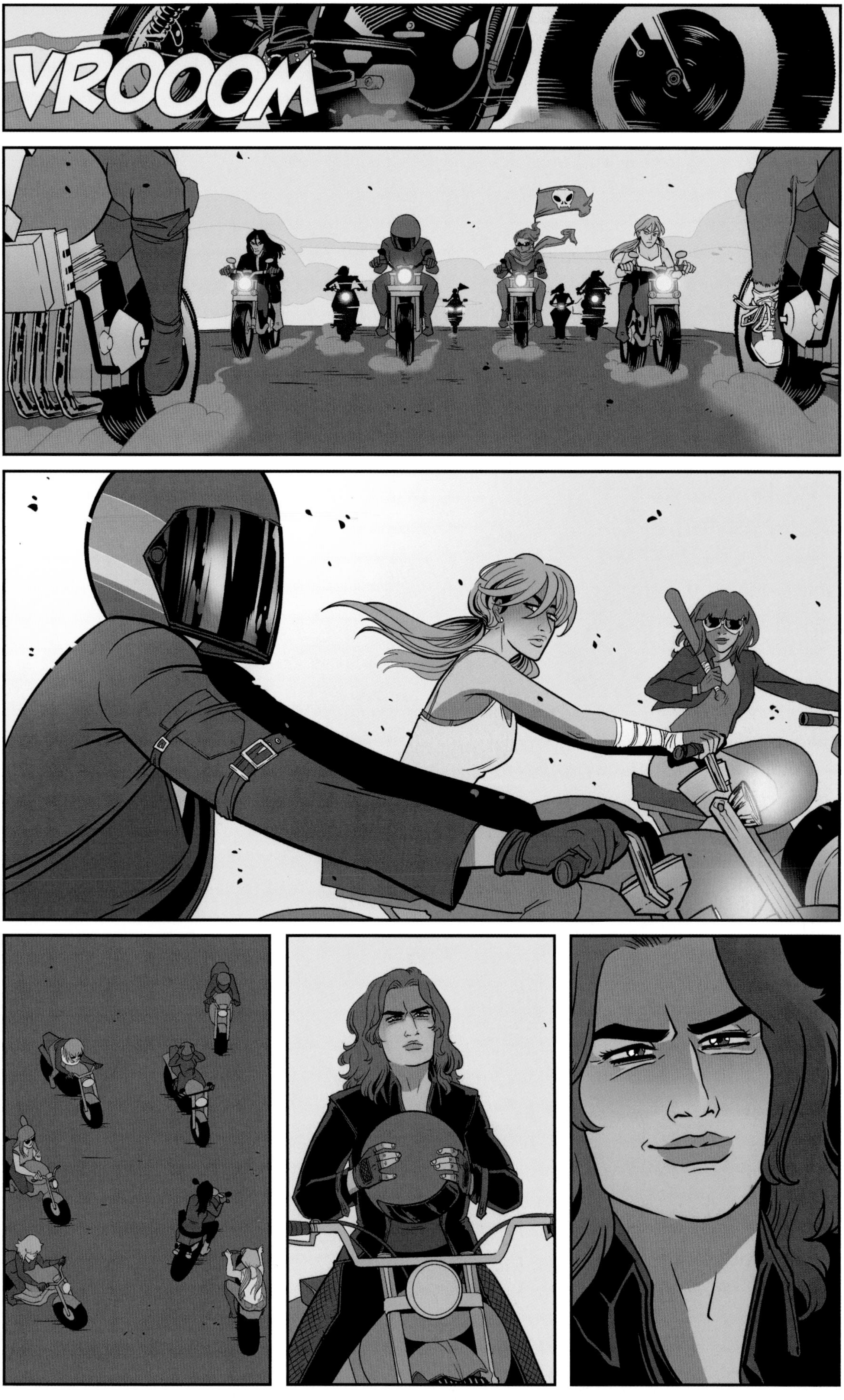
VROOOM

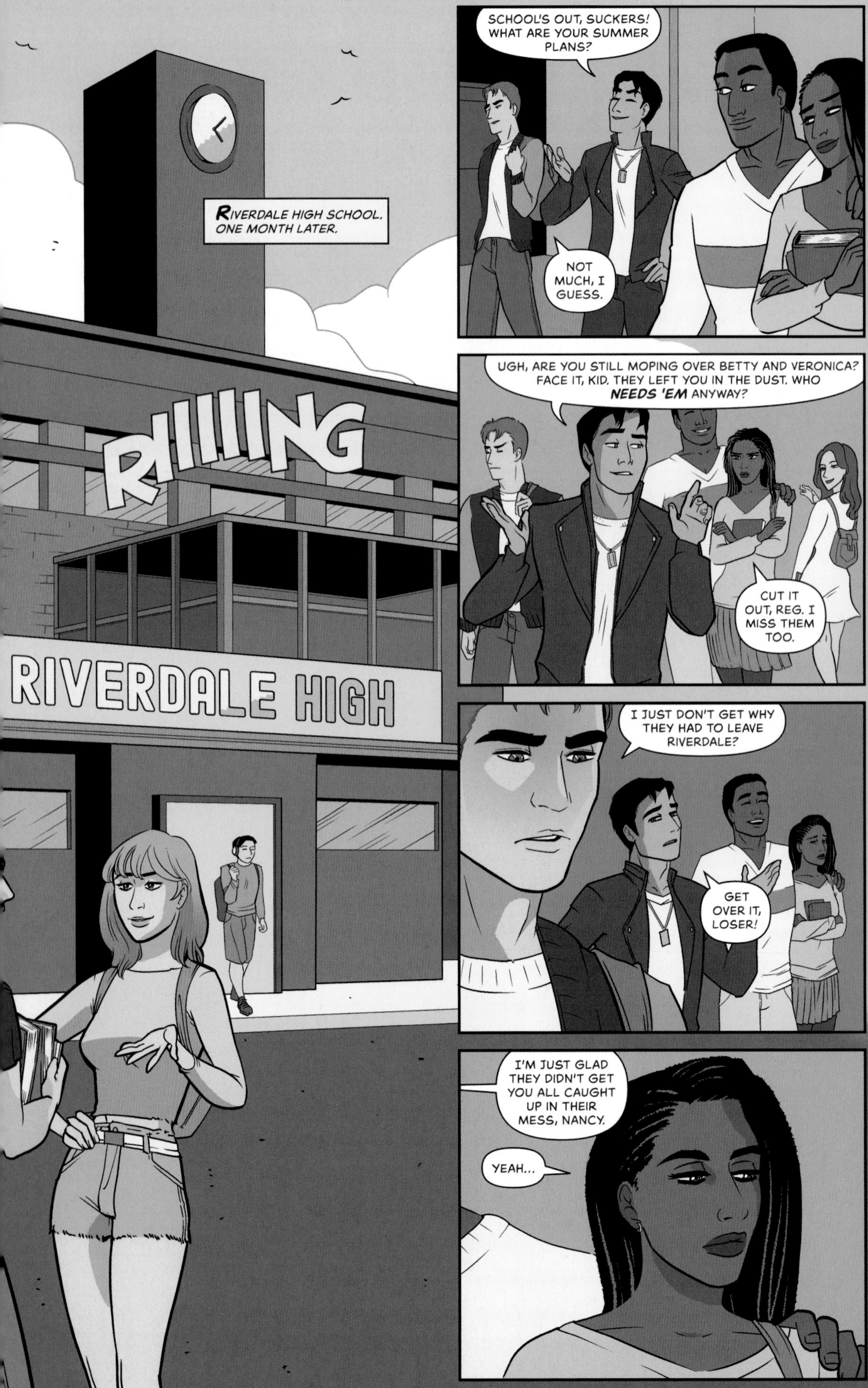
RIVERDALE HIGH SCHOOL. ONE MONTH LATER.
RIIIING
RIVERDALE HIGH
SCHOOL'S OUT, SUCKERS! WHAT ARE YOUR SUMMER PLANS?
NOT MUCH, I GUESS.
UGH, ARE YOU STILL MOPING OVER BETTY AND VERONICA? FACE IT, KID. THEY LEFT YOU IN THE DUST. WHO NEEDS 'EM ANYWAY?
CUT IT OUT, REG. I MISS THEM TOO.
I JUST DON'T GET WHY THEY HAD TO LEAVE RIVERDALE?
GET OVER IT, LOSER!
I'M JUST GLAD THEY DIDN'T GET YOU ALL CAUGHT UP IN THEIR MESS, NANCY.
YEAH...

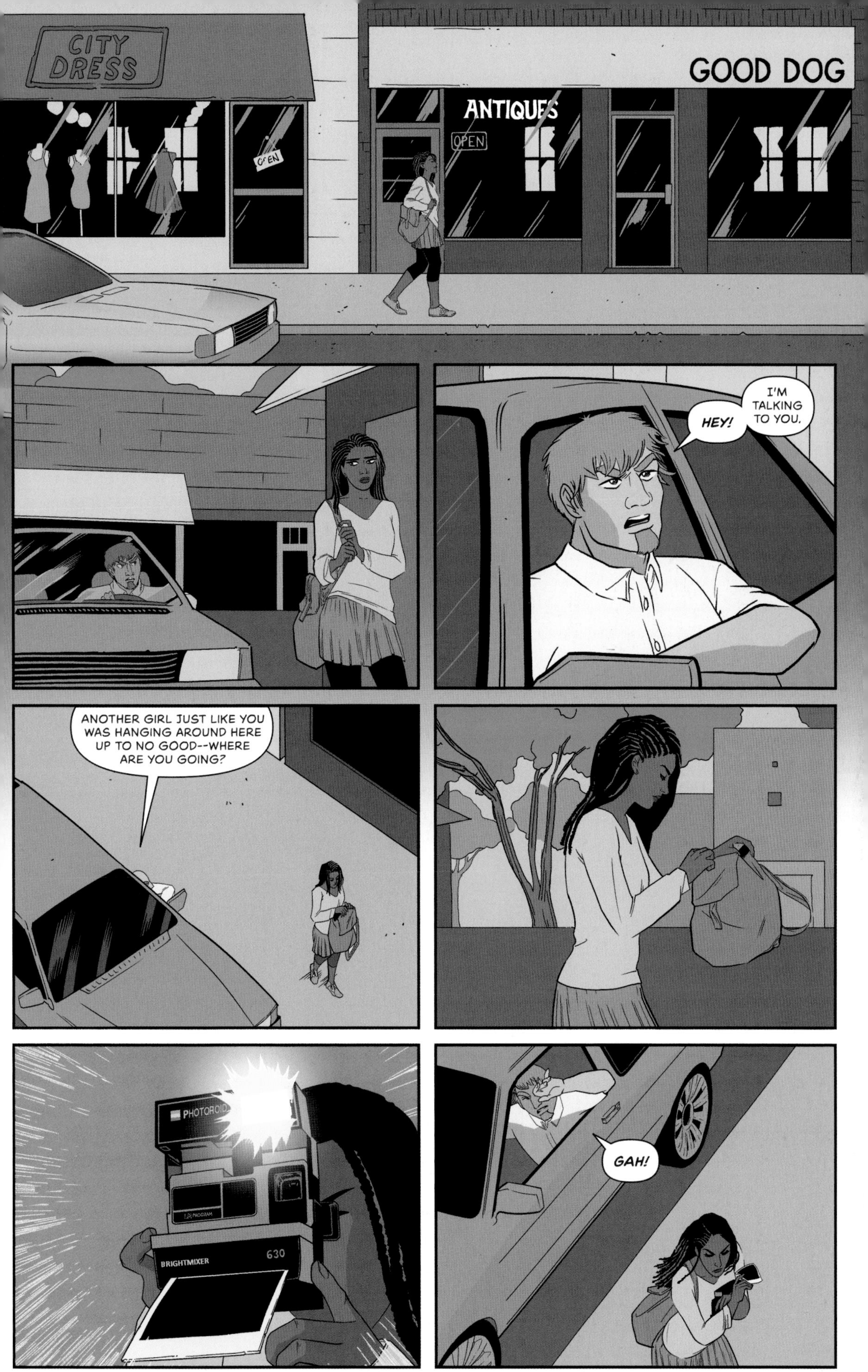
CITY DRESS
OPEN
GOOD DOG
ANTIQUES
OPEN
HEY!
I'M TALKING TO YOU.
ANOTHER GIRL JUST LIKE YOU WAS HANGING AROUND HERE UP TO NO GOOD--WHERE ARE YOU GOING?
PHOTOROID
BRIGHTMIXER
630
GAH!

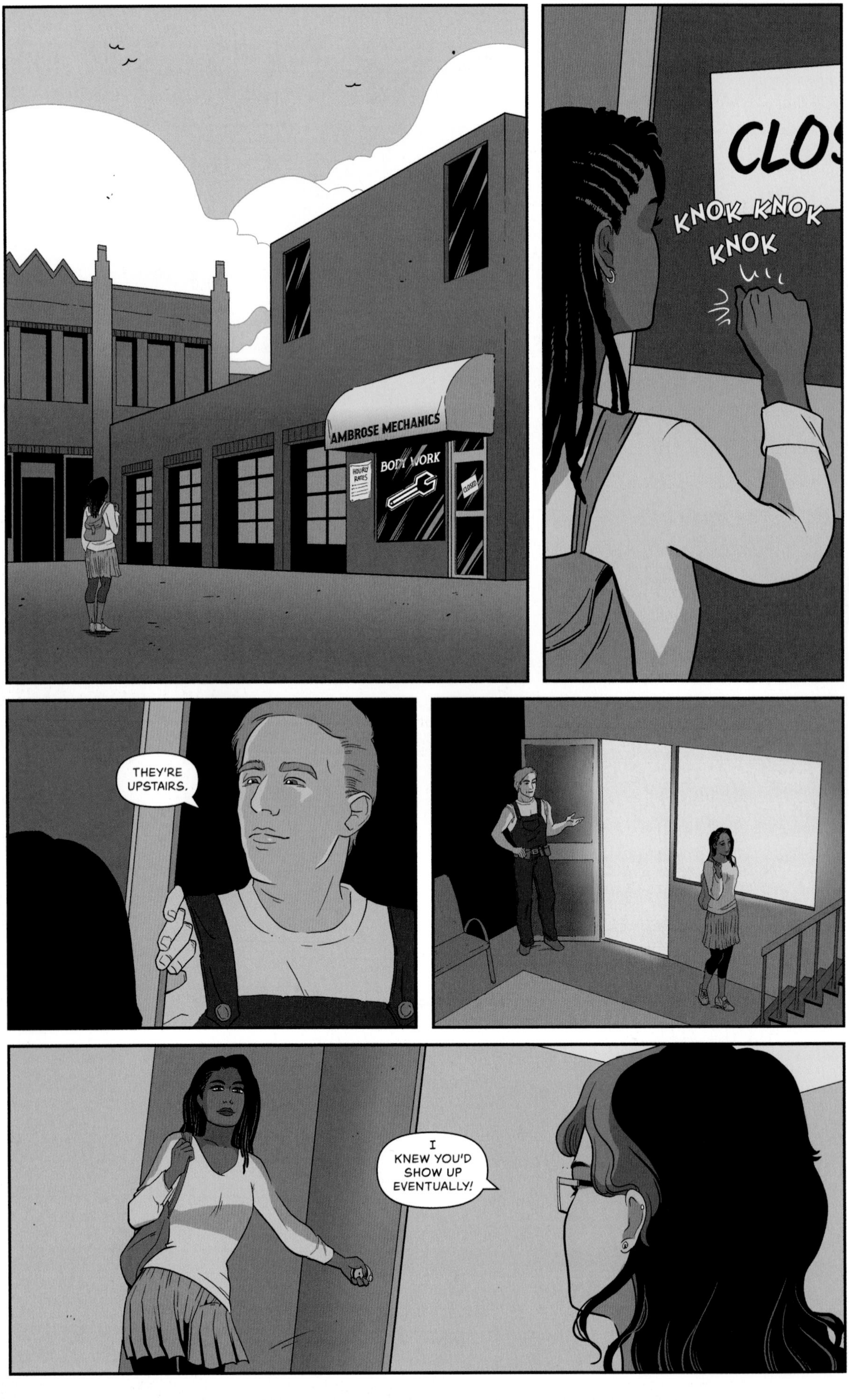
AMBROSE MECHANICS
BODY WORK
HOURLY RATES
CLOSED
CLOS
KNOK KNOK
KNOK
THEY'RE UPSTAIRS.
I KNEW YOU'D SHOW UP EVENTUALLY!

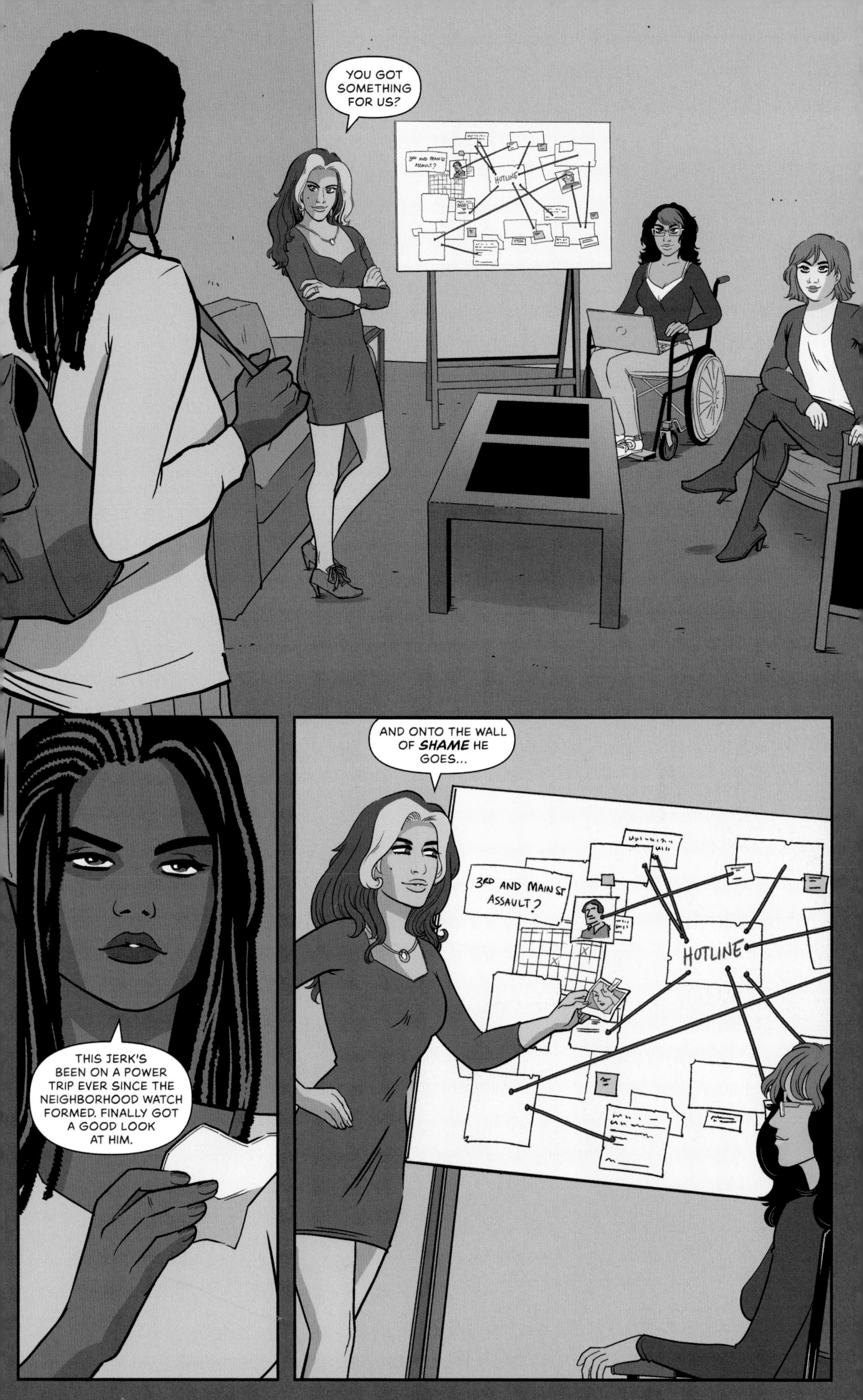
YOU GOT SOMETHING FOR US?
3RD AND MAIN ST ASSAULT?
HOTLINE
THIS JERK'S BEEN ON A POWER TRIP EVER SINCE THE NEIGHBORHOOD WATCH FORMED. FINALLY GOT A GOOD LOOK AT HIM.
AND ONTO THE WALL OF *SHAME* HE GOES...
3RD AND MAIN ST ASSAULT?
HOTLINE

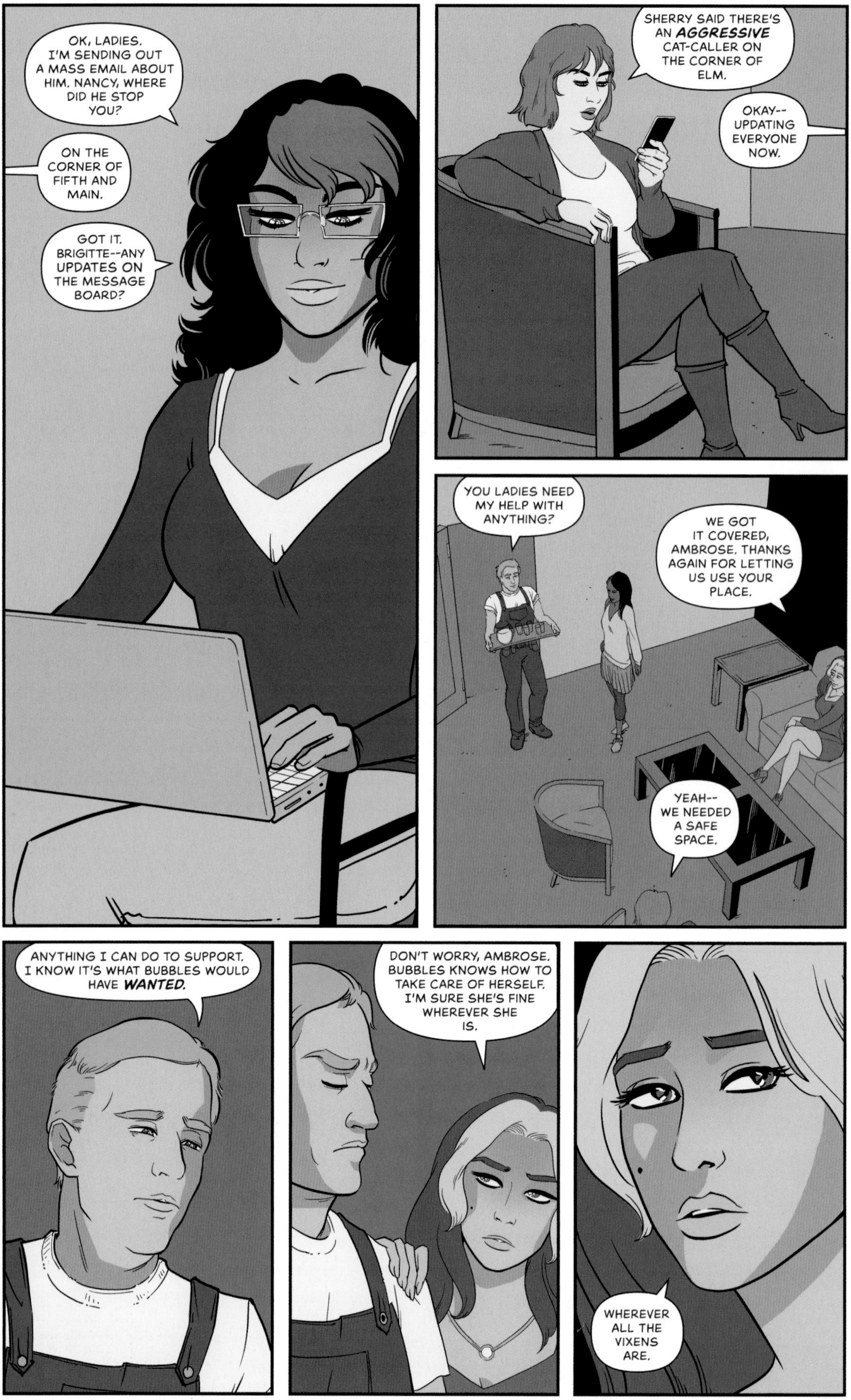
OK, LADIES. I'M SENDING OUT A MASS EMAIL ABOUT HIM. NANCY, WHERE DID HE STOP YOU?
ON THE CORNER OF FIFTH AND MAIN.
GOT IT. BRIGITTE--ANY UPDATES ON THE MESSAGE BOARD?
SHERRY SAID THERE'S AN **AGGRESSIVE** CAT-CALLER ON THE CORNER OF ELM.
OKAY--UPDATING EVERYONE NOW.
YOU LADIES NEED MY HELP WITH ANYTHING?
WE GOT IT COVERED, AMBROSE. THANKS AGAIN FOR LETTING US USE YOUR PLACE.
YEAH--WE NEEDED A SAFE SPACE.
ANYTHING I CAN DO TO SUPPORT. I KNOW IT'S WHAT BUBBLES WOULD HAVE **WANTED.**
DON'T WORRY, AMBROSE. BUBBLES KNOWS HOW TO TAKE CARE OF HERSELF. I'M SURE SHE'S FINE WHEREVER SHE IS.
WHEREVER ALL THE VIXENS ARE.

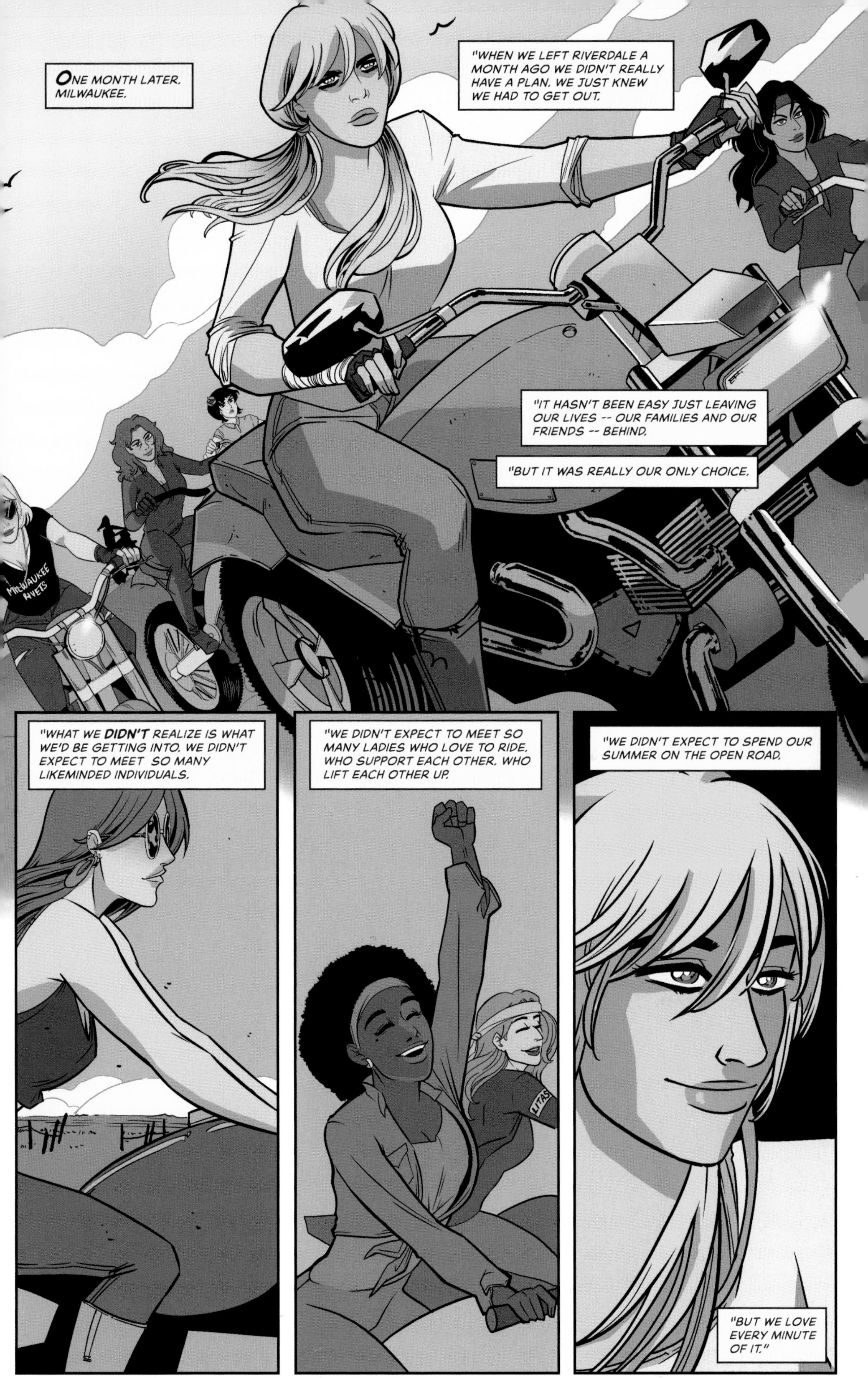
ONE MONTH LATER, MILWAUKEE.
"WHEN WE LEFT RIVERDALE A MONTH AGO WE DIDN'T REALLY HAVE A PLAN. WE JUST KNEW WE HAD TO GET OUT.
"IT HASN'T BEEN EASY JUST LEAVING OUR LIVES -- OUR FAMILIES AND OUR FRIENDS -- BEHIND.
"BUT IT WAS REALLY OUR ONLY CHOICE.
MILWAUKEE RIVETS
"WHAT WE DIDN'T REALIZE IS WHAT WE'D BE GETTING INTO. WE DIDN'T EXPECT TO MEET SO MANY LIKEMINDED INDIVIDUALS.
"WE DIDN'T EXPECT TO MEET SO MANY LADIES WHO LOVE TO RIDE, WHO SUPPORT EACH OTHER, WHO LIFT EACH OTHER UP.
LITAS
"WE DIDN'T EXPECT TO SPEND OUR SUMMER ON THE OPEN ROAD.
"BUT WE LOVE EVERY MINUTE OF IT."

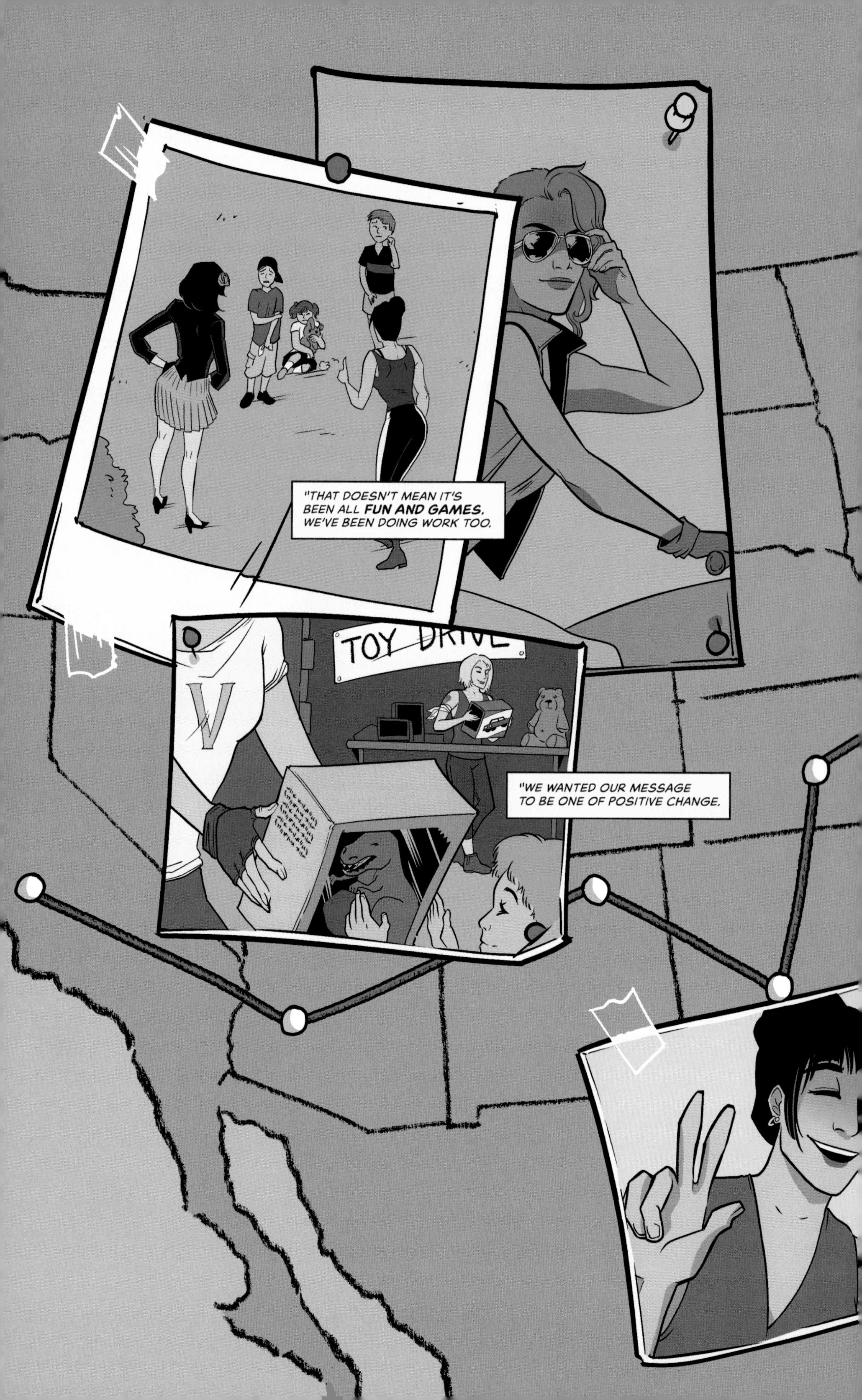
"THAT DOESN'T MEAN IT'S BEEN ALL **FUN AND GAMES.** WE'VE BEEN DOING WORK TOO.
TOY DRIVE
"WE WANTED OUR MESSAGE TO BE ONE OF POSITIVE CHANGE.

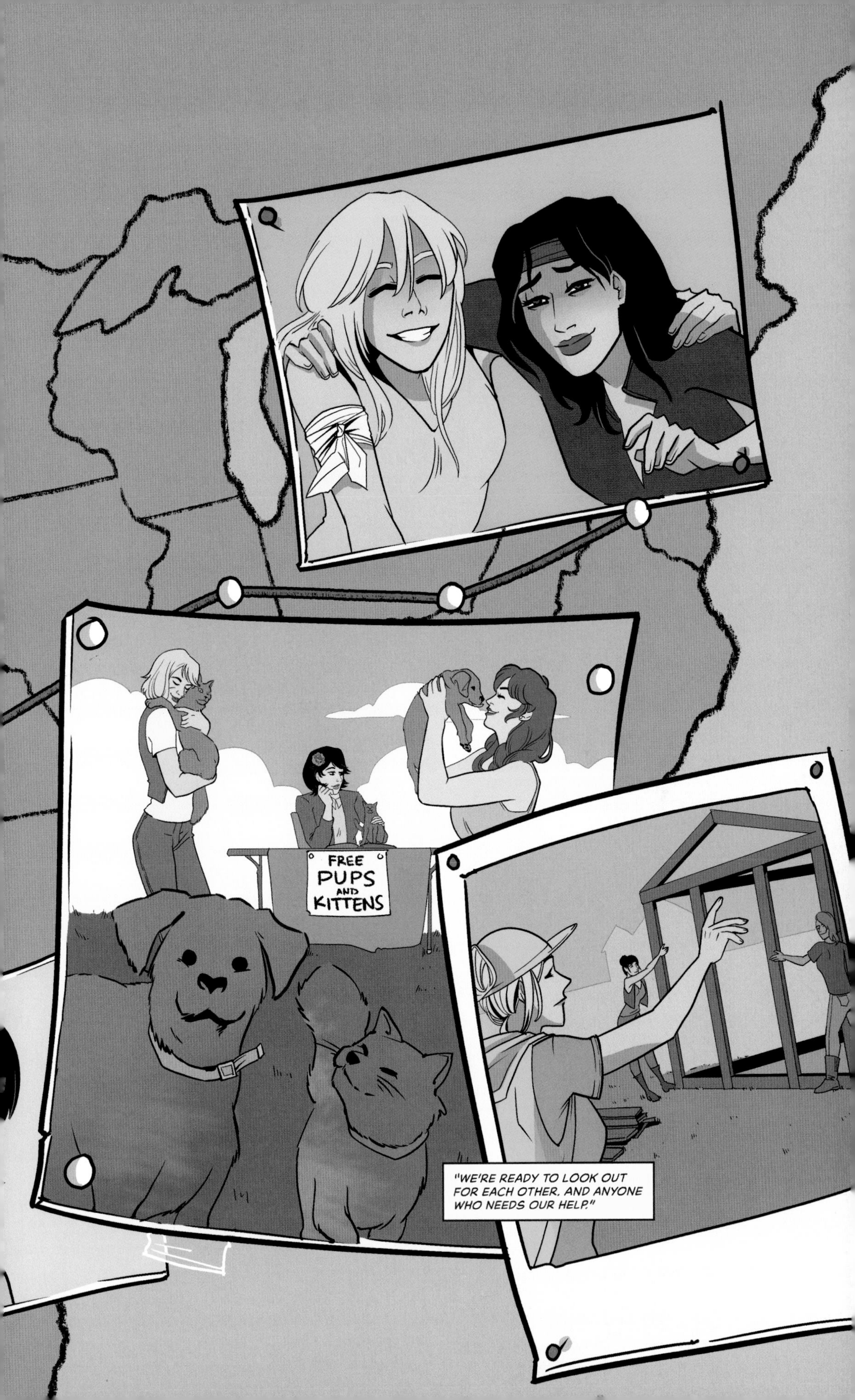
FREE
PUPS
AND
KITTENS
"WE'RE READY TO LOOK OUT FOR EACH OTHER. AND ANYONE WHO NEEDS OUR HELP."

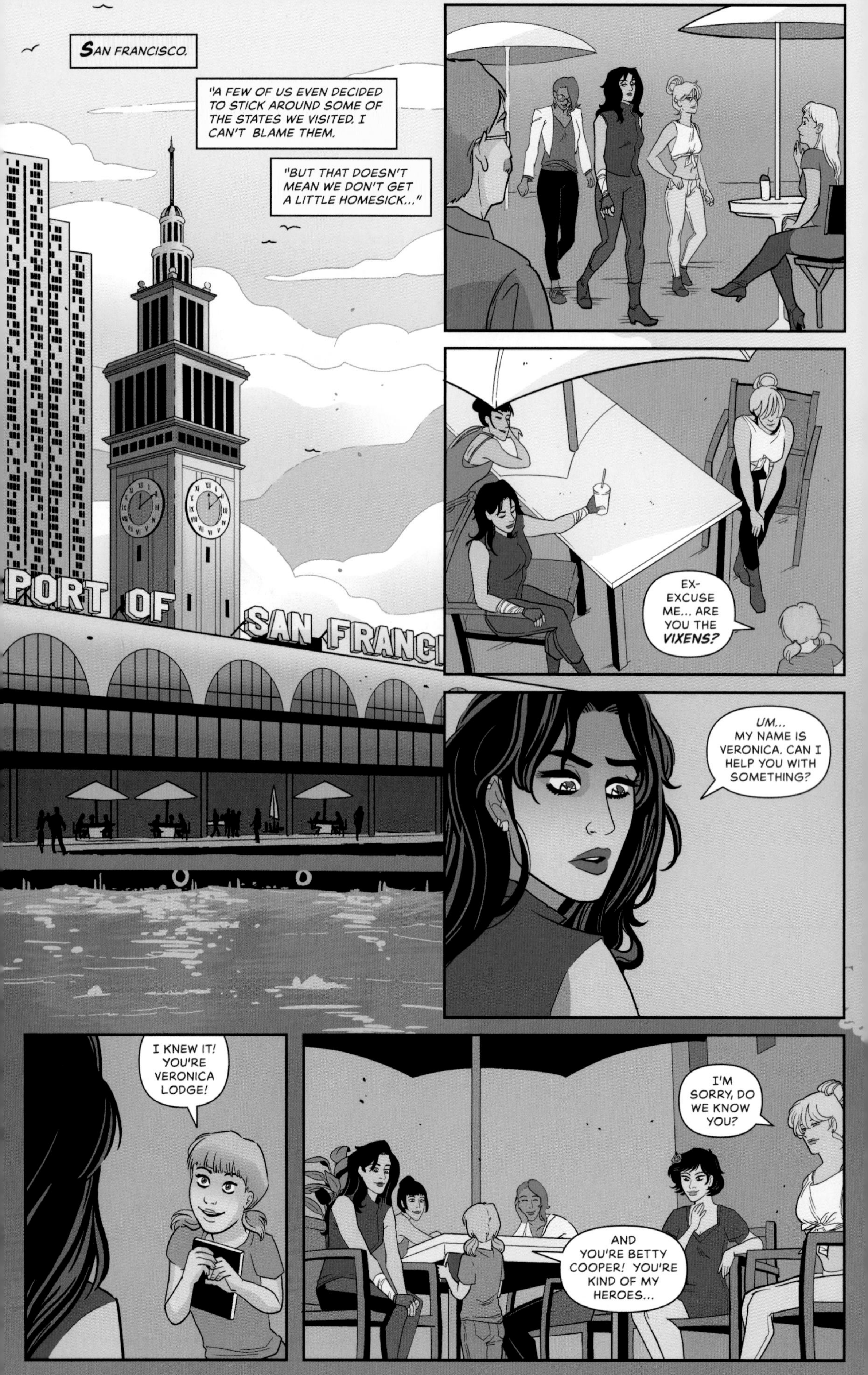
SAN FRANCISCO.
"A FEW OF US EVEN DECIDED TO STICK AROUND SOME OF THE STATES WE VISITED. I CAN'T BLAME THEM.
"BUT THAT DOESN'T MEAN WE DON'T GET A LITTLE HOMESICK..."
PORT OF SAN FRANCI
EX-EXCUSE ME... ARE YOU THE VIXENS?
UM... MY NAME IS VERONICA. CAN I HELP YOU WITH SOMETHING?
I KNEW IT! YOU'RE VERONICA LODGE!
I'M SORRY, DO WE KNOW YOU?
AND YOU'RE BETTY COOPER! YOU'RE KIND OF MY HEROES...

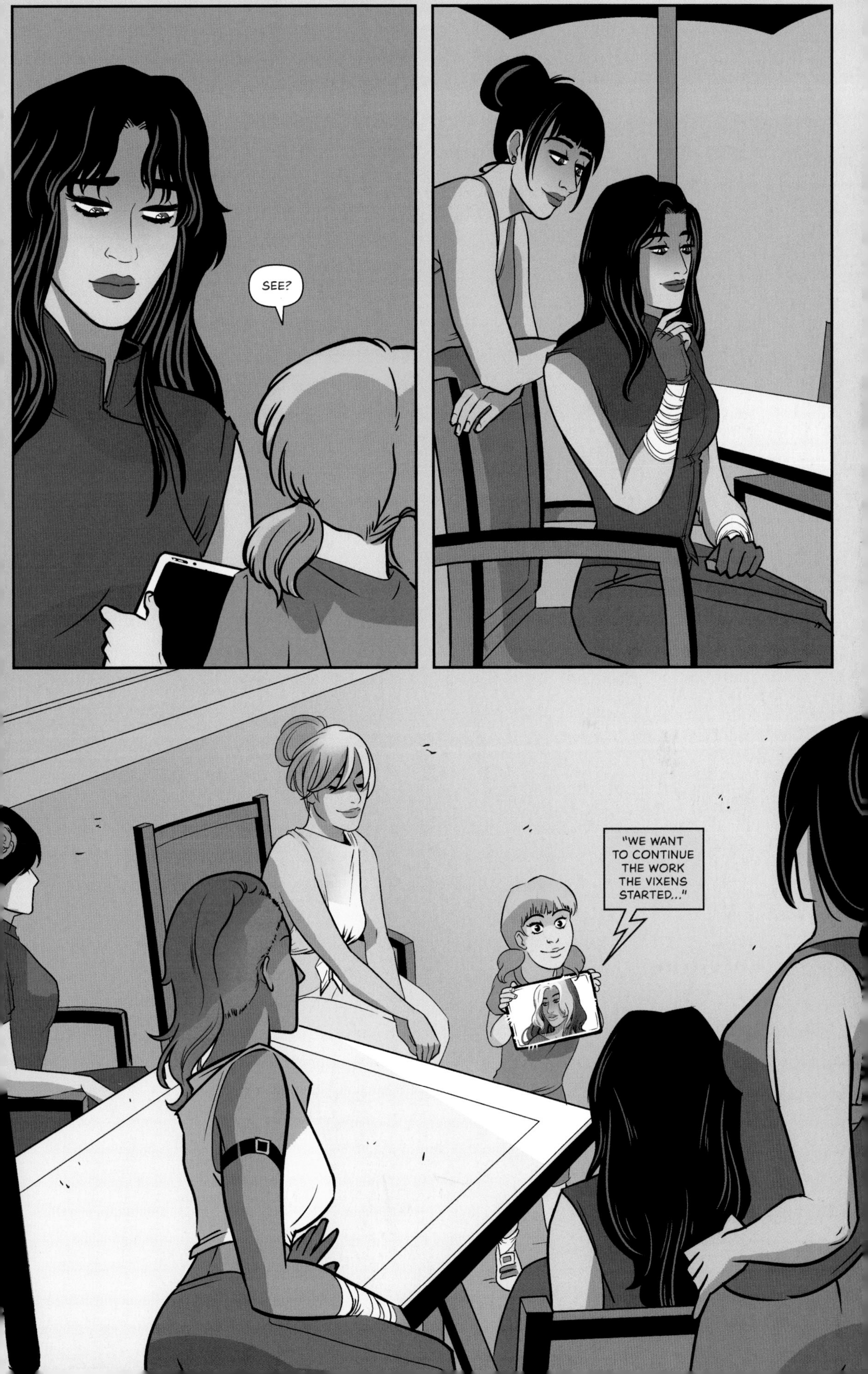
SEE?
"WE WANT TO CONTINUE THE WORK THE VIXENS STARTED..."

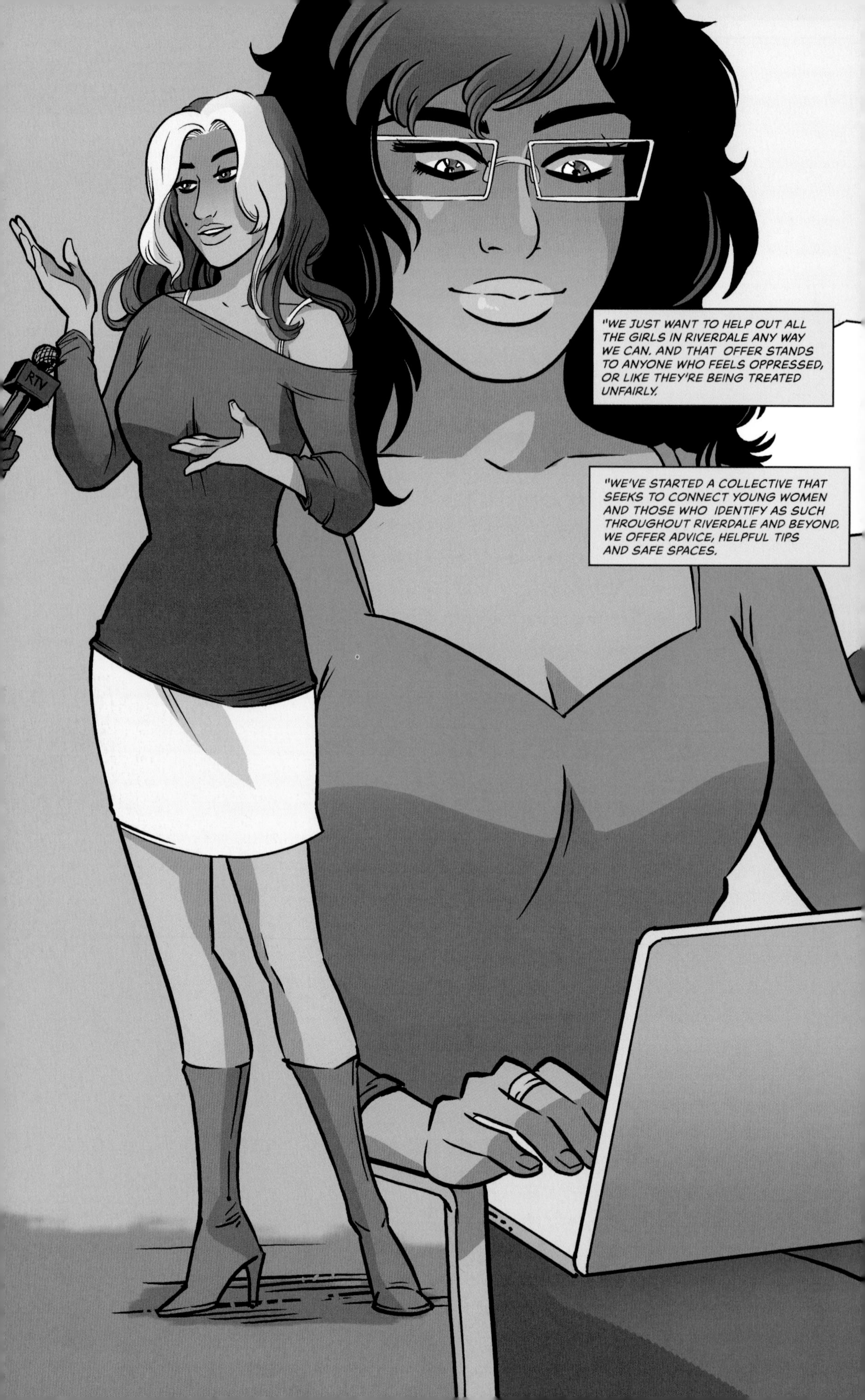
"WE JUST WANT TO HELP OUT ALL THE GIRLS IN RIVERDALE ANY WAY WE CAN. AND THAT OFFER STANDS TO ANYONE WHO FEELS OPPRESSED, OR LIKE THEY'RE BEING TREATED UNFAIRLY.
"WE'VE STARTED A COLLECTIVE THAT SEEKS TO CONNECT YOUNG WOMEN AND THOSE WHO IDENTIFY AS SUCH THROUGHOUT RIVERDALE AND BEYOND. WE OFFER ADVICE, HELPFUL TIPS AND SAFE SPACES.
RTV

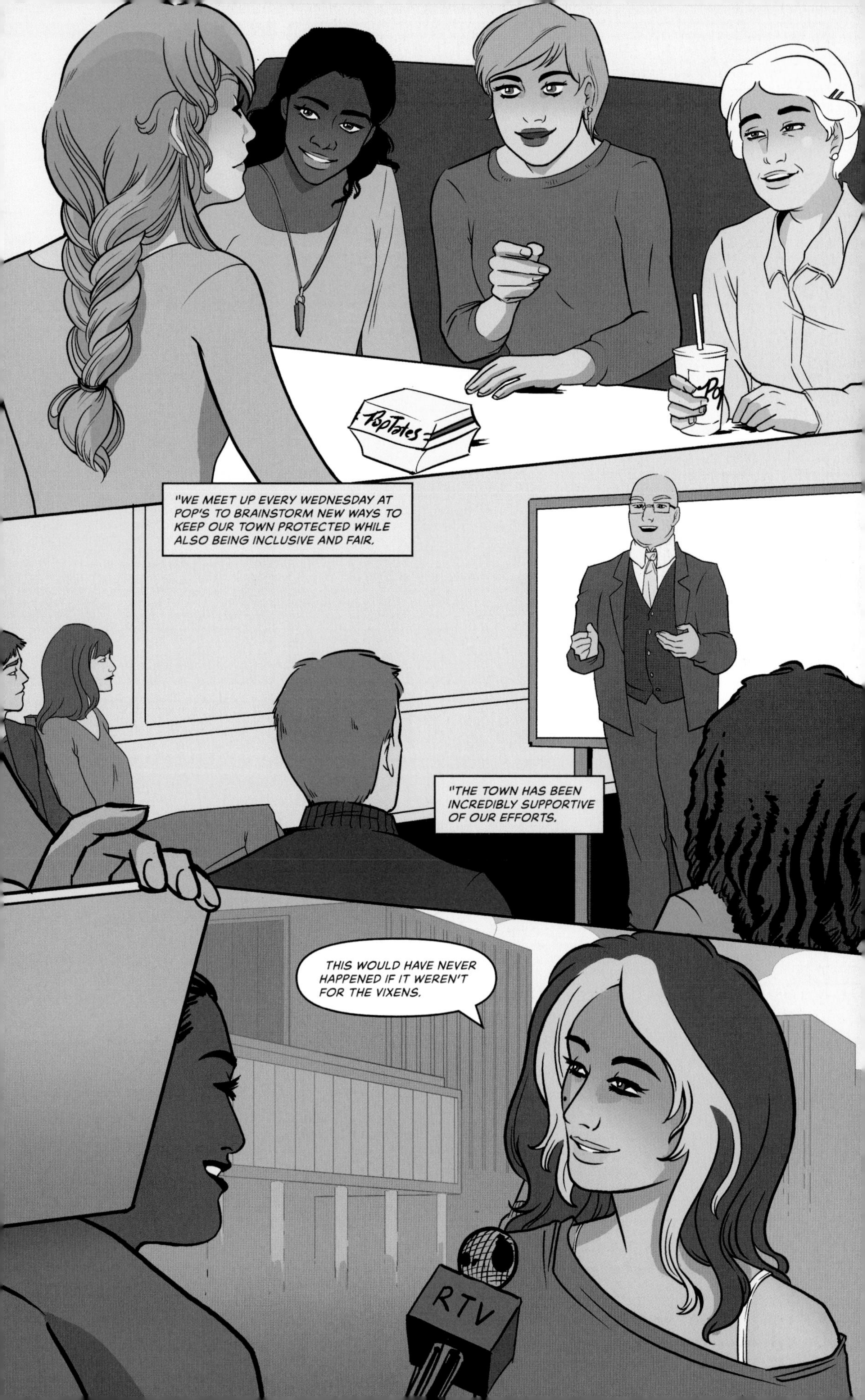
PopTates
Pop's
"WE MEET UP EVERY WEDNESDAY AT POP'S TO BRAINSTORM NEW WAYS TO KEEP OUR TOWN PROTECTED WHILE ALSO BEING INCLUSIVE AND FAIR.
"THE TOWN HAS BEEN INCREDIBLY SUPPORTIVE OF OUR EFFORTS.
THIS WOULD HAVE NEVER HAPPENED IF IT WEREN'T FOR THE VIXENS.
RTV

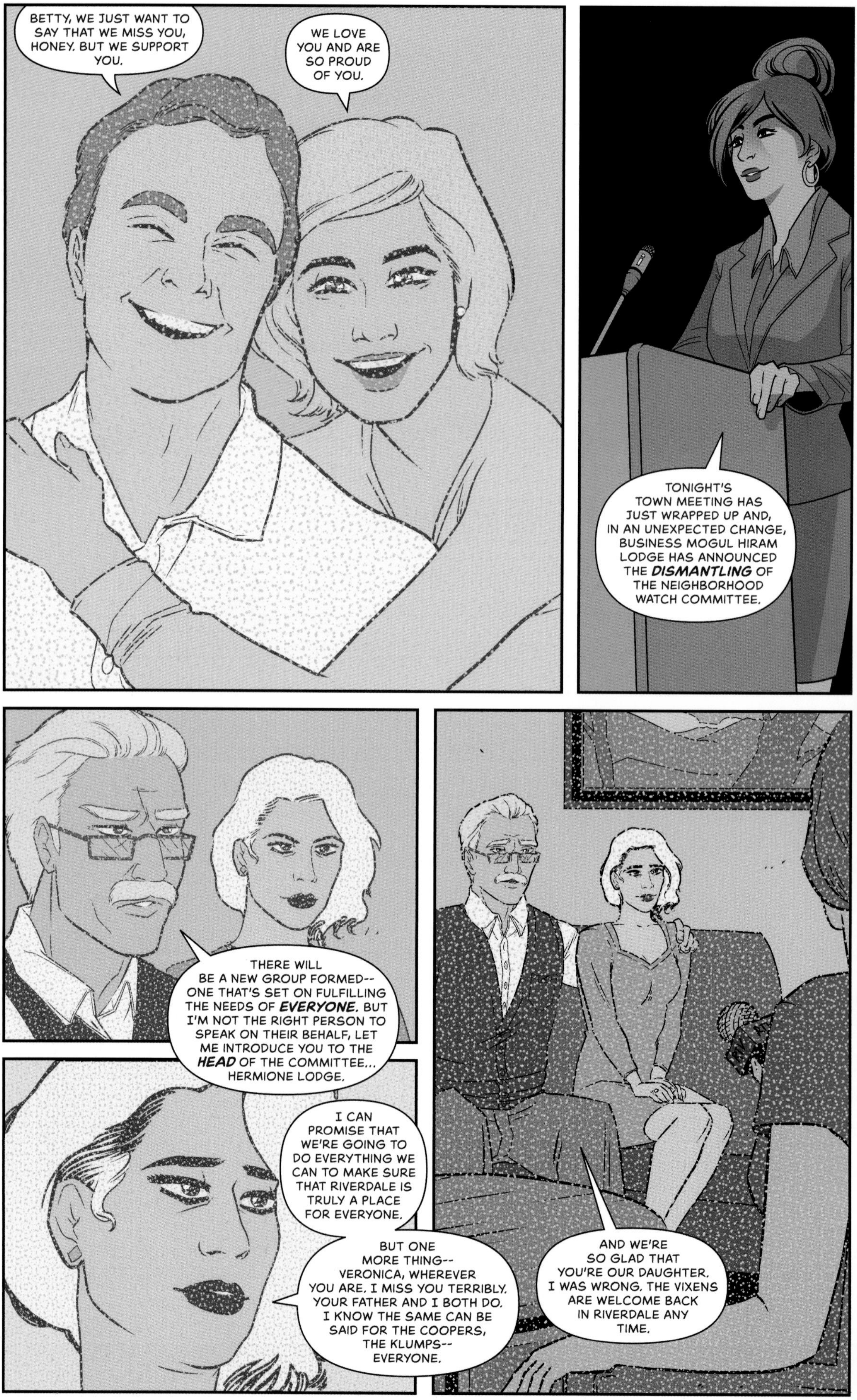
BETTY, WE JUST WANT TO SAY THAT WE MISS YOU, HONEY. BUT WE SUPPORT YOU.
WE LOVE YOU AND ARE SO PROUD OF YOU.
TONIGHT'S TOWN MEETING HAS JUST WRAPPED UP AND, IN AN UNEXPECTED CHANGE, BUSINESS MOGUL HIRAM LODGE HAS ANNOUNCED THE DISMANTLING OF THE NEIGHBORHOOD WATCH COMMITTEE.
THERE WILL BE A NEW GROUP FORMED--ONE THAT'S SET ON FULFILLING THE NEEDS OF EVERYONE. BUT I'M NOT THE RIGHT PERSON TO SPEAK ON THEIR BEHALF, LET ME INTRODUCE YOU TO THE HEAD OF THE COMMITTEE... HERMIONE LODGE.
I CAN PROMISE THAT WE'RE GOING TO DO EVERYTHING WE CAN TO MAKE SURE THAT RIVERDALE IS TRULY A PLACE FOR EVERYONE.
BUT ONE MORE THING--VERONICA, WHEREVER YOU ARE, I MISS YOU TERRIBLY. YOUR FATHER AND I BOTH DO. I KNOW THE SAME CAN BE SAID FOR THE COOPERS, THE KLUMPS--EVERYONE.
AND WE'RE SO GLAD THAT YOU'RE OUR DAUGHTER. I WAS WRONG. THE VIXENS ARE WELCOME BACK IN RIVERDALE ANY TIME.

"AND THAT'S THE NIGHTLY NEWS FROM RIVERDALE."

SO, WHERE ARE YOU GOING NOW?

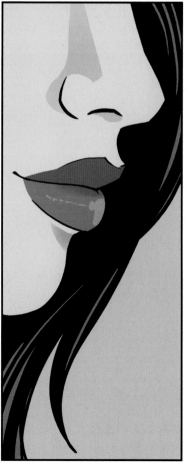

HOME.

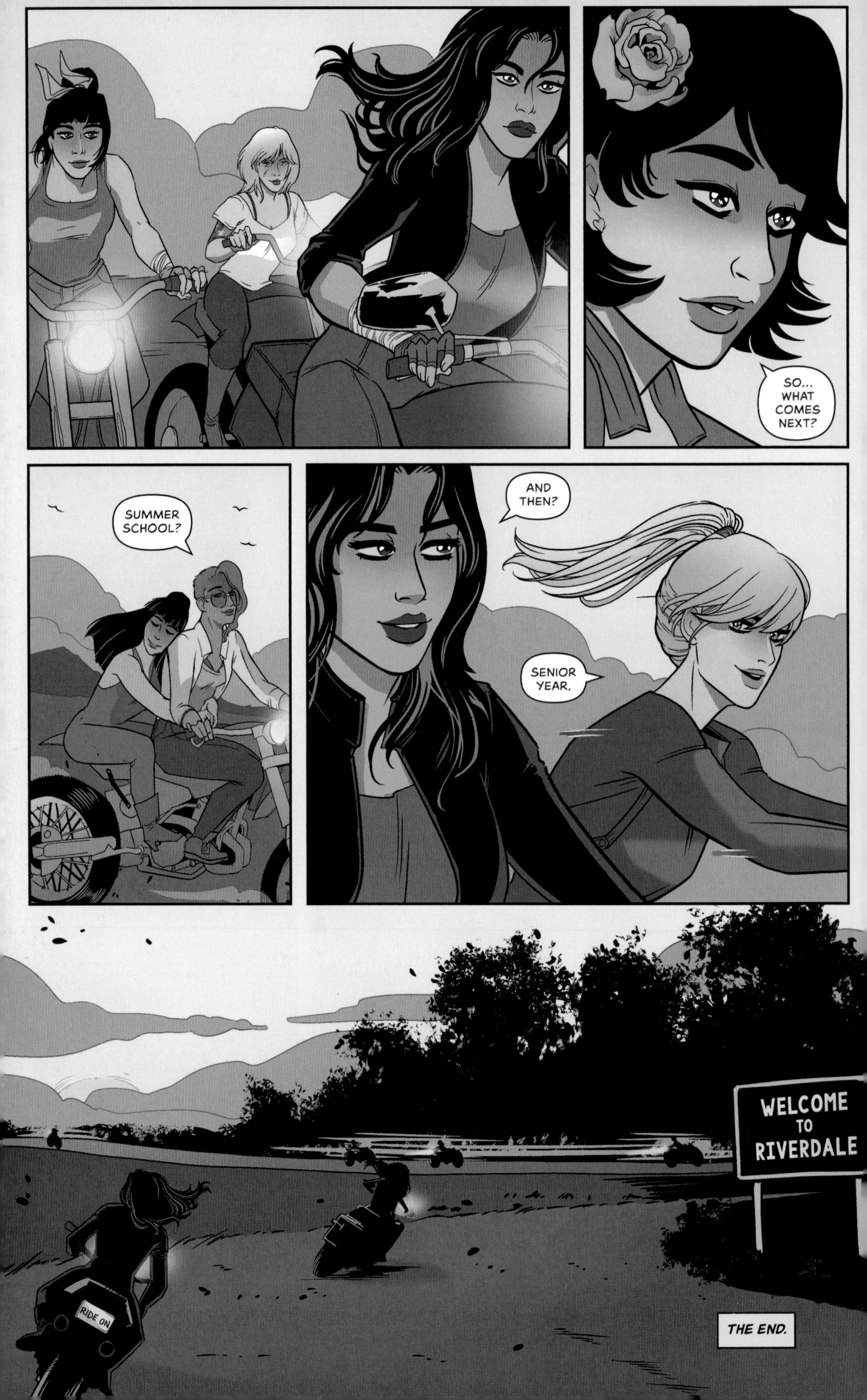
SO... WHAT COMES NEXT?
SUMMER SCHOOL?
AND THEN?
SENIOR YEAR.
WELCOME TO RIVERDALE
RIDE ON
THE END.

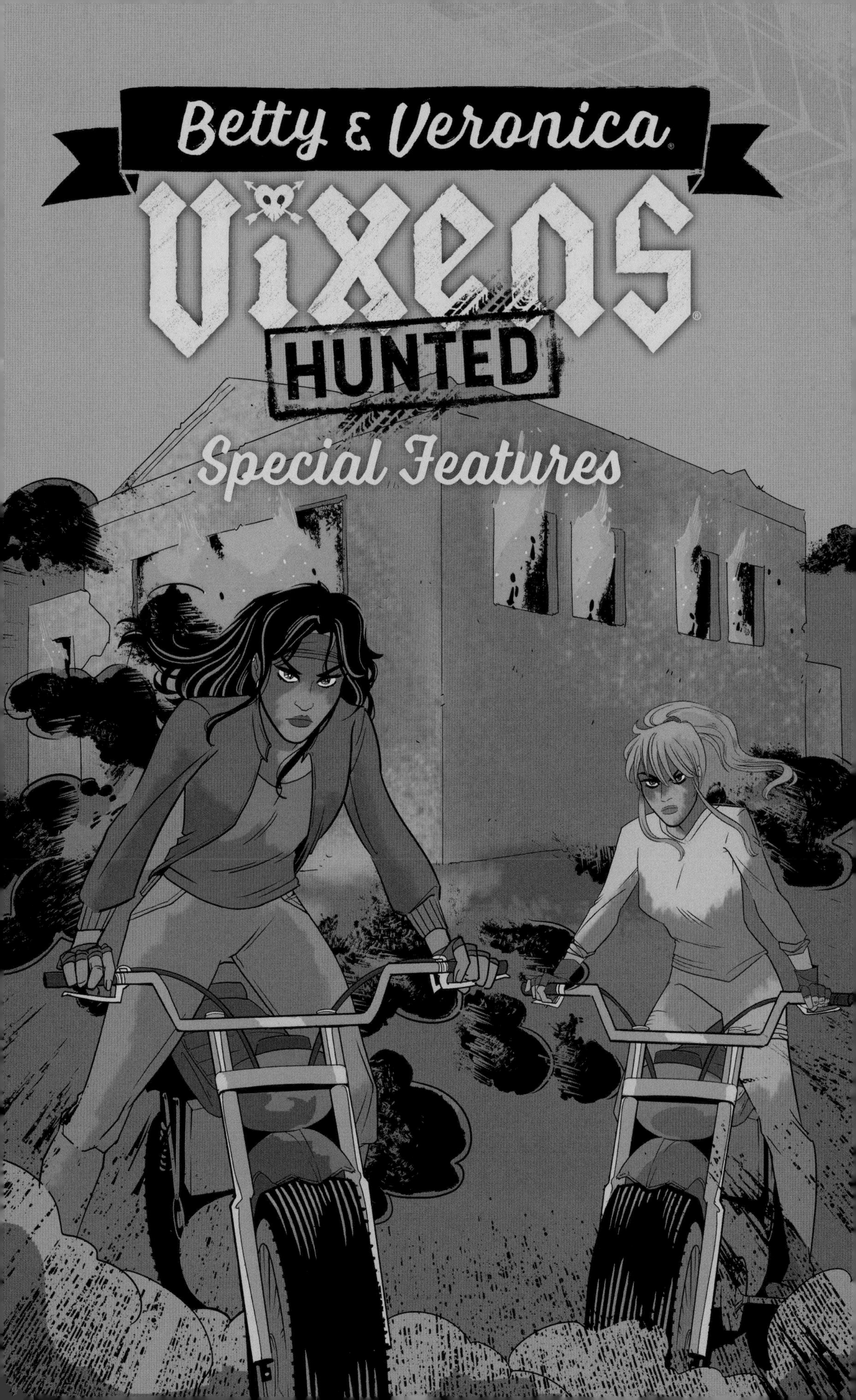
Betty & Veronica®
Vixens®
HUNTED
Special Features

Betty & Veronica®
Vixens® HUNTED
Variant Cover Gallery

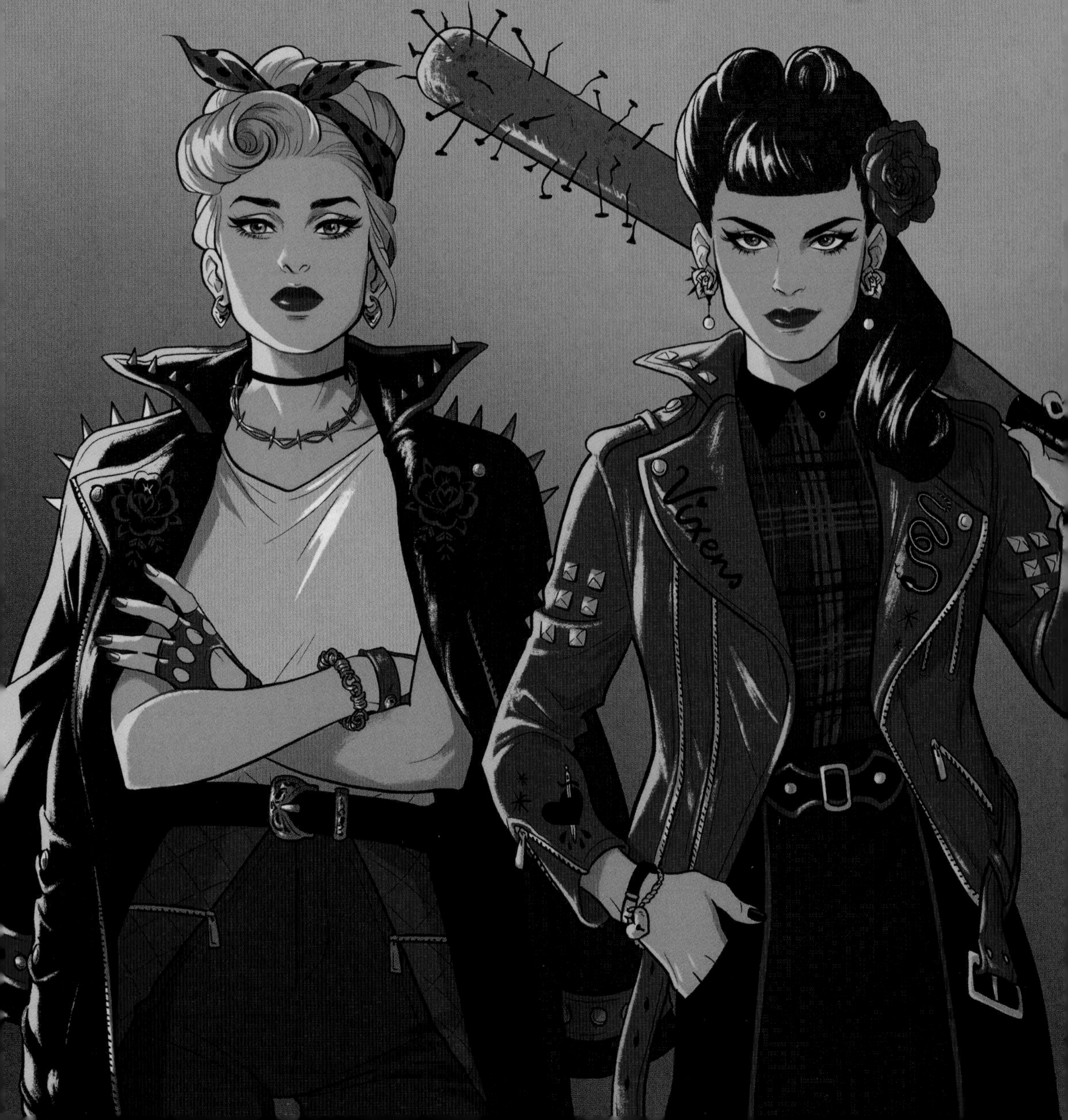
Vixens

Issue Six

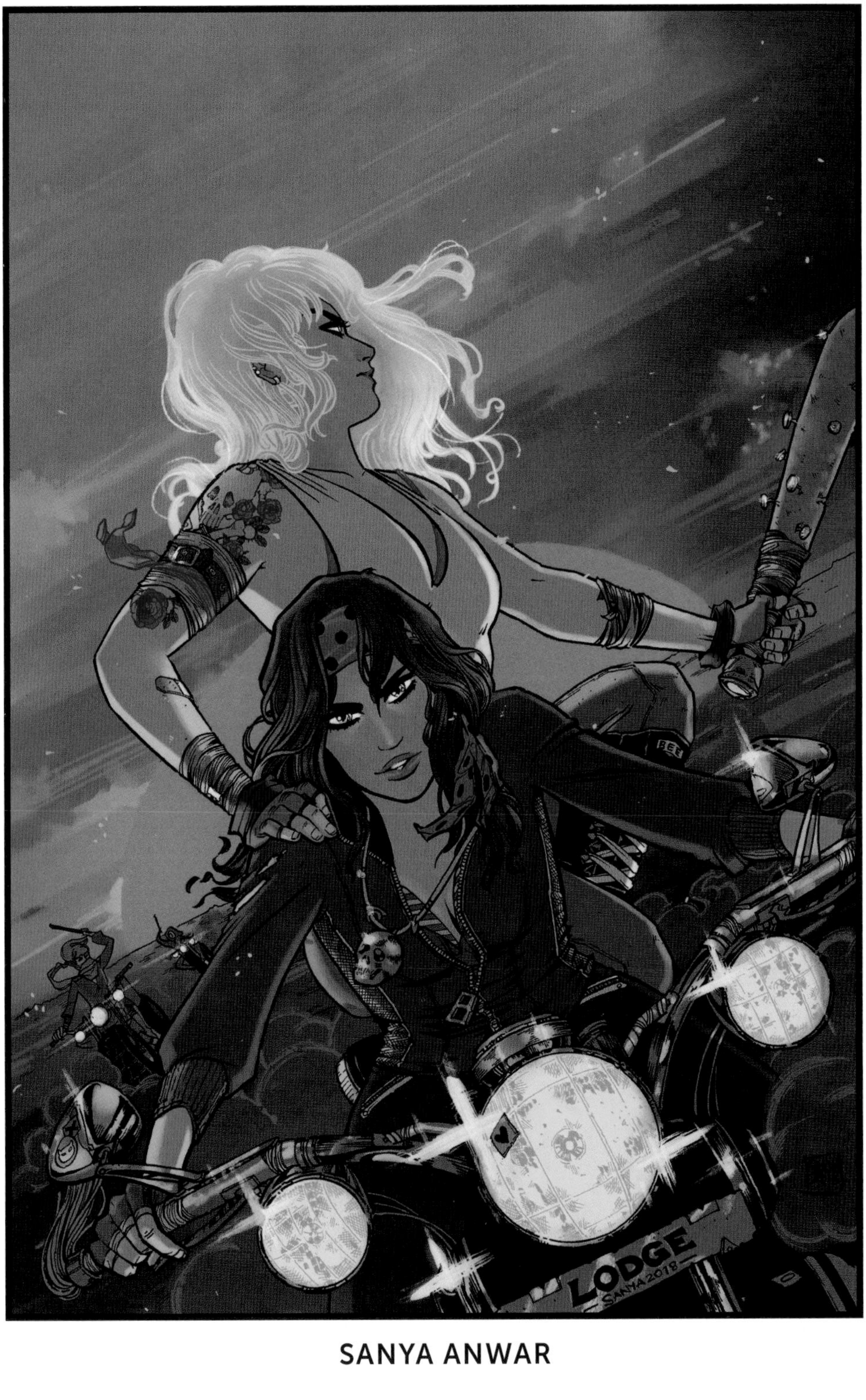
LODGE
SANYA 2018

SANYA ANWAR

Issue Six

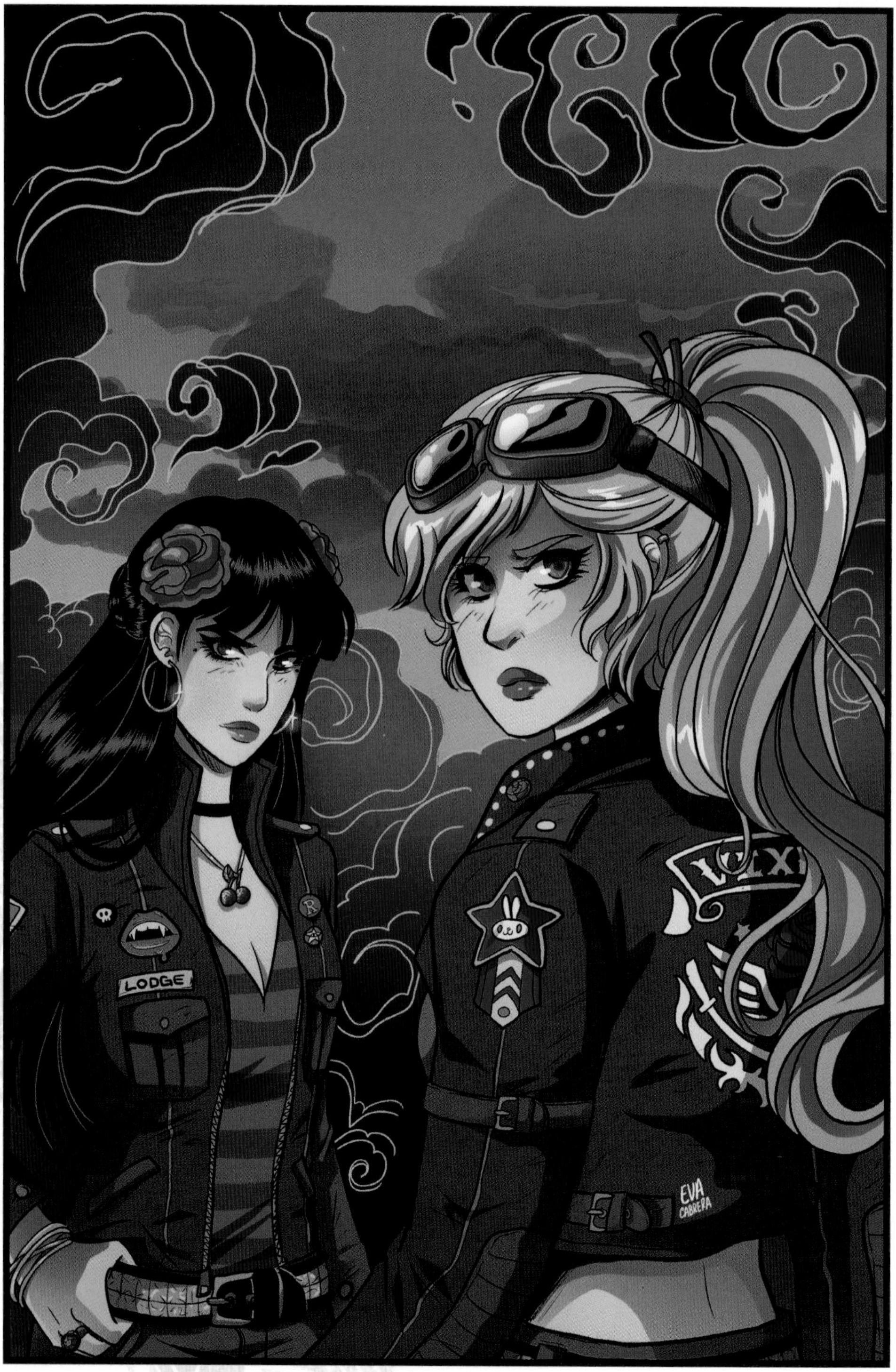

LODGE
EVA CABRERA

EVA CABRERA

Issue Seven

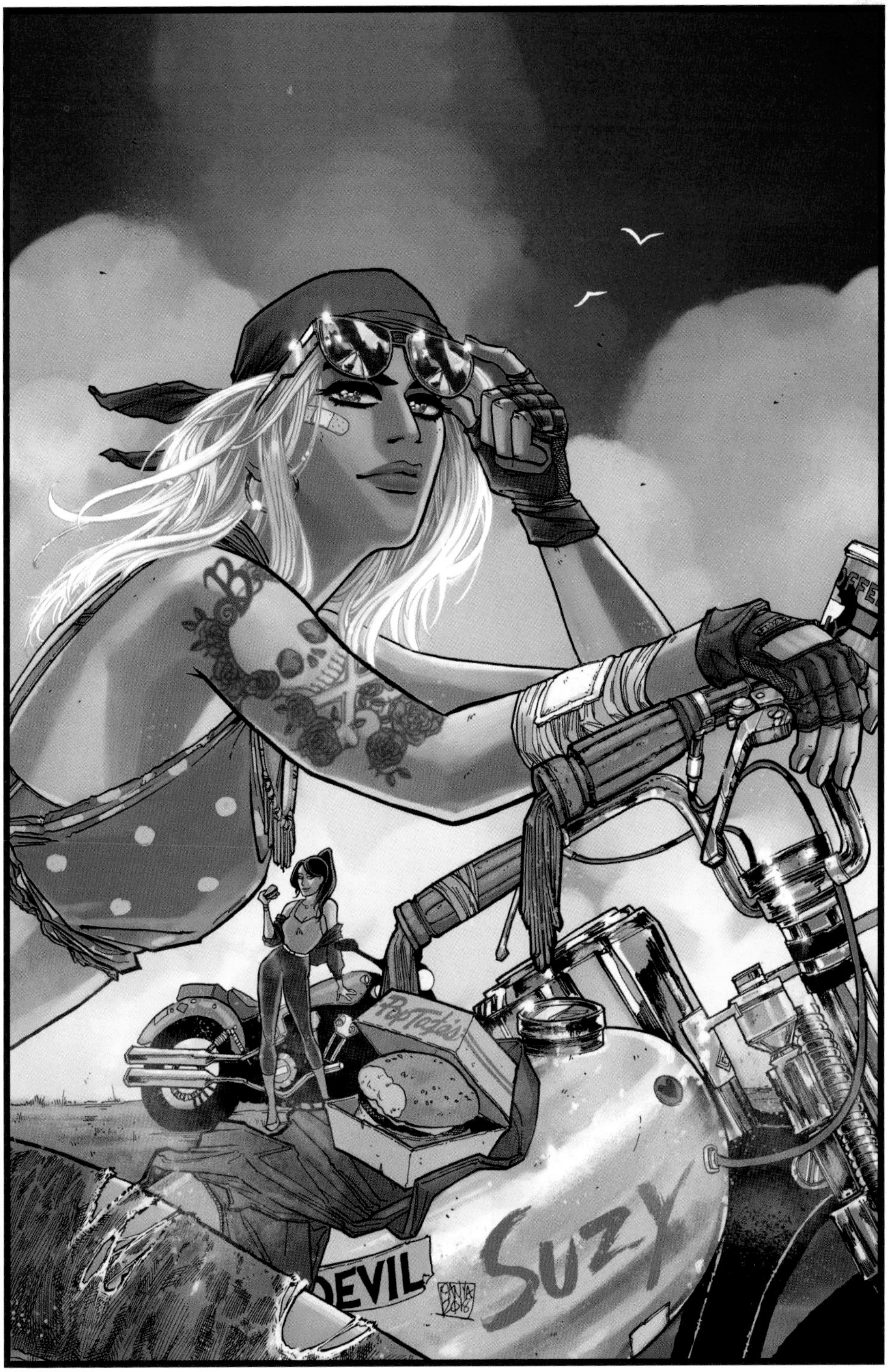
DEVIL
SUZY

SANYA ANWAR

Issue Seven

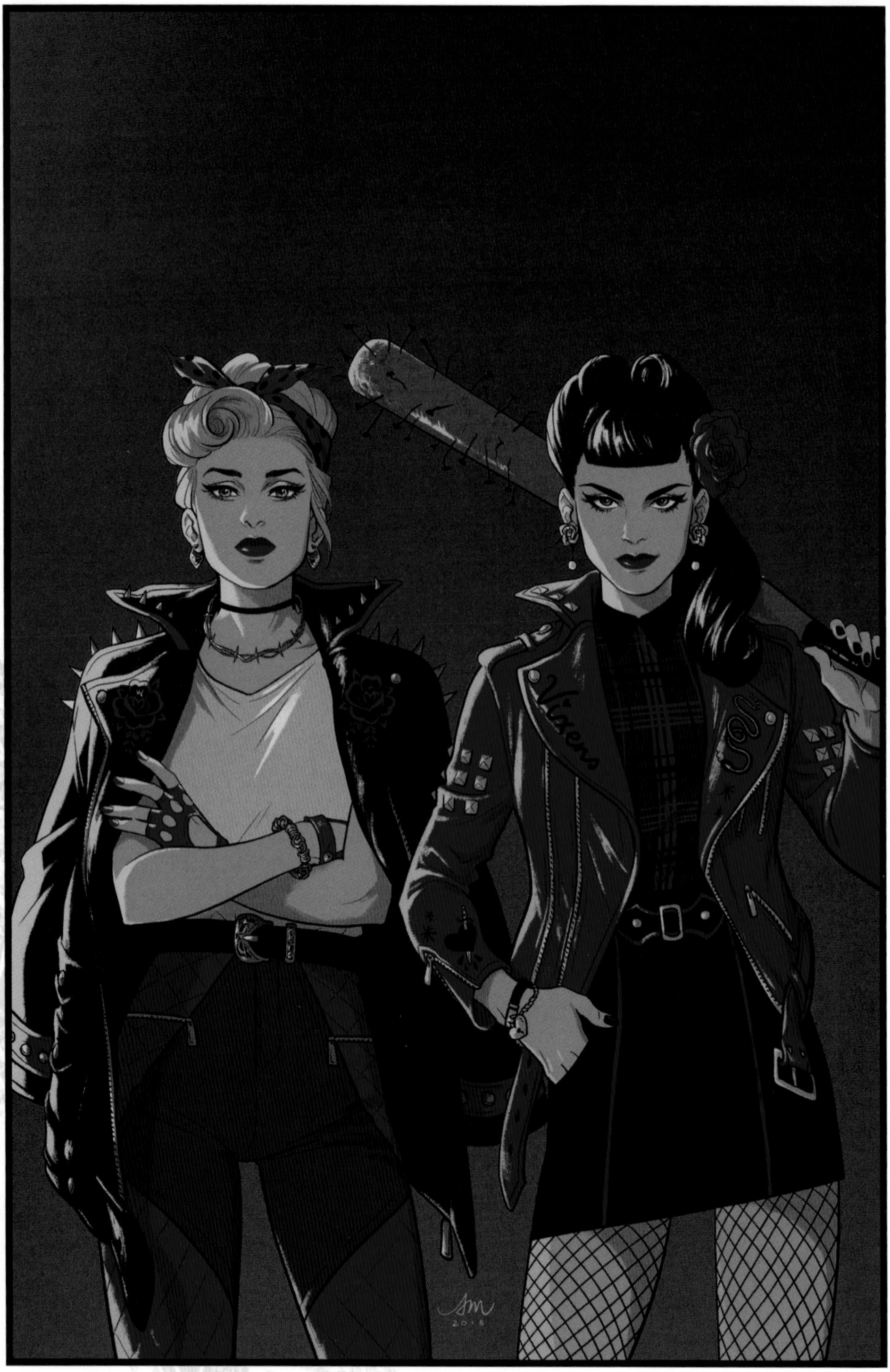

Vixens

AUDREY MOK

Issue Eight

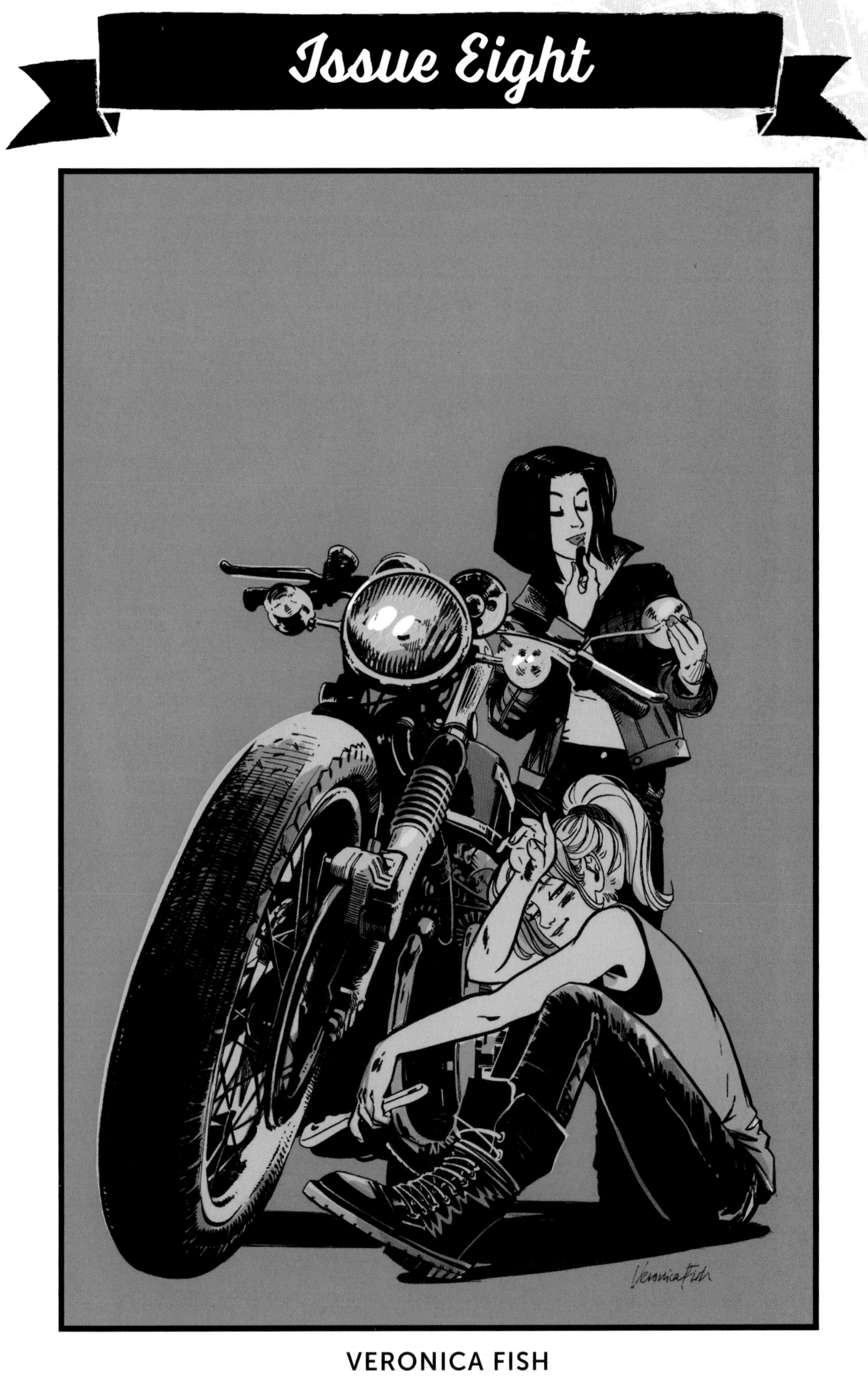
Veronica Fish

VERONICA FISH

Issue Eight

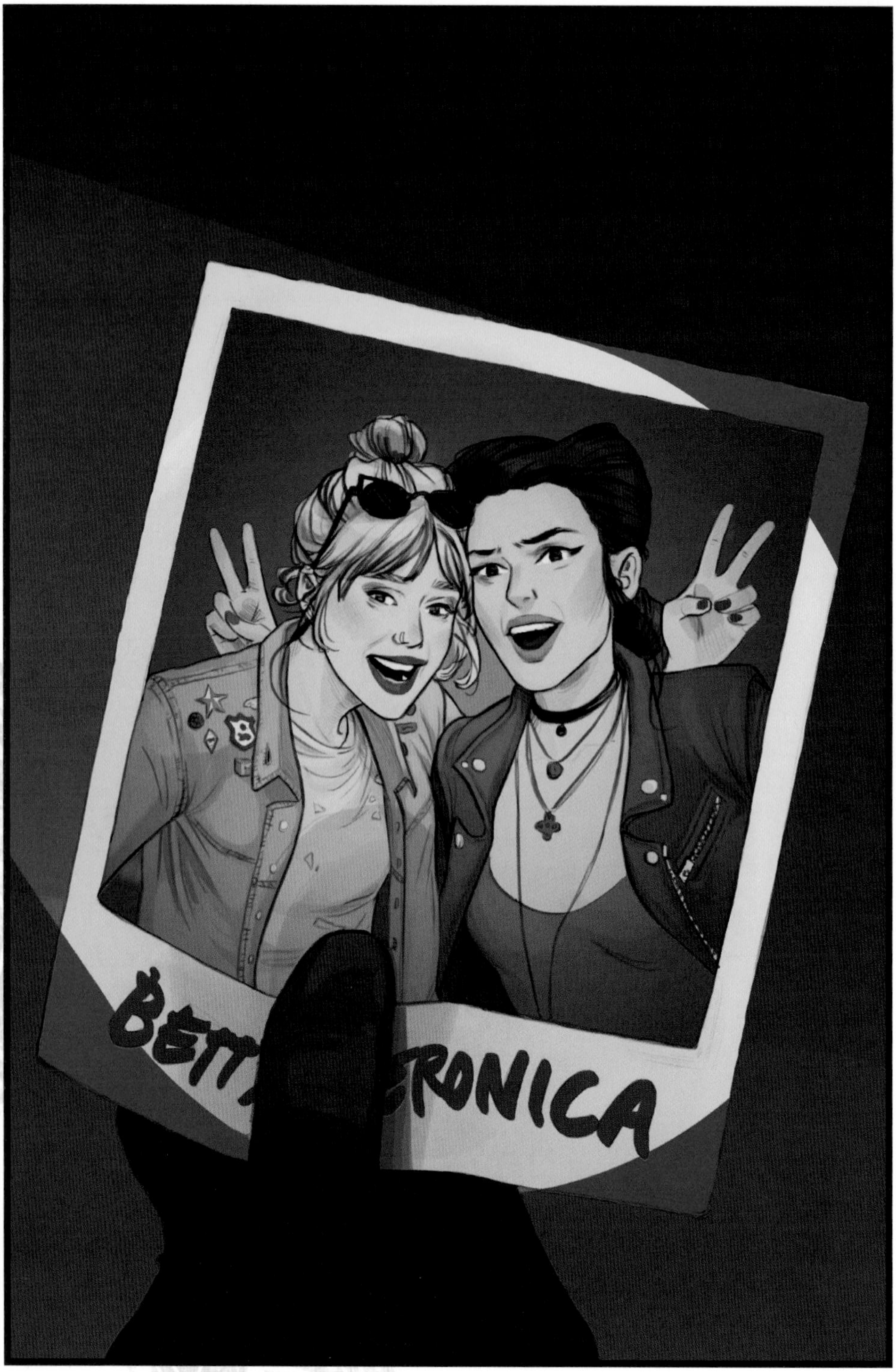
ERONICA

SANDRA LANZ

Issue Nine

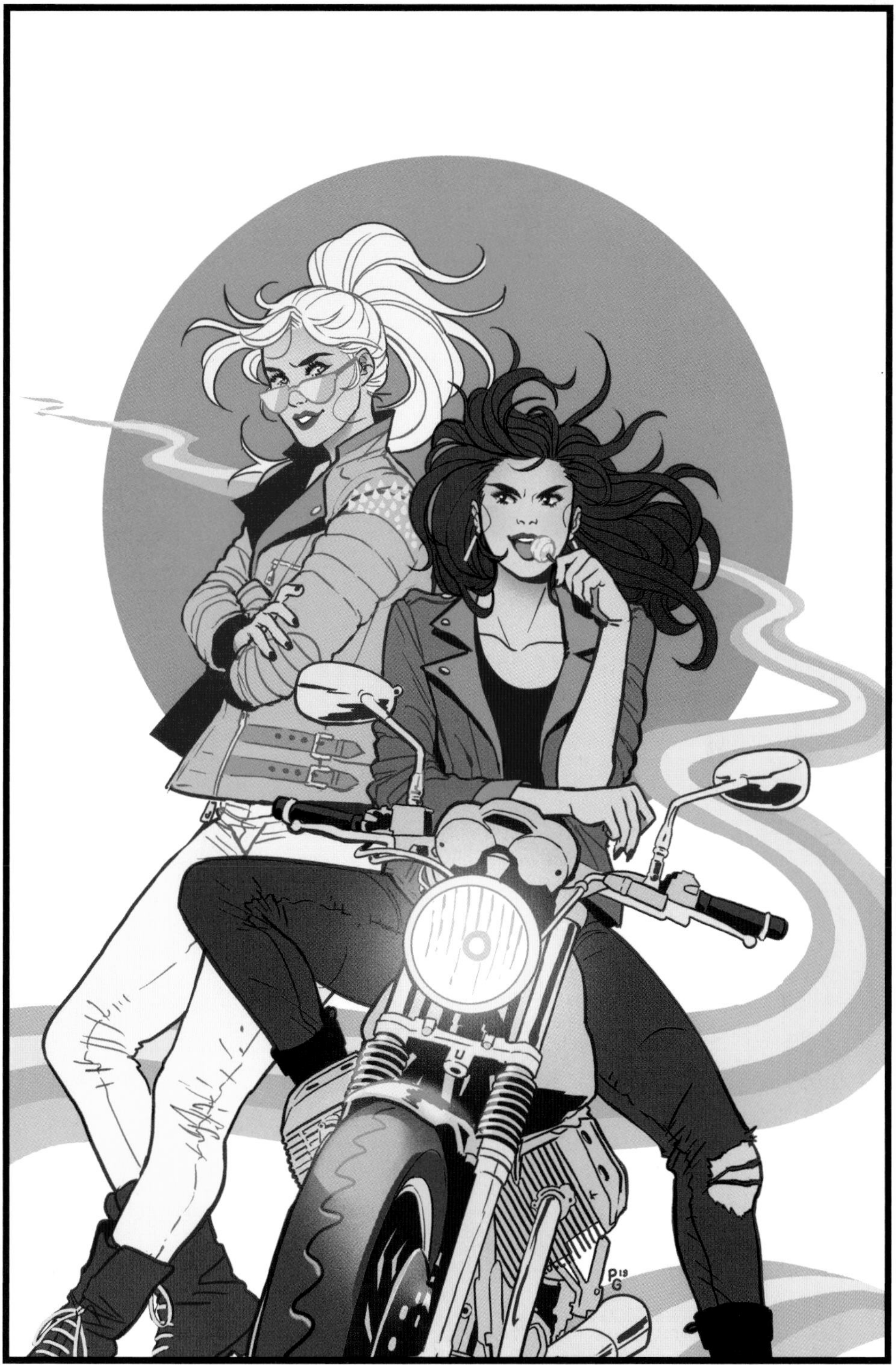

PAULINA GANUCHEAU

Issue Nine

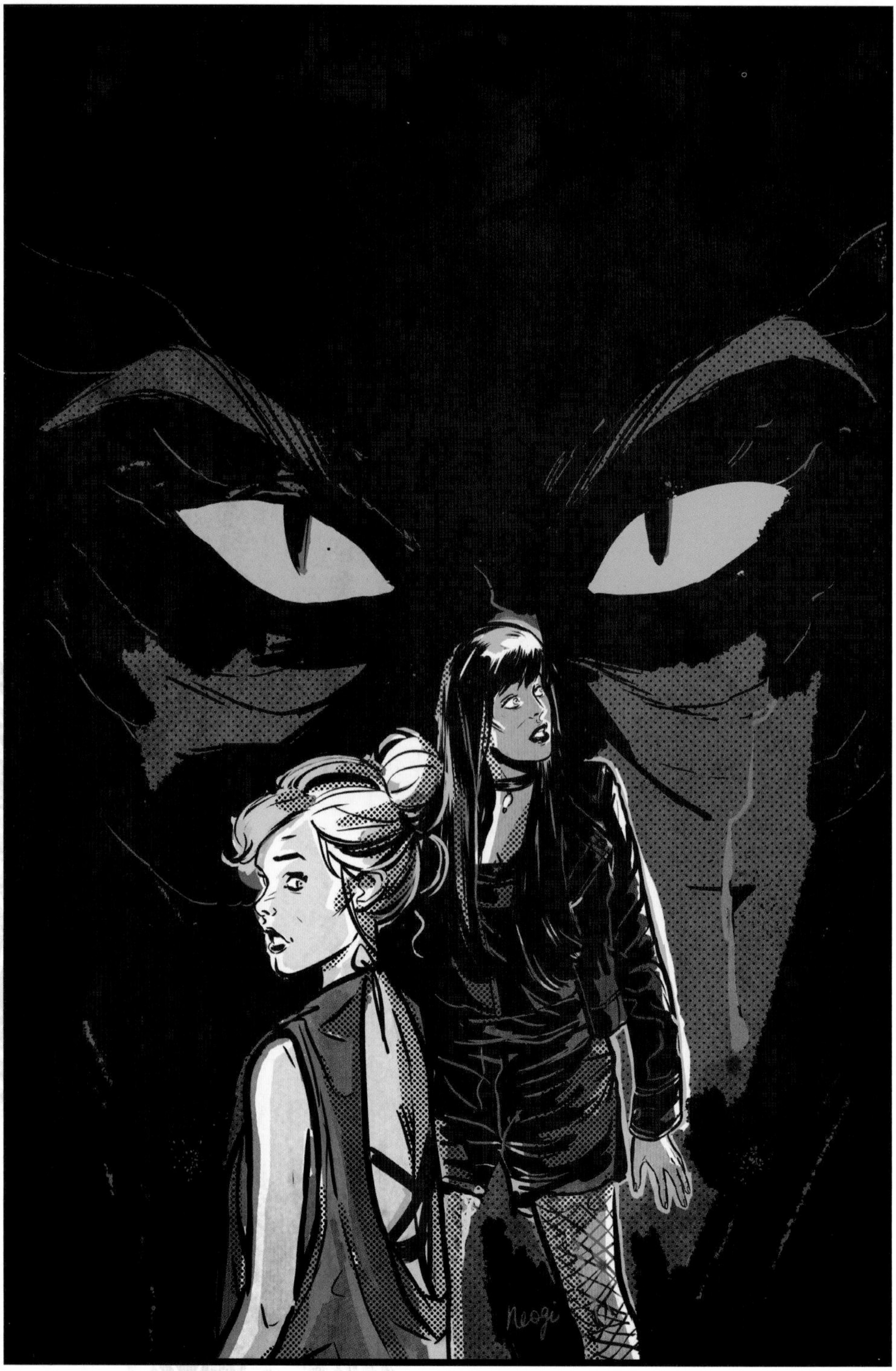
Neogi

DEVAKI NEOGI

Issue Ten

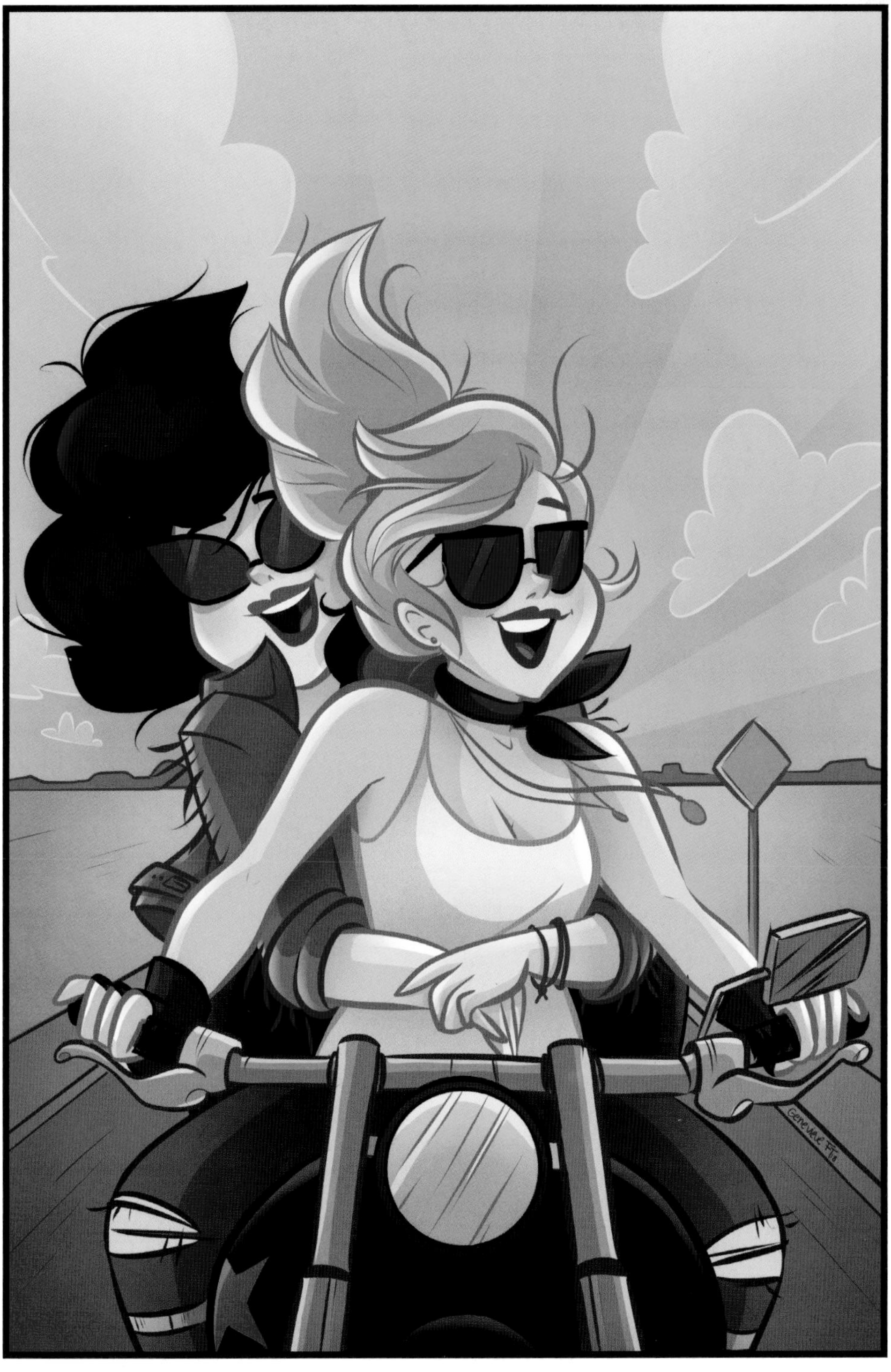

GENEVIEVE F.T.

Issue Ten

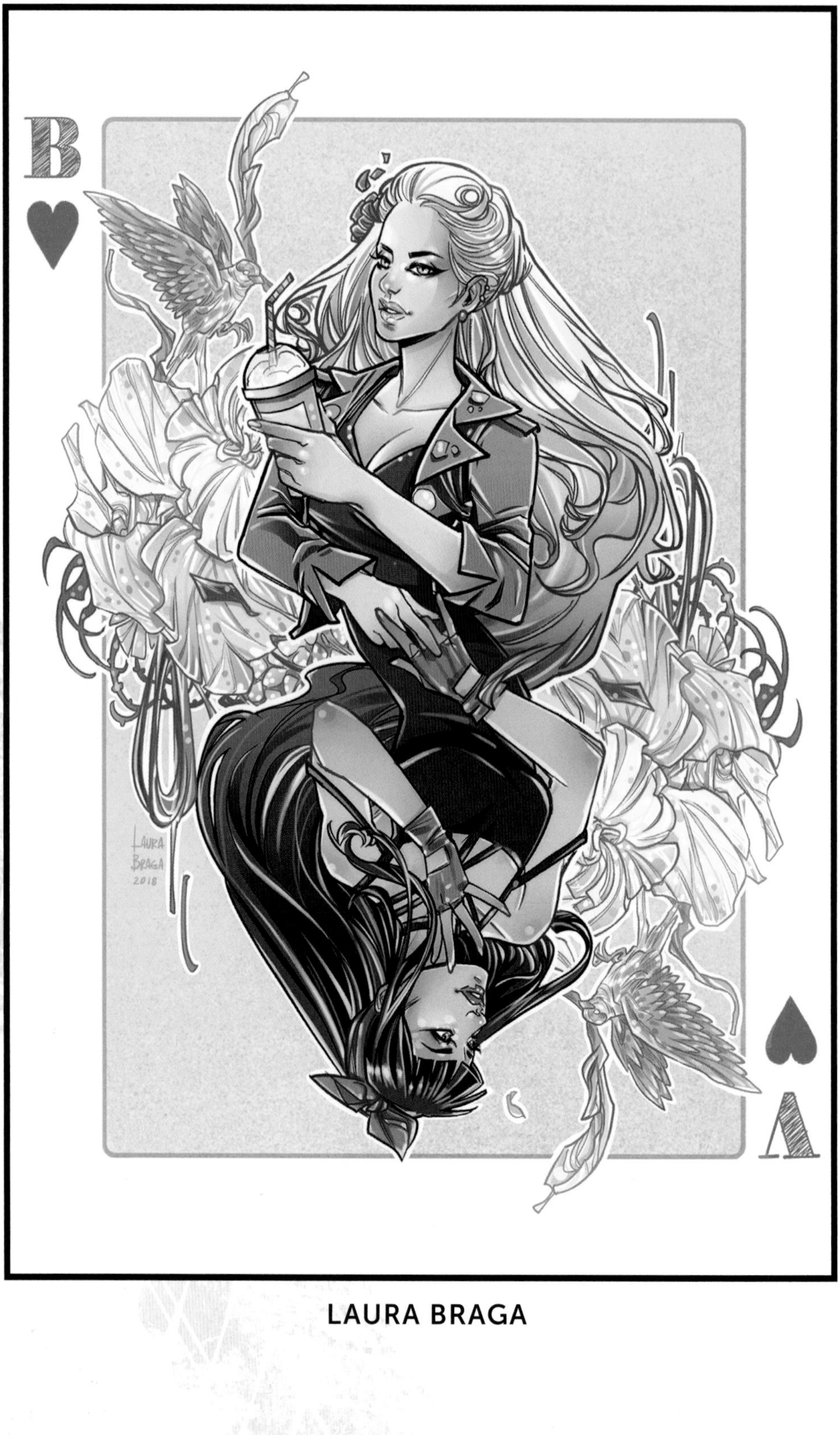

B
A
LAURA BRAGA 2018

LAURA BRAGA

Betty & Veronica® Vixens® HUNTED

Meet the Thrashers!

Much like the Southside Serpents that came before them, the Thrashers—while not a preexisting gang in Archie lore—are comprised of a group of characters pulled from the pages of some classic Archie comics. Named after their leader, Sassy Thrasher, these girls know how to throw down and do it in style! Here's a look at each of the characters and their origins:

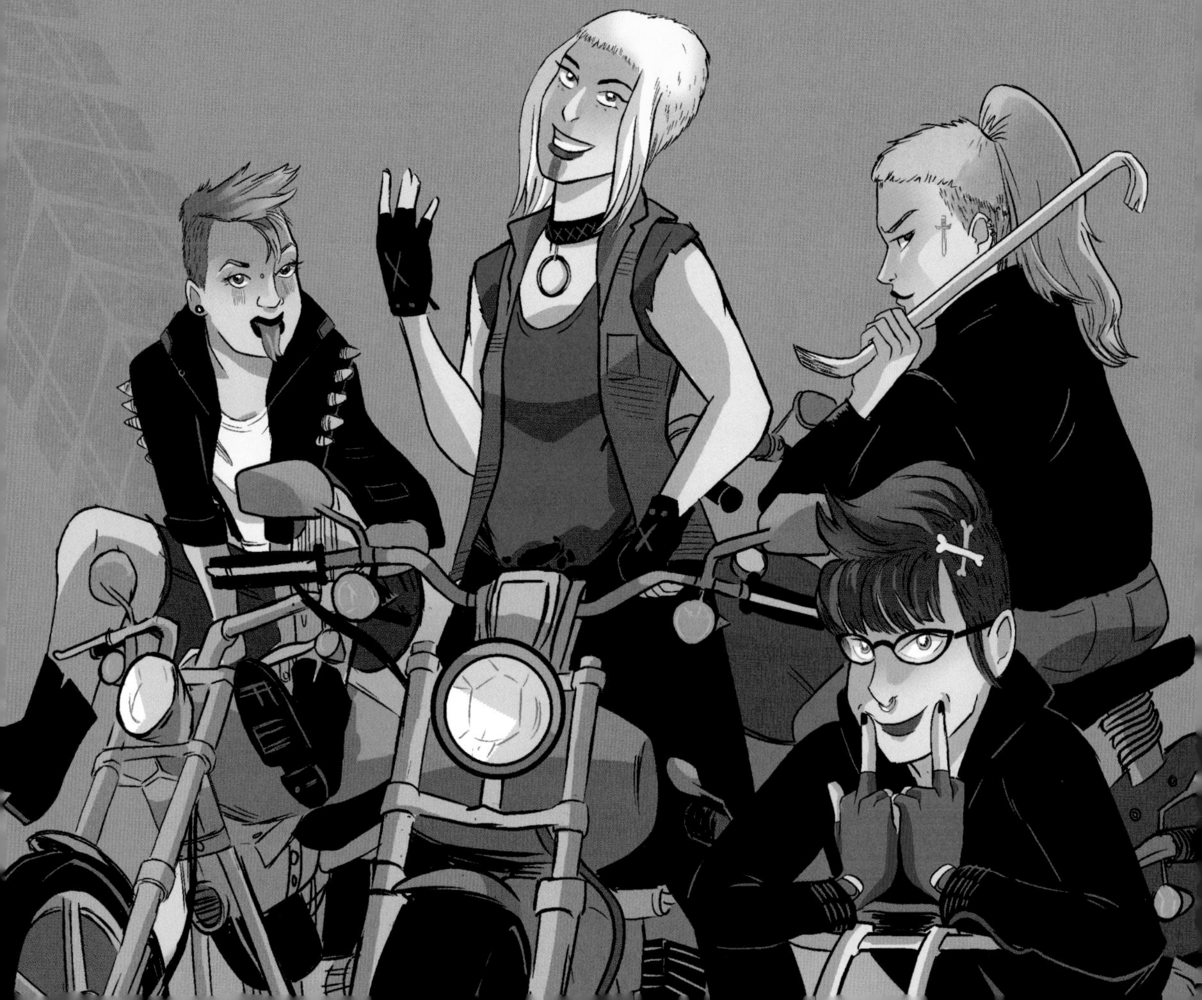

SASSY THRASHER

Then: Sassy Thrasher was a friend of Jughead Jones introduced in the late 1980s when Jughead got a "skate punk" makeover (yep—that happened!). Sassy was rebellious, fond of skateboarding and had a "don't mess with me" attitude—especially towards Archie and Reggie when they'd try to get her attention!

Now: Sassy's upgraded her skateboard for a two-wheeler—but her attitude has remained the same! She doesn't take anything from anyone and she makes sure people know it!

PEPPER SMITH

Then: Pepper Smith was Josie McCoy's best friend in the original 1960s comic *She's Josie*, known for her sharp wit and cynical nature. When Josie shifted gears and focused on the musical aspect of the Pussycats, Pepper was swapped out in favor of Valerie.

Now: Pepper's still got her sharp wit about her! Slightly quieter and less bold than her fellow Thrashers, she relies heavily her intellect and biting sarcasm.

CRICKET O'DELL

Then: Cricket O'Dell may have one of the most interesting back stories in Archie Comics. First introduced in 1962, Cricket is a friendly girl with a unique talent— she has the ability to sniff out money. Her nose can also determine whether treasure is genuine or not.

Now: While we didn't get to explore in-depth whether or not Cricket's talent is still intact, let's just say that the Thrashers didn't come face-to-face with the Vixens by accident—someone's nose may have sniffed out the likes of Veronica and Cheryl!

SUE STRINGLY

Then: Sue Stringly first appeared in the *Little Archie* comic. She was a poor little girl who's family lived in a shack near the railway tracks. Despite this, Sue was an upbeat, cheerful girl who never complained about her predicament. While most of the school students didn't want anything to do with her, eventually Sue became good friends with Little Archie and Veronica.

Now: Sue, like Evelyn, had an intimate connection with Archie and the gang before disappearing for some time. In fact, she may be the only person who knows Evelyn—and, more importantly, where Evelyn's been all this time. What the two got into together, however, remains a mystery.

Betty & Veronica Vixens HUNTED

Roller Derby

In issue #5 from volume 1 of *Vixens*, Cheryl Blossom joined the gang after showing off her chops both on and off the roller derby track. While the Pembrooke Punishers are a fictional team, the real River City Roller Derby from Richmond, VA made a very special cameo appearance. This led to even more real-world derby teams being featured each issue. Here's a recap of all the teams that have lent their support to this series:

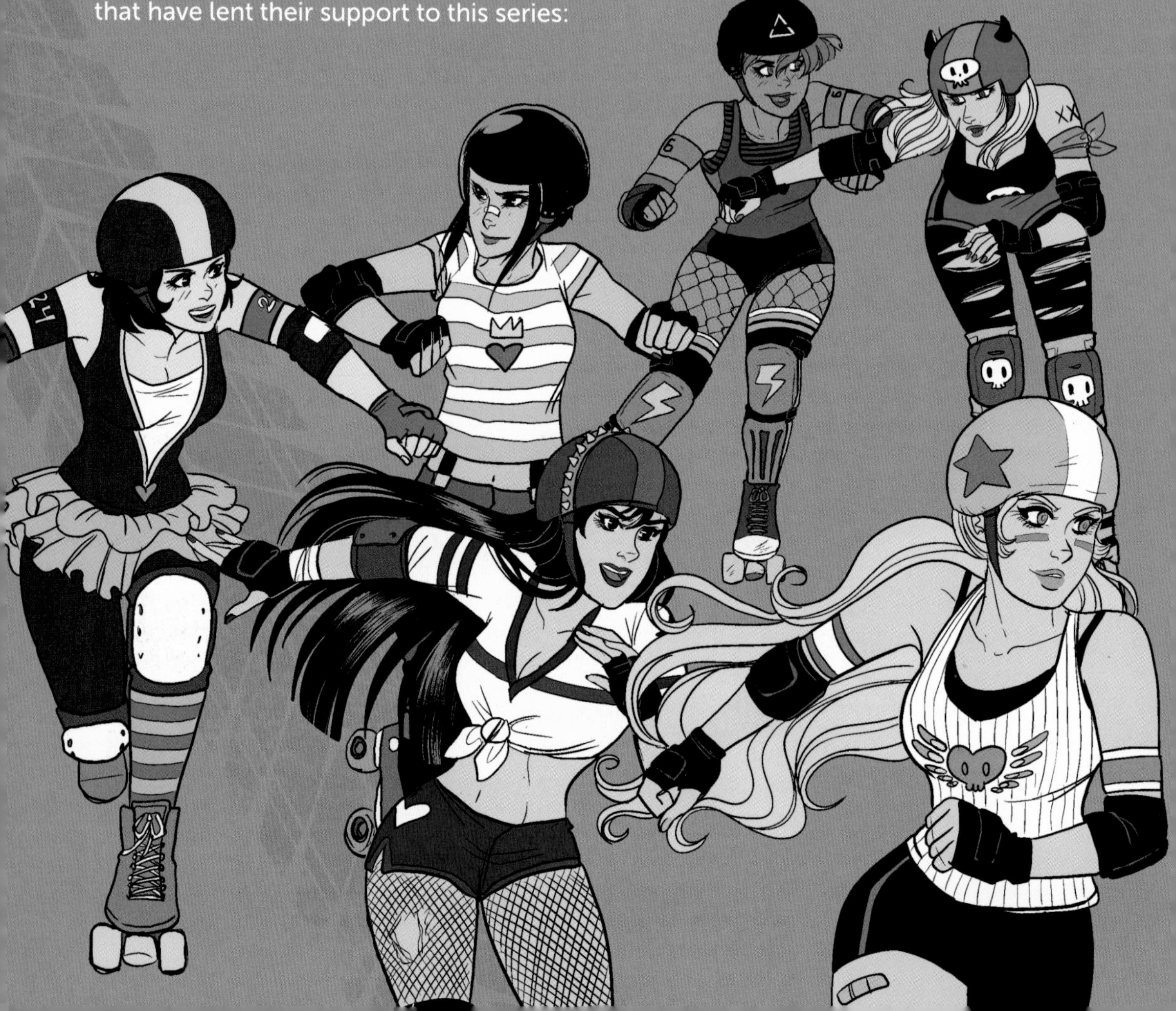

RIVER CITY ROLLER DERBY

Region: Richmond, VA
Battle Cry: "RCR! RCR! RCR! D!!!"

CHARM CITY ROLLER GIRLS

Region: Baltimore, MD
Battle Cry: "CCRG! CCRG! CCRG!"

STEEL CITY ROLLER DERBY

Region: Pittsburgh, PA
Battle Cry: "yinz! yinz! yinz!"

SAVANNAH DERBY DEVILS

Region: Savannah, GA
Battle Cry: "Raise Hell!"

SOUTHERN HARM DERBY DAMES

Region: South Atlanta, GA
Battle Cry: "Bless Your Heart!"

Southern HARM Derby Dames

COAL MINERS' DAUGHTERS

Region: Gillette, WY
Battle Cry: "CMD Boom!"

SINDERELLA #666
POCKET CHAOS #67
VANILLA WILD #35
GYPSY DANGER #19
TERMIKNITTER #45
DR.DEFIANCE #16
ANGRY BEAVER #14
OSAMA BIN LLAMA #6
DANGER NOODLE #321
TOXIC VIXEN #308
HOT MAMA SPEEDA #702
AMMOZON #55
THREATA VAN SUFFERIN #119
MAD DOG #42
MURDUSA #12
OBSIDIAN SIXX #18
WOUND HER WOMAN #1941
2018 COAL MINERS DAUGHTERS

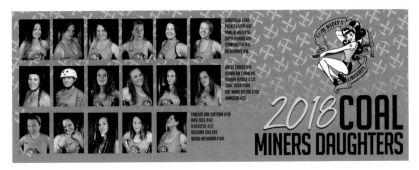

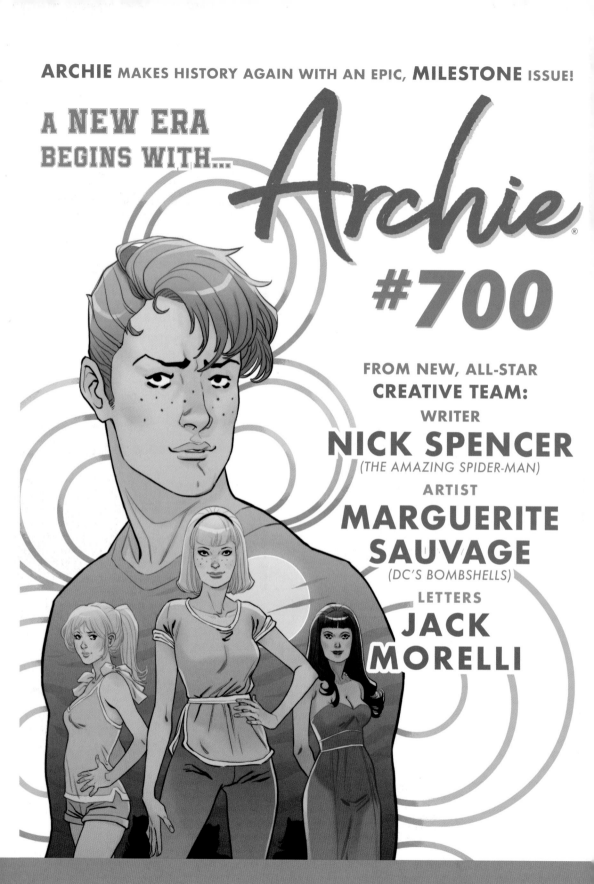

ARCHIE MAKES HISTORY AGAIN WITH AN EPIC, **MILESTONE** ISSUE!

A NEW ERA
BEGINS WITH...

Archie®
#700

FROM NEW, ALL-STAR
CREATIVE TEAM:
WRITER
NICK SPENCER
(THE AMAZING SPIDER-MAN)
ARTIST
**MARGUERITE
SAUVAGE**
(DC'S BOMBSHELLS)
LETTERS
**JACK
MORELLI**

SPECIAL PREVIEW

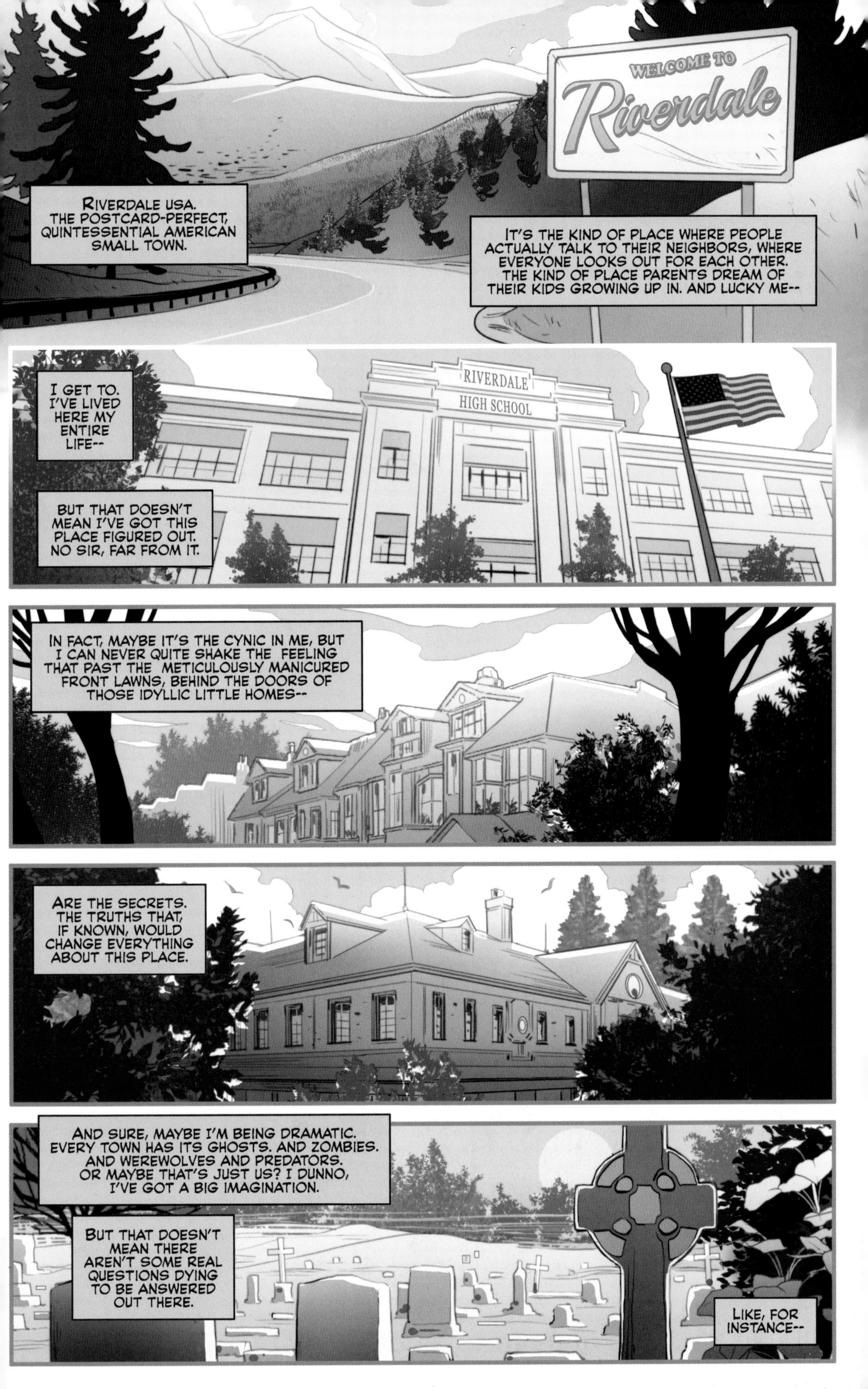
WELCOME TO
Riverdale
RIVERDALE USA. THE POSTCARD-PERFECT, QUINTESSENTIAL AMERICAN SMALL TOWN.
IT'S THE KIND OF PLACE WHERE PEOPLE ACTUALLY TALK TO THEIR NEIGHBORS, WHERE EVERYONE LOOKS OUT FOR EACH OTHER. THE KIND OF PLACE PARENTS DREAM OF THEIR KIDS GROWING UP IN. AND LUCKY ME--
RIVERDALE
HIGH SCHOOL
I GET TO. I'VE LIVED HERE MY ENTIRE LIFE--
BUT THAT DOESN'T MEAN I'VE GOT THIS PLACE FIGURED OUT. NO SIR, FAR FROM IT.
IN FACT, MAYBE IT'S THE CYNIC IN ME, BUT I CAN NEVER QUITE SHAKE THE FEELING THAT PAST THE METICULOUSLY MANICURED FRONT LAWNS, BEHIND THE DOORS OF THOSE IDYLLIC LITTLE HOMES--
ARE THE SECRETS. THE TRUTHS THAT, IF KNOWN, WOULD CHANGE EVERYTHING ABOUT THIS PLACE.
AND SURE, MAYBE I'M BEING DRAMATIC. EVERY TOWN HAS ITS GHOSTS. AND ZOMBIES. AND WEREWOLVES AND PREDATORS. OR MAYBE THAT'S JUST US? I DUNNO, I'VE GOT A BIG IMAGINATION.
BUT THAT DOESN'T MEAN THERE AREN'T SOME REAL QUESTIONS DYING TO BE ANSWERED OUT THERE.
LIKE, FOR INSTANCE--

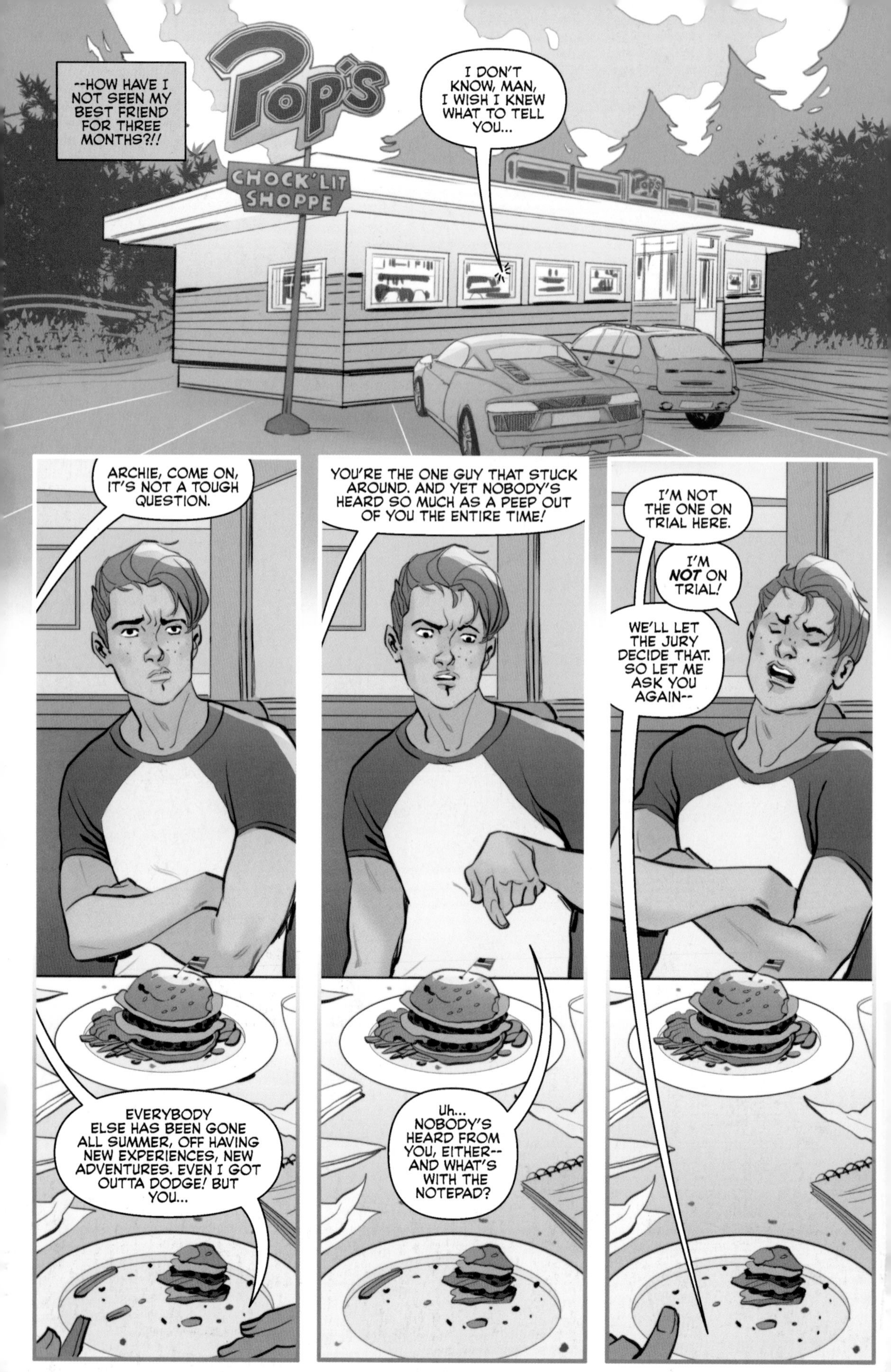
--HOW HAVE I NOT SEEN MY BEST FRIEND FOR THREE MONTHS?!!
POP'S
CHOCK'LIT SHOPPE
I DON'T KNOW, MAN, I WISH I KNEW WHAT TO TELL YOU...
ARCHIE, COME ON, IT'S NOT A TOUGH QUESTION.
EVERYBODY ELSE HAS BEEN GONE ALL SUMMER, OFF HAVING NEW EXPERIENCES, NEW ADVENTURES. EVEN I GOT OUTTA DODGE! BUT YOU...
YOU'RE THE ONE GUY THAT STUCK AROUND. AND YET NOBODY'S HEARD SO MUCH AS A PEEP OUT OF YOU THE ENTIRE TIME!
Uh... NOBODY'S HEARD FROM YOU, EITHER-- AND WHAT'S WITH THE NOTEPAD?
I'M NOT THE ONE ON TRIAL HERE.
I'M *NOT* ON TRIAL!
WE'LL LET THE JURY DECIDE THAT. SO LET ME ASK YOU AGAIN--

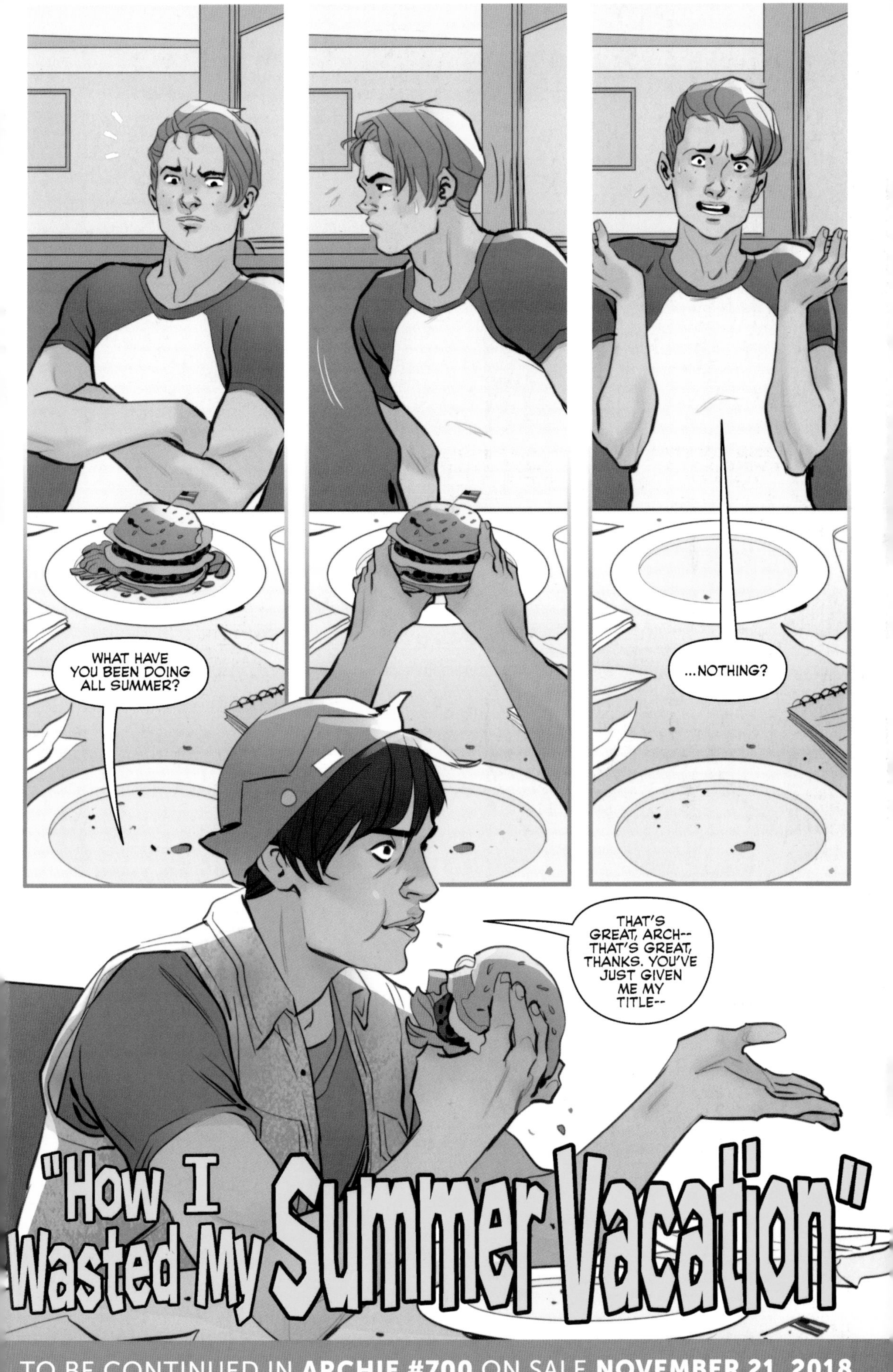
WHAT HAVE YOU BEEN DOING ALL SUMMER?
...NOTHING?
THAT'S GREAT, ARCH-- THAT'S GREAT, THANKS. YOU'VE JUST GIVEN ME MY TITLE--
"How I Wasted My Summer Vacation"

TO BE CONTINUED IN **ARCHIE #700** ON SALE **NOVEMBER 21, 2018**